Sweden: Social Democracy
in Practice

Sweden: Social Democracy in Practice

HENRY MILNER

Oxford University Press

Oxford University Press, Walton Street, Oxford OX2 6DP
Oxford New York Toronto
Delhi Bombay Calcutta Madras Karachi
Petaling Jaya Singapore Hong Kong Tokyo
Nairobi Dar es Salaam Cape Town
Melbourne Auckland
and associated companies in
Berlin Ibadan

Oxford is a trade mark of Oxford University Press

Published in the United States
by Oxford University Press, New York

First published 1989
First issued in paperback 1990
Reprinted 1990

British Library Cataloguing in Publication Data
Milner, Henry
Sweden: social democracy in practice.
1. Sweden. Politics
I. Title
320.9485
ISBN 0–19–827856–X

Library of Congress Cataloging-in-Publication Data
Milner, Henry.
Sweden: social democracy in practice / Henry Milner.
Bibliography. Includes index.
1. Sweden—Economic policy. 2. Sweden—Politics and
government—1973– 3. Sweden—Social policy. I. Title.
HC375.M5 1989 361.6'5'09485—dc19 88–27156
ISBN 0–19–827856–X

Printed in Great Britain
by Biddles Ltd.
Guildford and King's Lynn

This book is dedicated to BERNT CARLSSON 1938-88: peace-maker, social-democratic statesman, scholar, and friend, who died on 21 December on Pan Am Flight 103 on his way to New York for the signing of the Namibia Accords he had laboured to achieve as UN Under General Secretary for Namibia.

We his friends, the Swedish nation, indeed mankind itself, are immensely the poorer for his loss.

PREFACE

Question: how does someone with no background in Swedish studies and only a rudimentary grasp of the language write a book about Swedish social democracy? Answer: rather apologetically. The story begins around 1983. I had been writing mainly about Quebec and Canadian politics for more than a decade. The 'new politics' of 'left-wing nationalism', as I had termed it in previous books, was waning. The Parti Québécois and its allies among trade unionists and intellectuals, which had during that decade dominated Quebec political life under the banner of social democracy as well as nationalism, were losing steam.

I was at the time completing a book on the aborted modernization of Quebec's educational structures. A vicious strike that pitted public-sector employees led by the teachers against the Parti Québécois government not only sounded the death-knell for that reform but, ultimately, for the cohesion and credibility of the social-democratic alliance. Yet how could a simple dispute over wages and working conditions bring down a movement united around the grand principles of social solidarity and national liberation?

The existing literature on social democracy in Quebec was of no help in answering the question, consisting as it does largely of Marxist dismissals of social democracy as 'capitalism with a human face'. Without spelling it out clearly at first, I set about coming to terms with social democracy in both theory and practice. The absence of North American practical experience meant that the starting point had to be in Europe. Completion of the project entailed gaining familiarity with recent European experience, especially in the Nordic and German-speaking countries. It also meant going back to the basics in the burgeoning field of economic policy analysis.

A sabbatical year was planned for 1985–6: the logical site was Stockholm. Where better to explore social democracy than in the country ruled longest by social democrats? Of course, other, more mundane, factors entered into the choice:

the availability of an office at the political science department at the University of Stockholm, an apartment at the nearby Wenner-Gren Center for visiting researchers, a place at the Rödaberg English-language public school for the 13-year-old.

Though excited at the prospect of our year abroad, nothing prepared us for the fact that we were about to commence an involvement with Sweden and the Swedes of which this book is but one manifestation. Upon our arrival, my wife, Frances Boylston, enrolled in the International Graduate School, a multidisciplinary programme in Scandinavian studies, which included intensive Swedish language instruction. I set about systematically reading about social democracy and methods of economic-policy analysis.

In our everyday lives we were living not only among but, increasingly, as Swedes. Imperceptibly our interests shifted. Canada was very far away: social democracy as abstraction gave way to social democracy as a way of life. My readings focused increasingly on Sweden, supplemented by discussions with knowledgeable Swedes. The insights Frances and I shared daily as we compared notes on what we were learning and experiencing began to find their way into a series of written reflections; though it was only months later that these emerged as themes of systematic research and writing. It goes almost without saying that the most important contributor to this book, from before its conception through every stage of research and writing, right to the proof-reading and indexing, is Frances Boylston.

In virtually every conceivable way I found myself in ideal circumstances for writing what became this book. This was largely due to the very nature of Swedish society as we were coming to understand it: its openness to the world outside it and its preoccupation with accumulating and disseminating practical knowledge. Few if any countries afford a comparably hospitable context. I discovered a vast English-language literature on the relevant aspects of Swedish society in easily accessible libraries and through various research organizations happily disposed to make their publications available to me. The Swedes I approached for interviews or materials were invariably open, courteous, immensely helpful in directing me toward the required sources of information—and spoke excellent English. Of course I also benefited from fortunate circumstances: especially the welcome accorded to me by the Stockholm University political science department which served as home base. For this and much else we are indebted to its respected chairman Olof Ruin, whose wise counsel and friendship, and that of his wife Inger, were a constant source of sustenance.

It was readily apparent that Swedish social democracy was not virgin territory: there was no shortage of knowledge nor knowledgeable persons when it came to Swedish policy and politics. It was not until the spring of 1986 that I hesitatingly began to view the information accumulated and ideas being gathered as lending themselves to a book focusing on Sweden, rather than forming part of the background material for a more general survey of social democracy and its application to Canadian experience.

The introduction of this book begins with the reasoning that induced me to tackle Swedish social democracy in and of itself. The key to understanding social democracy is to approach it as a social system, a system of complementary rational choices made by human beings through common institutions. For all the insights and information provided, neither general comparative works, nor ones that treat specific aspects of Swedish policies and politics, can get at this essential complementarity. And for reasons explored in the Introduction, such an approach was largely absent from the more general recent works on Swedish society by Swedes as well as foreigners.

The most decisive Swedish influence upon my choosing to write the book I did, and on the content that went into it, was the labour economist Gösta Rehn. My limited readings on this side of the Atlantic had already drawn my attention to the post-war Swedish economic-policy model associated with Rehn. To my happy surprise I found Gösta Rehn still very active: when not in continental Europe or North America giving papers and lecturing, he could be found—and often was by me—in his office at the Swedish Institute for Social Research at Stockholm University..

At various points along the way, Swedish colleagues and friends were kind enough to read all or part of the manuscript.

This was an invaluable service they rendered, for, however much I could go to secondary sources for my data, I needed continuously to bounce my impressions off knowledgeable Swedes. Gösta Rehn's scrutiny of my work was by far the most thorough, his suggested changes the most extensive and most valuable. His thoroughness is, in part, an expression of his personality—prototypical Swede in his practicality and unsentimentality when it comes to addressing social reality, so as to improve upon it. Moreover, Rehn is a practising economist, with an economist's less than reverent attitude toward the rhetorical flourishes those of us schooled in other social sciences have been known to affect.

Most important of course was that much of what I was writing about was the product of his efforts—along with those of his colleagues, as he always insists. For those crucial twenty post-war years he was at the very centre of economic policy making in Sweden, and, for the twenty years since, an active participant in the debate surrounding those policies both at home and abroad. The middle chapters of this book stand largely as a tribute to his ideas and achievements.

Another important influence in this early period was Bernt Carlsson, at this time serving as Swedish State Secretary for Nordic Affairs. Bernt is well known as a leading figure in international and Swedish social-democratic circles; he is also among the most knowledgeable of Swedish social-democratic intellectuals. Tomas Lundén, the director of the International Graduate School, Bengt Strieffert, secretary-general of the Nordic Association of Canadian Studies, and Darcy Thorpe of the Canadian Embassy, all of whom we came to number among our friends, were especially helpful at this early stage, sending me out in appropriate directions and helping open doors.

Not that the doors needed much opening. In the course of a year, I had useful discussions with scores of highly knowledgeable persons. In the labour movement these included Rehn's famous collaborator Rudolph Meidner and their successors at LO, Anna Hedborg, Anders Bäckström, and Dan Andersson; while in government, Lars Heikensten and Mikael Suhlman in finance, State Secretary Sverker Gustafsson and Gunnel Stenqvist in education and culture, and Hans Dahlgren and Agneta Mödig Tham in the Prime Minister's office were especially obliging. On the business side, I profited from a number of useful discussions with leading economists at policy-research centres including Gunnar Eliasson, head of IUI, Hans Soderström of SNS, Hans de Geer and Nils Elvander of FÅ Rådet, as well as Erik Lundberg, now with the SE Bank, Kurt-Staffan Giesecke, president of Trygg-Hansa Insurance and former director of the Employers' Federation (SAF), and vice president Berth Jönsson, and Karl Köhler of Volvo.

Among the many academics whose suggestions and help proved most welcome are Michele Micheletti, Björn Wittröck, Donald Lavery, Victor Pestoff, Diane Sainsbury, Sven Olsson, Anders Mellbourn, Eskil Wadensjö, Elias Berg, and Ingemar Fägerlund of Stockholm University; Agne Gustafsson, Björn Beckman, Håkan Magnussen, and Lars Lindvahl of Lund University, Pavel Pelikkan of IUI, Gudmund Hernes of the University of Oslo, Katarina Engberg of the Swedish Institute of International Affairs, Anders Bröström and Jan Lindhagen of the Arbetslivscentrum, Per Stava of the Norwegian Institute for Regional Research, Per K. Madsen of the University of Copenhagen, and Connie Wall of the Stockholm International Peace Research Institute. In my investigation of politics and parties, I benefited from discussions with opinion-researcher Hans Zetterberg, now editor of the Stockholm daily, *Svenska Dagbladet*, Elizabeth Crona, Bengt Jönsson, and Anders Jönsson, journalists at the same paper, Kevin Dome, *Financial Times'* correspondent, Christina Tallberg, social-democratic member of the Stockholm Regional Council, George Dannels, director of the Moderate Party, Olof Öhman and Margerita Töngren at Stockholm City Hall, and Annika Öhgren of the National Labour Market Board. Friends in Sweden whose contributions merit special mention are Suzanne Dansereau Forslund, Sigrid Lenntörp, Håkan Blömberg, Marsha Wåhlström, Karen von Vietinghoff, Pierre and Monique Bélanger, and Ingar Palmlund.

Extra-special thanks are in order to those Swedes who read all or large parts of the draft manuscript: Björn Beckman, Bengt Metelius, Tomas Lundén, and Olof and Inger Ruin, as well as Kevin Henley, Peter Findlay, and Arthur Milner on this side of the Atlantic. Other non-Swedes whose comments and suggestions proved helpful include Gordon Laxer, Robert Campbell, Kent Weaver, David and Pam Tucker, John Richards, Mario Iaccobacci, Ivo Duchacek, and Bryan Campbell. Lars Malmström, Maria MacMillan, Sylvia Geerts, and Ambassador Ola Ullsten at the Swedish Embassy in Ottawa were very helpful indeed, as were Lena Daun of the Swedish Institute and Henry Hardy, Anne Kitson, and Janet Moth at Oxford University Press. An earlier draft of chapter 1, published in December 1987 in *Scandinavian Political Studies*, as well as several academic papers which presented the main themes of the early chapters, drew many useful comments, which, along with those of other contributors too numerous to mention, are hereby gratefully, if anonymously, acknowledged.

The above explains how the content—for which I of course take full responsibility—found its way to the pages that follow. A word about form is also in order. Readability of text was a constant preoccupation. Every effort was made to remove unnecessary abstractions and ambiguities, to make points clearly and succinctly. There are necessarily a great many references in a work of this scope, but the number has been kept within reasonable bounds. Repetitive references have been avoided, as have most references to contemporary news reports in newspapers, magazine articles, or press services like the Swedish International Press Bureau (SIP Newsletter). Footnotes have been kept to a minimum to avoid breaking up the text.

The same consideration prevailed in the approach to quantitative data which necessarily abounds in a book about social democracy in practice. Numerical figures tend to weigh down text. Nevertheless, considerable effort was expended at maintaining the lightness of the text into which the numbers were incorporated, rather than relegating the figures to tables and graphs.

The reasoning behind this choice has to do with the synthesis of form and content. Tables and graphs break up the text, taking the reader's attention from it to the illustrated figures—thus interrupting the flow of the argument—losing the 'fit' of the parts to the whole. The central theme running through this book is that the various elements of social democracy as practised in Sweden are complementary: they make sense because they fit together. A table is selective, it excludes by its very nature; in contrast, continuing print is inclusive.

There are two tables in this book, setting out rudimentary up-to-date demographic and economic facts about Sweden and placing them in comparative context. They come right at the beginning. Armed with these figures, the reader should be able to read the chapters that follow without unwanted interruptions, assuming that the writing and content is sufficiently engaging not to lead him or her to want interrupting. If that is indeed the case, then this book is worthy of those without whose contributions it could never have written.

Montreal, April 1988

CONTENTS

Table 1. *Sweden in Comparative Perspective*[a]

	Sweden	OECD Europe[b]	Rank in OECD
Population	8,415,000	407,500,000	
Area (km²)	450,000		
Inhabitants per km² (UK = 230, US = 26)	19		
Exchange rate: UK £1.00 = 10.39 kr. US $1.00[c] = 6.35 kr.			
GDP per capita (kr.)	119,000		6[d]
GDP growth in 1987 (%)	2.8	2.5	
GDP growth 1980–7[e] (%)	113.6	114.2	
CPI 1987[e]	167	165.8	
Industrial Production[e]	115	107.7	
Life Expectancy:			
Men	74		2
Women	80		2
Infant Mortality[f]	5.9		2
Consumer goods (per 1,000 people):			
Telephones (1984)	890		1
Motor vehicles (1985)	405		7
Television sets (1983)	390		5
Paper (tonnes consumed)	232		2
Labour force participation (%, 1986)	82.0	66.1	
Unemployment (%)	2.5	11.7	
Tax rates (single earner, 1986):			
Average	62	46	
Marginal	73	62	
GNP, % distribution by use:			
Private consumption	52.0	60.0	
Public consumption	26.9	18.5	
Gross investments	19.1	20.4	
Private sector	3.5		
Public sector	3.9		
Housing	4.2		

[a] Figures given are for 1987, unless otherwise indicated.
[b] Includes all 19 Western European nations (including Turkey).
[c] To take purchasing power parities into account, we note that $1.00 worth of a representative basket of goods and services in the US cost $1.37 in Sweden.
[d] This 'OECD' average also includes US, Canada, Japan, Australia, and New Zealand. This figure is for 1985 and was calculated in US dollars, ignoring purchasing power parities.
[e] 1980 = 100.
[f] In first year per 1,000 live births.

Sources: OECD: *Employment Outlook* (1987), and *Main Economic Indicators* (1988); *Statistical Abstract of Sweden* (1988).

Table 2. *The Swedish Economy at a Glance*[a]

The Labour Market		
Total Workforce		4,421,000
Employed Men		2,256,000
Employed Women		2,081,000
(of which) Part-time[b]		
Men		134,000[c]
Women		870,000
Private Sector		2,352,000[c]
Public Sector		1,638,000
Agriculture, Forestry, and Fishing		171,000
Manufacturing and Mining		1,013,000
Construction		278,000
Wholesale and Retail Trade, etc.		606,000
Communications		310,000
Banking and Insurance		330,000
Government and Related Services		1,627,000

Imports and Exports
Total Exports 281 billion kr.
Total Imports 257 billion kr.

Major Export Markets	Exports (%)	Imports (%)
EEC	51	57.3
W. Germany	11.9	21.8
UK	10.2	9.1
Denmark	7.4	6.7
France	5.4	5.1
Norway	10.8	5.9
US	10.7	6.9
Finland	6.2	6.9
Japan	1.5	6.0

The Central Government Budget	
Revenues (%)	
Income taxes, etc.	25.5
Value added taxes	23.4
Payroll fees	17.9
Other	31.3
Deficit	1.9
Major Expenditures (%)	
Department of Social Affairs	27.4
Department of Education and Culture	13.1
Department of Defence	8.5
Department of Labour	7.0
Interest on the National Debt	15.1
Balance of Trade	+24.0 billion kr.
Balance on Current Account[d]	−4.8 billion kr.

[a] Figures given are for 1987, unless otherwise indicated.
[b] Less than 35 hours per week.
[c] 1986
[d] Equals balance of trade adjusted for net balance on services, tourism, shipping, aid to developing nations, etc.

Sources: Statistical Abstract of Sweden (1988), and OECD: *Main Economic Indicators* (1988).

ABBREVIATIONS

ABF	Workers' Educational Association (Arbetarnas Bildningsförbund).
AMS	Swedish Labour Market Board (Arbetsmarknadsstyrelsen).
AMU	Labour Market Training Board (Arbetsmarknadsutbildning).
ATP	Supplementary Pension Programme (Allmän Tilläggspension).
KF	Co-operative Union and Wholesale Society (Kooperativa Förbundet).
KFO	Co-operative Negotiations Association (Kooperationens Forhändlingsorganisation).
KTF	Federation of Salaried Local Government Employees (Kommunaltjänstemannakartellen).
LF	Federation of Swedish County Councils (Landstingsförbundet).
LO	Confederation of Swedish Trade Unions (Landsorganisationen i Sverige).
LRF	Federation of Swedish Farmers (Lantbrukarnas Riksförbund).
MBL	Law on Co-determination (Lag om Medbestämmande i Arbetslivet).
OECD	Organization for Economic Co-operation and Development.
PTK	Federation of Salaried Employees in Industry and Services (Privattjänstemannakartellen).
SACO/SR	Swedish Confederation of Professional Associations/Federation of Civil Servants (Centralorganisationen Sveriges Akedemikers Centralorganisationentatsjänstemannens Riksförbundet).

SAF	Swedish Employers' Confederation (Svenska Arbetsgivareforeningen).
SAP	Swedish Social Democratic Party (Sveriges Socialdemokratiska Arbetarepartiet).
SAV	National Agency of Government Employers (Statens Arbetsgivarverk).
SFO	Employers' Association for Companies in Joint Ownership (Arbetsgivareforeningen for Samfällt ägda Företag).
SI	Federation of Swedish Industries (Sveriges Industriförbund).
SIF	Swedish Union of Clerical and Technical Employees in Industry (Svenska Industritjänstemannaförbundet).
SIFO	Swedish Institute of Public Opinion Research (Svenska Institutet för Opinionsundersökningar).
TCO	Central Organization of Salaried Workers (Tjänstemännens Centralorganisation).
VPK	Left Party Communists (Vänsterpartiet Kommunisterna).

Introduction

Writing is a social act of communication between author and reader. I cannot help but suppose that something of the same sensibilities that led the author to write this book also led the reader to pick it up. I presume the reader would rather live in a society (and, more distantly, a world) in which everyone has enough to live decently, a contribution to make (that is, a good job), and the freedom to speak and think and live as he or she chooses. This sensibility I term—for lack of a definition that will come later—social-democratic.

The reader, presumably, is also sceptical of promised egalitarian paradises that, on examination, turn out to be sterile if not destructive, where small privileged groups rule—rather ineffectively—in the name of equality. He/she has begun to look seriously at the neo-conservative (neo-liberal in Europe) contention that equality and markets don't mix. How else to react, after all, to the democratic left's political and intellectual battering by the economic crisis this past decade: its ablest practitioners forced to admit that it knew how to distribute wealth but not how to create it; and even that modest claim undermined by critics who spied leaks in the redistributive bucket, the contents of which, in large part, found their way to others than the needy for whom they were intended?

But however telling some of these points, the reader remains unconverted to the sanctification of self-interest preached by today's apostles of the market, such as Hayek, Friedman, Nozick, Gilder, and their acolytes in Washington, London, Paris, and Bonn. Heart still on the left, the reader dutifully votes for liberal democrats in the US, Labour in the UK, and the NDP in English Canada. But the act is a passive one; illusions are gone. The 'system' gives every indication of being here to stay: after all, even social democrats in office don't establish social democracies—as post-1982 France under Mitterrand, or Spain under Gonzales, or Italy under Craxi demonstrate.

This suspicion of the 'system' sounds almost Marxist, but the reader, still impressed by the analytical skill of certain Marxists, has come to learn that, politically, Western Marxism serves primarily as a convenient means of avoiding responsibility for changing a system that one uncompromisingly rejects. When it comes to alternatives to the system they abhor, most Marxists have little idea of where they really want to go and none of how to get there; and those that do, prescribe a cure worse than the disease.

Years ago, the reader formed a positive image of life in Scandinavia; it even became a kind of unconscious model. But this too has faded: the picture of workers building a Volvo as a team after cycling to work through an unspoiled natural environment seems to have given way to one of suicidal tax evaders. Yet it is not so much the 'Scandinavian model' as the very idea of a real alternative to the 'system' that has been tarnished. The reader sympathizes with those who would be the conscience of Western society, whether in the peace movement, among Church activists, environmentalists, or other groups—and joins them, now and then, in opposing racism, nuclear arms, and acid rain—but knows that attacking corporations for putting profits before people, while true, is also entirely beside the point.

The point is that, for the time being, capitalism appears to be delivering the goods, whatever one may think of the value of much of what it produces and however unfairly it distributes it. It works because its principles correspond sufficiently to the way people act in their regular lives. A viable social system can be built only on the way people do behave—not on the way we want them to behave. Any realizable alternative to the 'system' must deliver the goods, that is, in the Western world at the end of the 1980s, foster a degree of economic growth comparable to that under American-style capitalism. Only thus can it reasonably hope to retain the requisite continuing popular support for democratic programmes of redistribution. And so, in spite of ourselves, we, reader and author, find it difficult to counter the 'common sense' dictum that nations that intervene in the marketplace to promote equality will inevitably fall behind those that do not. We end up quintessential late twentieth-century political men and women: social democrats in our hearts; neo-conservatives in our heads.

But is this the only viable choice? Can we not be social democrats in our heads too? Is a hard-headed economic justification of social democracy a contradiction in terms? In the post-recession 1980s, only the foolish or naïve are anything but sceptical of any claims to the contrary. But, armed with such scepticism, we should be all the more prepared to examine a claim that social democracy indeed delivers the goods on its merits.

In this spirit, then, we revisit social democracy in theory and—most importantly—practice. This is not a work of moral philosophy. No attempt is made to prove that social democracy is morally superior. I simply take it for granted that it is. Those who believe that human beings are ennobled by the misery and suffering of the economic struggle for 'survival of the fittest' are unlikely even to consider the arguments of a book such as this. Social democracy stands or falls on its practicability: that it can and does work.

For these purposes, however, a compilation of statistics about 'quality of life' in Sweden or anywhere else will not suffice. Statistics can be challenged, either by other statistics or by alternative analyses of historical trends. The most positive of indicators can be dismissed as partial, temporary, or exceptions that prove the rule. Statistics serve best when they back up arguments that ultimately rest or fall on their underlying logic. It is the logic that is at the base of a social system's economic stability and growth that we must comprehend. The inescapable question it poses can be phrased as follows: do the people living within a given system act in a way complementary to the logic which governs its structure, that is, does it make sense for individuals to *choose* to act in a way the system requires them to for it to work effectively? Capitalism, as practised, say, in the US—alas, many of us would say—passes this test. At the end of the Reagan era, Americans continue to largely act and think in a manner not inconsistent with the way their socio-economic system expects

Soviet-style socialism—despite the efforts of Mikhail
v—does not. In their everyday lives, as producers
ially as consumers, people in the USSR and its
~~satellites~~ are necessarily engaged in an effort to beat the
system's governing logic. Overregulation and repression are
the inevitable result.

This book poses—and answers—this question with respect
to social democracy. It argues that social democracy works as
a social system because the way people in it choose to act and
think corresponds quite adequately to the way the logic of the
system calls for them to think and act. Values and institutions
'fit'. Beginning in chapter 1 at the level of the economy, and
working through major areas of policy and belief, I try to
show that social democracy is a system of human relations—
rather than a mere package of government policies—different
in kind from both competitive capitalism and state socialism.

WHAT SOCIAL DEMOCRACY IS AND IS NOT

We can begin with a list of the principles commonly associated
with social democracy. Furness and Tilton stress six fundamental values: 'equality, freedom, democracy, solidarity,
security and efficiency' (Furness and Tilton, 1979: 38). Similarly, the six basic principles here proposed as governing human
relations in a modern social democracy are the following:

1. Economic well-being. The fruits of economic prosperity
are to be distributed fairly, and in such a way as not to
undermine that prosperity.

2. Work. Since human beings seek to live productively, fair
distribution is to be effected through decently remunerated
employment rather than simply cash or services.

3. Social solidarity. Individuals are members of communities
through ties of culture and history. Members have reciprocal
rights and obligations over and above the right of all human
beings to be treated with tolerance and compassion without
distinction as to race, sex, disability, etc.

4. Democracy. A society of justice must follow rules, without
which it degenerates into a jungle in which the 'fittest' prosper.
Democracy entails that the rules to be obeyed—by leaders

and followers alike—result from decisions made by the people themselves through free elections that fully safeguard fundamental political freedoms.

5. Participation. Especially in modern societies with complex systems of economic co-ordination, democracy entails active decentralized decision-making and employee participation in management.

6. Access to information. Democratic participation requires open and informed discussion, that is, a free and responsible press, an informed, well-educated citizenry, full public access to information based on data reliably gathered and presented, and publicly accountable independent boards of inquiry into matters of controversy.

(A final principle could be added: respect for the environment. Through creative decentralized planning, social democracy protects and enhances the natural environment as vital to human existence. Fostering the survival of the planet through aid to development and weapons reductions is an extension of this principle.[1])

The above listing is not meant to suggest that adherence to one or more of these principles is exclusive to social democrats. What the list suggests, and what the rest of this book seeks to demonstrate, is that social democracy can and does constitute a functioning social system in which these principles correspond to the way the people choose to act and live. In the present intellectual climate especially, such a demonstration hinges on—as chapter 1 is entitled—the economics of social democracy: the reconciliation of the twin goals expressed in the first principle, equality and efficiency. Yet, as the remaining chapters show, the realization of these two supposedly contradictory goals is interdependent with the realization of the

[1] Respect for the environment is treated parenthetically because it is of a somewhat different order than the others. In Sweden, environmental preservation, like armed neutrality and generous foreign aid, generally enjoys sufficient organizational and public support for it to be regarded more as an external 'given' than as integrated into the system of institutionalized trade-offs. The great 1970s debate over nuclear energy in the end served to underscore this fact, as did the determined but reasoned and largely non-partisan response to the Chernobyl disaster, which has led to a plan to rapidly phase out nuclear power. This is not to suggest that political discussion ignores environmental issues—quite the contrary, as evidenced in the 1988 election campaign—but rather that the parties and organizations largely share the same perspective. In 1988 the powerful Swedish Employers' Confederation (SAF) appointed a leading ecologist as its full-time environmental adviser.

goals expressed in the other principles. Thus to talk economics is, simultaneously, to talk attitudes and values as well as structures and policies.

At the philosophical core of social democracy is the third principle, social solidarity. A social-democratic society is constituted not of winners and losers in a competitive struggle, but of members of a community. Respecting each other, they respect their common institutions, and the rules that govern them. Rather than something external, these rules are regarded as products of the community, collectively constructed. Expectations are clear: everyone is to be treated fairly. One does not 'free ride' on personal channels of influence or access, nor abuse or steal public property.

If it stresses values, the above list leaves out programmatic goals commonly associated with the Left. The most glaring omission concerns 'ownership of the means of production'. Academics and journalists like to draw political maps on which the left is inhabited by those who scorn private property as exploitation and the right by those who prize it as the basis of human freedom. A convenient distinction, perhaps, but in fact not an especially helpful one. The same is true of workers' ownership of enterprise. Logic and experience teaches that not only private firms but also state-owned and worker-owned ones can inhibit rather than foster equality and solidarity. Finally, the rule of thumb that social democrats favour union demands also proves inadequate.

Social-democratic parties operationalize the above principles in what is here termed a 'labour programme for society'. But only under certain conditions can specific trade-union demands be expected to correspond to such a programme. The words of one especially perceptive Marxist sum up the practical consequences of reducing a labour programme to union demands: 'Defense of obsolete plants and inefficient industries for the sake of maintaining jobs has been an almost irresistible stance to the Left, with inevitable detrimental effects for economic welfare. . . . [It] has turned into a major barrier to investment that would improve productivity, increase output, raise wages, and/or reduce working time' (Przeworski, 1985: 217). Przeworski admits further that Marxism has little to contribute to a labour strategy:

Marx's economics, even its most sophisticated version, is not a helpful tool for addressing workers' distributional claims within capitalism. . . . Dreams of utopia cannot be a substitute for the struggle to make capitalism more efficient and humane. Poverty and oppression are here and they will not be alleviated by the possibility of a better future (Przeworski, 1985: 206).

A labour programme for society is diminished in his terminology to 'a struggle to make capitalism more efficient and humane': so be it. For it is indeed fundamentally at odds with the 'class politics' advocated by less perceptive Marxists. Class politics put into application results in labour's collective withdrawal from any possible share in overall responsibility for the well-being of the greater society: just as business cannot do right; labour cannot do wrong. A labour programme for society, on the contrary, entails the acknowledged assumption of that responsibility: labour is concerned not merely with equality and redistribution but with efficiency and economic growth.

In that context, equality is both absolute—in guaranteeing decent work and living conditions for all—and relative: the degree to which income and resources can be redistributed without undermining growth cannot be determined in advance. Nor is it unrelated to the level achieved by the nation's neighbours and trading partners, which itself is linked to the size and openness of its economy. But while the level of redistribution attainable at any given moment is always relative to that of comparable nations, social democracy—as opposed to liberalism, which seeks to maximize individual economic freedom while maintaining certain basic minimums of equality—never rests on its laurels with regard to equality. Perhaps the simplest definition of social democracy is that it seeks to maximize equality with the free, active, and continuing support of the population, which it can only do by maintaining growth through an efficient market for goods, capital, and labour. In the long run, such support cannot be won by a series of slogans, however well-meaning, but by demonstrable proof of success at delivering the goods.

SWEDEN AS MODEL

From this perspective, it is on its right flank that social democracy is most exposed: the capacity of an egalitarian society to achieve and maintain respectable economic growth. As the ideological spectrum of Western thought shifted to the right in the late 1970s, pushing egalitarian aspirations to the margins, the economic thinking associated with neo-conservatism came to occupy the mainstream. Any attempt at redistribution—or in fact any state 'interference' with the economy—beyond that needed to maintain order, it insists, places an added cost on the productive system, reducing efficiency. In the long run, either society will get poorer, or it will get more unequal.

If this is true, then social democracy is indeed doomed. On this question the real battle is joined, and the terrain on which attacks are launched is frequently a Scandinavian one: Sweden as self-contradiction versus Sweden as model (e.g. Shenfield, 1980; Schwartz, 1980). Yet why should we choose Sweden here? Several questions lie within this simple query. At its most superficial level, the answer is obvious: Sweden, detractors and admirers agree, is the site of the longest and fullest expression of social-democratic politics in practice. Yet why not a composite of several societies, including Norway and Austria along with Sweden, to really grasp the dynamics of social democracy?

The answer underlies our approach to the principles of social democracy, viewed not as distant ideals, but as the operational goals of a functioning social system. As a system of institutionalized relationships among individuals and groups—or institutions—linked by common values, a social system must be understood as an organic whole, its viability ultimately resting upon that link, the 'fit' between the expectations and actions of real people living out their lives in a real society. To be meaningful, an analysis must seek above all else to come to terms with the overall workings of an existing society in which social-democratic values are dominant. Relevant facts from comparable societies need to be brought in—but not at the cost of losing sight of the threads binding the social system.[2]

This said, it remains true that selecting Sweden as exemplary of social democracy necessarily gives rise to ambiguity. First, the term 'social-democratic' is intimately associated with Sweden's leading political party, the official name of which is the Social Democratic Labour Party of Sweden (SAP). Indeed the link between Sweden's historical values and the SAP, as we shall see in chapter 2, is in no sense coincidental. Though we will use the term 'solidaristic market economy' when referring to its economic relations and institutions, to invent a term other than social democracy for the system as an entity would be artificial and inappropriate. As one commentator recently put it:

Anyone who visits Sweden will quickly recognize that the influence of Social Democratic thinking extends beyond the 45 percent of the adult population who vote for the Social Democrats. To a remarkable extent, the Swedish Social Democrats have been able to define the problems on the political agenda and the terms in which these problems have been discussed by all major political parties. It is in this sense that social democracy might be described as the hegemonic force in postwar Swedish politics (Kesselman *et al.*, 1987: 529).

To dispel any possible ambiguity, it should be clearly understood that, as a social system, social democracy does not necessarily conform to programmes, policies, or even stated ideological principles of the Social Democratic Party of Sweden (or any other party going by that name) at any given time. The question is not whether Social Democrats see their programme reflected in the analysis provided here, but whether they, like others, see in it the Sweden they know. From this perspective, Sweden remained social-democratic when the Swedish Social Democrats' 'bourgeois' (a non-derogatory term in Sweden) opponents held power from 1976 to 1982, just as, say, Spain's social system was not transformed with the arrival to power of Felipe Gonzales's Socialists in the 1980s.

There is another side to the question 'why Sweden?' Since

---

[2] This approach serves to distinguish this book from other recent works (such as Heckscher, 1984, and Esping-Andersen, 1985), which compare Scandinavian experience.

almost everyone seems to be familiar with the Swedish model, what possible new light could such a piece of work shed? In fact much of what is taken as common knowledge about Sweden is partial, coloured by ideologies of the right or far left, each with its own reason for proving that a 'middle way' does not èxist. In addition, positive reports by outsiders are often of limited value. Typically, what impresses visitors is the extensive network of services, especially those provided to the weakest in society. An image is created out of a composite of such reports—in themselves not inaccurate—which is false in that it is partial, since it leaves out underlying economic trade-offs and cultural expectations.

On the other hand, home-grown Swedish observers have a tendency to assume as givens non-quantifiable values embedded into patterns of human relations that underlie Swedish social democracy. Unaware of these assumptions, outsiders generally take Swedish commentaries—especially the self-critical ones commonplace in the Swedish media—at face value, a tendency that has significantly skewed the discussion. These combined tendencies have etched out of contemporary events a stereotypical international image of Sweden.

Encountering economic problems unknown to them for a generation in the late 1970s, Swedes began to question widely held assumptions. There followed a spate of articles in the international press that took Swedish self-criticism out of its own cultural context and, often gleefully, announced the death of the Swedish model. For example, as the title of an April 1981 piece in *Forbes* put it, Sweden's middle road had led to a 'dead end'. Even after the economic troubles that gave rise to them receded, the residues of these inappropriate obituaries continued widely to affect perceptions. Ideologically grounded expectations from right and left that Sweden *should* fail (e.g. Parkin, 1971), combined with unfounded conclusions from recent experience that it *has* failed, for several years deflected observers from arriving at more appropriate conclusions.

The resilience Sweden's economy in fact demonstrated under strain justifies our turning back to the 'Swedish model' in the post-crisis 1980s. Explaining that resilience serves to enhance our understanding of social democracy as a system once we penetrate beneath the stereotype. The problems, the doubts encountered—doubts that parallel those of social democrats everywhere—and Sweden's ability to address them, make the 'Swedish model' more rather than less relevant. The final section of this Introduction suggests an explanation for that resilience and, in so doing, sets in context the argument, subject matter, and order of presentation in the chapters that follow. Before doing so, however, given the misinterpretations they have sometimes invited, a brief overview of recent Swedish economic developments within the wider international context is in order.

THE DECLINE OF THE SWEDISH MODEL

In the 1960s few doubted that Sweden was creating a prosperous society in which everyone had enough to eat, a job, and a decent place to live, and where differences in income and education were being relentlessly narrowed. This was the period of triumphant reform liberalism: continued economic progress seemed certain; ideology was coming to the end of its usefulness. Scandinavian accomplishments were regarded as impressive but not extraordinary: a signpost of things which lay a relatively short way down the road. Sweden was, as an American academic subtitled his book, 'Prototype of Modern Society' (Tomasson, 1970).

Then came the Vietnam War, the 'new left', and the end of 'the end of ideology'. In Britain, Labour intellectuals who had tended to accept Crosland's (1956) endorsement of the Swedish approach, came increasingly, after their party's defeat in 1970, to distinguish their 'socialist' goals from those of 'reformist' Scandinavians (Castles, 1978: ix). In Sweden itself demand for change grew stronger and shriller. The well-worn mechanisms of change through consensus seemed too slow. Left-wing critics (e.g. in Fry, 1979) spoke derisively of capitalism with a human face. The nuclear power issue threw a new destabilizing element into the political formula, undermining the ruling Social Democratic bloc. Moreover, governments were unusually weak by Swedish standards in this critical period. The new constitution had checked the electoral system's tendency to favour the largest party with additional seats, as well as shortened the term of office to three years. The 1973–6 parliament was split evenly down the middle between the Social-Democrat-led ruling coalition and its bourgeois opponents. And the 1976 election brought power to the latter—an inexperienced coalition far from unanimous on major policy questions—at exactly the worst moment.

Sweden's relatively poor economic performance starting in the mid-seventies was due, as one observer put it, to 'a considered and competently executed strategic miscalculation' (Scharpf, 1981: 30). Profits had soared from 1972 to 1974, after having been slowly declining for the previous decade. Labour, bolstered by a growing public-service white-collar sector, responded with high wage and fringe-benefit demands. The policy-makers—following OECD advice most other members chose to ignore—shortsightedly adopted a wage-led demand-expansion strategy in an effort to 'bridge over' the 1975 world recession which followed upon the first OPEC 'oil shock'. The timing could not have been worse. The recession lasted longer than expected and Sweden found itself priced out of a shrinking market and then plunged into recession just as the international market improved in 1979. In power in unwonted hard times, the untried bourgeois coalition lacked both the requisite social support and coherence of purpose to risk incurring public displeasure at the start of its mandate by raising taxes—as many expected the SAP to have done. Instead, the new government borrowed heavily on the international market, seriously weakening Sweden's balance-of-payments position.

The attitudes of the business community hardened in this period, emboldened by the political reverses suffered by the Social Democrats. Small businessmen especially were already smarting over the deprecation of their role in some of the labour movement rhetoric of the early 1970s, especially that surrounding the debate (recounted in chapter 5) over industrial democracy and the wage-earner funds. The climate was hardly conducive to joint action to face up to the economic problems precipitated by the second oil shock of 1978–9. The old consensus had been tarnished. Some for the first time began to question the long-term viability of their societal institutions.

In retrospect, however, it is doubtful that the soul-searching among intellectuals and the doubts of businessmen about the welfare state significantly affected popular attitudes. The SAP vote never shifted more than a few percentage points and, judging by their reported attitude toward taxes, Swedes were, if anything, less dissatisfied than before.[3] This reasonableness was demonstrated by the willingness of Swedish workers and pensioners to transfer some of their purchasing power to producing corporations when, in 1982, the new SAP government responded to Sweden's weakened international position by significantly reducing the exchange rate of the Swedish currency beyond that already effected by their predecessors.

While the confidence of the pre-OPEC days has yet to be fully restored—especially as far as small business is concerned—objectively speaking, Sweden's economic performance has regained its bearings. By the mid 1980s, profit levels had returned to those of the late 1960s. Sweden's 1987 unemployment rate stood at 2 per cent.[4] But low unemployment in itself is not a reliable indicator of economic success. Even in its worst days of crisis, Sweden's annual unemployment rate never exceeded the (1983) level of 3.5 per cent. Reacting to the recession, the bourgeois government had provided subsidies to threatened companies, primarily in steel and shipbuilding, measures previously out of keeping with Swedish practice.[5] The result was a significant and worrisome rise in the total public-sector deficit to a high of 6 per cent of GDP in 1982 with a corresponding deterioration in the external curent account balance (Ministry of Finance, 1986: 34). Critics (e.g. Örtengren, 1984) maintained that these and other

[3] In 1981, 36 per cent of Swedes found their tax burden unreasonable as compared to 41 per cent in 1968 (Hadenius, 1985).

[4] Sweden, unlike Austria, West Germany, and especially Switzerland—the only nation (aside from Norway) with a lower rate of unemployment—does not treat immigrants as 'guest workers' to be shipped home as employment possibilities decline. Moreover, Sweden has the highest labour participation rate in the Western world, primarily as a result of the fact that 70 per cent of women are employed outside the home, and it has not, like Switzerland, sought to entice women to withdraw back into the kitchen.

[5] As a rule, the subsidies were conditional on the company's restructuring its operations in an effort to conform to new market conditions.

measures they termed politically motivated, designed to disguise the unemployment rate, impeded Sweden's economic recovery.

The subsidy programmes have since been phased out. While there continues to be the high level of expenditures on 'active' labour market programmes described in detail in chapter 4, this practice began early in the 1960s. Moreover, these programmes cannot be regarded as disguised unemployment since they bring into the labour market some, such as the handicapped, who would otherwise remain outside it, and retrain many who are already employed so that they can move to expanding sectors of the economy. Disguised unemployment may be an apt term for incentives for early retirement and similar practices; but these appear, on the whole, to be less widespread in Sweden than in comparable nations (Auer, 1988).

Other basic indicators taken from the latest budget statement are, on balance, quite encouraging. Inflation is still within tolerable limits: the figure for 1985 was 5.5 per cent; in 1986 it went down to 3.3 per cent, thanks to cheap oil and the low dollar, while in 1987 it just topped 5 per cent. The consolidated public-sector deficit shrank to less than 1 per cent of GDP by 1987. It had been as high as 6 per cent of GDP in 1982. Annual economic growth from 1983 through 1987 averaged a respectable, though hardly inspiring, 2.3 per cent. Yet with industry operating at effectively full capacity, such figures correspond to an essentially sound industrial structure, one better positioned to face the next economic recession than the last one. The SAP government refused to bail out financially troubled shipyards, namely those at Uddevalla and the huge Kockums plant in Malmö, taking advantage of the desire of Volvo and SAAB-Scania respectively to step in with new plants and thus take advantage of the regions' skilled workers and economic infrastructure.

In addition, Sweden's population, which was older than that of most European nations in the 1960s, is now slightly decreasing in average age. And, with its housing stock, schools, and hospitals relatively new, Sweden's rate of increase in demand for state expenditure on services is expected to decrease until at least the year 2000 (Snickars and Axelsson,

1984). Thus, despite some belt-tightening, the new conditions forced no appreciable retreat in egalitarian policies and services. As we shall see in chapter 7, Sweden remains the Western society with the lowest levels of income inequality and the highest proportion (of GDP) of public expenditures on health and education and related programmes (Heidenheimer *et al.*, 1983; Castles, 1978:57-92). Writing early in 1988, one finds it hard to dispute that Sweden has succeeded at reconciling equitable distribution with continued economic growth.

Of course, some do. Lingering memories of the crisis and high unemployment in Europe lead some to see contradictions beneath the surface, and view as temporary the present prosperity and consensus. Economic statistics alone cannot demonstrate the underlying soundness, though they have impressed critical observers such as *Business Week* (4 Aug. 1986), *The Economist* (7 Mar. and 1 Aug. 1987), and the Brookings Institution (Bosworth and Rivlin, 1986). The Swedish economy's ability to rebound after just about everything outside its control that could go wrong did go wrong in the late 1970s certainly indicates a resilience few had anticipated only a few years earlier.

To account for this resilience is to set the 'Swedish model' against the conventional economic wisdom of the day. It is possible, it would seem, to escape the imprisonment to which we are condemned under the dictates of the laws of the 'dismal' science of economics. As we shall see, Sweden provides unrivalled public services irrespective of income and has probably the highest level of marginal taxation and lowest level of income inequality among Western nations. Its undeniable economic success makes it, in the words of *The Economist*, an 'economic paradox . . . it ought to be suffering from an acute bout of "eurosclerosis" with rigid labour markets and arthritic industry'. Indeed. Swedes should, according to prevailing economic wisdom, work, study, and train less, be more reluctant to accept positions of responsibility, and emigrate in droves to nations with low taxes and high salary differentials. Of course, in nostalgic comparison to the 'good old days', many Swedes will insist that this is all true. But in fact, as these informed foreign observers admit—shaking their heads

all the while—comparatively speaking, Swedes in fact neither
work, study, or accept responsibility less, nor emigrate more.
It shouldn't work; but it does.

THE SWEDISH PARADOX

Up-to-date statistics and common-sense observation depict a
society that has found a viable mean between equitable
distribution *and* solid economic performance. Enterprise and
innovation are successfully promoted, with the result that
Sweden's large industrial enterprises, such as Volvo, Elec-
trolux, ASEA, Saab-Scania, Ericsson, and SKF, 'win' in
the highly competitive international economic environment
(Lewis, 1986). Yet, in their relationships with the institutions
of their community, people in Sweden are treated as equals
rather than as winners and losers in a competitive jungle. This
basic attitude of solidarity is built into the many programmes
outlined in the chapters to follow, but also in observable
everyday acts. As a rule, Swedes do not try to cut corners, to
take advantage of their positions to arrange special deals, to
'free ride' on the backs of others. That this is so is bespoken
by the living environment that greets the visitor. Relatively
absent are signs of decay, crass advertising, litter, poor
workmanship, and other manifestations of the culture of the
'fast buck'.

   The research in this book was initially stimulated by a
question that repeatedly posed itself to this visitor. How did
this society keep the values governing human interaction in
these two spheres of activity, one competitive and the other
non-competitive or solidaristic, from spilling over on to the
other? As I delved further into the economics of social
democracy I discovered that posing the question this way in
fact pointed toward an explanation of Sweden's apparent
success at reconciling equality and efficiency and thus making
social democracy possible. The key lay in *the complementary
rather than contradictory relationship of the two spheres.* For Swedes, it
would appear, the very possibility of maintaining a community
where basic human relations are based on social solidarity
and not subject to the laws of the economic jungle is understood

as conditional upon the community's 'fitness' at surviving in the international economic jungle.

Conversely, the institutionalized social solidarity around them enables Swedes to feel secure and thus prepared to follow the market in the promising directions it opens up. It amounts to people deciding to respect two fundamental principles simultaneously. First, actions and policies designed to meet socially necessary goals are not to be subverted into means of furthering particular gains. Second, the market's functions of channelling capital, labour, and knowledge to where it can best contribute to the competitiveness of Swedish industry are to be fostered rather than inhibited—even when this entails a considerable concentration of economic power.

But values are not rational artefacts. In the values that govern their relations with others, people do not make fine, logical distinctions between spheres of activities. Why should one regard everyone outside one's family and circle of friends solidaristically rather than in the competitive manner a Volvo employee regards Mercedes Benz? Conversely, why should Volvo's unions not extend the solidarity principle to feather-bedding for the benefit of fellow members, or, given that neither socioeconomic position nor place in the community will be very much affected, why should its engineers not simply rest on past laurels and acquired rights? What is it about Swedish values that inhibits such spill-over?

When one poses the question this way, one realizes how little there is of use in the conventional analysis of right and left. Both, from opposite perspectives, preclude asking such a question, since neither can envisage the very possibility of complementarity. But what of the more subtle criticism which dismisses Swedish social democracy as 'culturally specific', a product of uniquely Swedish (and Norwegian) circumstances and applicable only there? In one sense, the assertion is true. Swedish-style social democracy cannot serve as a relevant model under all circumstances. One reason for looking at Sweden intensively is to identify those conditions conducive to social democracy. But while the combination of circumstances and characteristics is unique to Sweden, the specific characteristics and concrete circumstances themselves are not 'culturally specific' but the expression of developments shared to varying degrees with other societies.

The first of the relevant characteristics is to be found in the simple fact of size, the importance of which is too often neglected in comparative political analysis (Dahl, 1970). Both the Soviet Union and Iceland are independent states; we refer to Soviet or Icelandic society: but we are hardly talking about the same kinds of entities. Social democracy as analysed here has emerged only within the context of relatively small and culturally homogeneous societies. Such a society has two crucial characteristics: *one*, a single predominant national culture making possible a societal consensus over key issues, and, *two*, central to that cultural consensus, a sense of common vulnerability in the face of external forces (Katzenstein, 1985; Cameron, 1984). Together they constitute what might be termed the 'small country mentality'.

In a small, homogeneous industrial society, the value placed upon market-imposed efficiency logically enters as something both given *and* external, intrinsic to the international economic environment that no small industrial society can alter. Such a nation's long-term prosperity is conditional on the success of its enterprises in an internationally competitive market. This is an objective fact, but, more important, it can become a subjective one, an assumption rooted deep in the culture. International competitiveness based on free trade is then valued universally, but also instrumentally, as a *means* of securing those values intrinsic to the culture without spilling over and, ultimately, replacing them.[6] The expression of this small country mentality in the structures, orientations, and relationships of business organizations is the main theme of chapter 1. Starting from the idea of complementarity outlined here, the chapter develops a theory of economic relations under social democracy at both the macro and the micro levels, distinguishing those which constitute a 'solidaristic market economy' from both a traditional *laissez-faire* economy and a state-controlled one. In so doing, chapter 1 sets out the theoretical underpinnings of the policies and institutions

[6] One can readily see in the cultural consensus to achieve and maintain international competitiveness through concerted effort something analogous to the corporate culture of the large Japanese firms (Self, 1985: 122).

described in the chapters that follow. It builds on the insights of social scientists working in this field in the last twenty years by adding a link in the chain of logic tying values, institutional structures, and policy choices in a social-democratic social system.

Small size and relative cultural homogeneity are conducive to solidaristic values; their expression takes place within a particular historical setting. Chapter 2 looks directly at the origins and evolution of the values underlying the economic relations described. The latter part of the chapter goes on to assess the part played by the political process through the actions and teachings of the SAP and the other political parties in shaping these institutions and cultural values.

But values are not learned so much as lived. Chapter 3 portrays the network of ubiquitous voluntary organizations, among which the political parties constitute but one category among many, which communicate and re-enforce cultural values through their activities. The wide range of publicly oriented private activities on the part of Swedish voluntary associations are seen to constitute a kind of 'buffer zone' between the marketplace on the one side, and the state bureaucracy on the other. Membership on publicly mandated boards, agencies, and commissions by representatives of interest organizations, and the provision by those organizations themselves of important services in spheres such as housing, recreation, and adult education and retraining, are viewed as mitigating both the narrow self-interestedness of the market and the mechanistic inefficiency of bureaucratic regulation. The most important arena of interest-group co-operation, that of collective bargaining, is the focus of the latter part of the chapter.

The next two chapters set out the main features of Swedish economic institutions and policies. Chapter 4 examines the famous combination of wage solidarity and active labour market policy, the main components of Sweden's post-war strategy for full employment. The success of these policies is seen to vindicate the participation of labour and business with government in their implementation and, more profoundly, the principle of concerted participation itself. Chapter 5 looks at the two other, more controversial, aspects of the Swedish economic model, namely collective capital formation and employee participation in corporate decision-making. Both of these issues came to a head in 1982–3 over the establishment of the hotly disputed wage-earner funds, and the chapter describes the controversy, noting the contrast between the hostility toward the principle of the funds and the acceptance of their actual application. A similar point is made with regard to the contrast between the tensions raised by employee-participation (co-determination) laws and their application in an impressive series of innovations in workplace reorganization.

Chapter 6 returns to values but within a narrower policy framework, looking at Sweden's approach to the dissemination of knowledge. To that end, it sets out relevant policies in education, research and development, culture, and the mass media, stressing the role they play in making possible coherent informed democratic choice by individuals at the various levels of political and organizational decision-making consistent with the functioning of institutions described in the earlier chapters.

Chapter 7 explores the level and quality of public services. Two principles are identified as guiding Swedish social policies: the participation of representative organizations in the formation and implementation of policy, and universality. Universality means that all Swedes, whatever their position in society, have to rely on the same network of services and thus have a stake in their quality and accessibility. The chapter goes on to assess the results of Swedish social and housing policies, comparing outcomes on redistribution of wealth and level and quality of services in Sweden with those of other nations. It then considers the effects of the welfare state from the standpoint of its critics, testing for evidence of a 'dark side' of social democracy in manifestations of alienation, passivity, dependence, or the breakdown of social institutions and values.

While these global attacks are found to be baseless, the chapter concludes by examining the more serious questions posed by critics. Is the Swedish paradox viable? Can it continue to reconcile equality and efficiency? The answer turns out to be yes—for at least the time being: the pieces of the puzzle assembled in the earlier chapters fit—for now. That fit brings into one cohesive whole the six principles of social democracy: economic well-being, work, social solidarity, democracy, participation, and access to knowledge.

The conclusion restates the key elements of the social democratic system as they operate in contemporary Sweden and goes from there to consider the future prospects of social democracy in Sweden in light of recent challenges.[7] Objectively speaking, the prognosis is seen to be positive: domestic conditions favourable to social democracy are secure, though there are some clouds on the horizon. But subjectively? The complementarity at the base of the system means that in every generation the different groups must relearn how to live with compromise, and together maintain and develop the structures to bring it about. Business leaders have to live with the fact that, for all their economic importance, predominant socio-political power normally lies in the hands of representatives of labour; and labour must recurrently temper the egalitarian idealism of its most dedicated adherents with the realization that the 'exploitation' of the market economy is a precondition for economic prosperity, which is, in turn, a precondition for the maintenance of the solidarity at the base of social democracy.

The resilience of social democracy in Sweden, it is concluded, is secure as long as the key actors—and the people as a whole—continue to choose to act in accordance with its precepts. Hence, the institutions and policies to be put to the test will most likely be neither economic nor even social, but rather cultural. As long as Swedes remain active users of knowledge rather than mere consumers, it is argued, social democracy is secure in Sweden—though it has a long and hard road ahead of it in other societies with comparable economic development, but more passive consumerist cultural orientation.

---

[7] Eastern European developments at the end of the 1980s suggest that state socialism is unravelling not only in practice but as an ideal. As a consequence, social democracy may be left as the only alternative to competitive capitalism.

I

The Economics of Social Democracy

Having briefly outlined the central argument of the book, we now proceed to the key explanatory concepts. The goal is to set these arguments in a theoretical context, to construct a series of connected hypotheses describing how and explaining why social democracy succeeds when and where it does. In the end, the extent to which the application of these hypotheses stands up to examination determines whether the conceptual analysis that follows is but a series of observations connected by wishful thoughts or a viable explanation of a real social system in operation.

While various economic policies are frequently associated with it, social-democratic economics cannot be said to exist as a distinct body of literature. When it comes to modern economic systems, it is often presumed that there are only two basic types: capitalist (or 'market'), and socialist (or 'command') economies. The economic institutions and policies of states governed by social-democratic parties are treated as specific 'mixes' of those of market and command economies. When successfully applied, these hybrid economic programmes are heralded to have found a 'middle way' (Childs, 1936; 1985). Yet even those who portray social-democratic programmes in such sympathetic terms implicitly concede that they are *ad hoc* in nature, lacking an intrinsic economic logic of their own. As such, they invariably find themselves on the defensive, attacked—as noted in the Introduction—by critics of the right and far left, both of whom—for their own reasons—see such middle ground as inherently unstable.

But what if developed social-democratic economies, rather than consisting merely of a mix of state planning and market capitalism, in fact operate according to an economic logic of their own? In the Introduction we suggested a link between the resilience of the Swedish economy and the complementarity of its social and economic institutions. In this chapter we return to this fundamental idea, first proceeding through the relevant literature in the developing field of comparative political economy to further refine our analytical framework. To begin, we take a short detour out of economics to an approach that emerged in the 1960s when European social scientists, dissatisfied with the 'pluralist' framework that dominated American political sociology, began to develop an alternative.

CORPORATISM AND SOCIAL DEMOCRACY

Basing his work on Norwegian experience, Stein Rokkan argued that interest organizations in Europe, rather than competing for the favours of a 'neutral' elected government as the 'pluralist' framework assumed, more typically co-operated among themselves and were incorporated by government directly into the decision-making process (Rokkan, 1966). By the latter 1970s, a burgeoning literature had built such insights into a sophisticated theoretical framework commonly termed 'corporatist'. In the process it developed a multi-level analytical framework based on an 'ideal type', with corporatist social systems on one end of a continuum, and pluralist ones on the other (Jordan, 1984). Societies such as Austria, Norway, and Sweden are generally regarded as on the corporatist end of the continuum (Lehmbruch, 1984). A corporatist society, simply defined, is one in which policy is the outcome not of competing interests mediated by the state, but of 'concertation' (Goldthorpe, 1984), a 'social partnership' between 'peak' or encompassing representative organizations (Schmitter, 1981). A fruitful application of these ideas to Norway and Denmark in particular around the term 'the negotiated economy' is to be found in the work of Hernes and his collaborators (Nielson and Pedersen, 1988).

The term 'corporatist' is, unfortunately, reminiscent of anti-democratic pre-war ideologies. (It is probably why some writers prefer the term 'neo-corporatist', a cumbersome practice we shall not take up here.) Moreover, Marxist-inclined critics have seized on this connection by insisting on viewing concertation primarily in light of the social control function performed by organizational élites over the membership (Offe, 1981; Panitch, 1981), especially in the labour movement. Thus certain defenders of these very same arrangements in social-democratic countries reject the term 'corporatist' *per se*, preferring often less accessible terminology which lays stress on the active role of mass organizations, such as 'historic compromise—[and] distribution of power resources—between classes' (Korpi, 1978; 1980), or 'political unionism' (Higgins, 1985), or which, in Esping-Andersen's (1985) less happy terminology, attributes the success of the Swedish Social Democratic party to its ability to 'reproduce the social-democratic class base'.[1] Yet despite these terminological shortcomings, much progress has been made, resulting mainly from the changed context. In continental Europe the uto-pianism of left-wing intellectuals of an earlier decade has given way to a practicality and pragmatism that has, by and large, paved the way for fruitful advances in political economy whether the adopted framework is termed corporatist or something else. As they have developed, corporatist ideas have crossed beyond the boundaries of academic social science to enter the standard framework of economic policy analysis. The OECD, perhaps the most important arbiter among the varying approaches to comparative public policy analysis in the industrialized nations, describes the framework for 'structural adaptation' which 'pervades much of [the OECD's] work' as '"positive adjustment policies" . . . shorthand for an economic policy approach that enhances a country's ability to adapt to change by moving its economic resources out of declining industries, occupations, and areas into new ones so as to remain competitive and productive . . .'. The OECD's corporatist orientation could hardly be more explicit, as it continues: 'It implies also a high degree of social consensus between the social partners and in the society more generally.'[2]

Partly because of the generosity of research institutions associated with the OECD and member states, there is significant ongoing effort to identify the relationship between

[1] Esping-Andersen nobly seeks to defend Scandinavian social democracy against Marxist attacks; unfortunately, he fights the battle largely on their barely accessible linguistic terrain.

[2] The quote is from the standard (undated) OECD introductory brochure.

the degree of such corporatist social consensus in societies and their economic performance. Their work serves to explode the assumption of neo-conservatives of a necessary contradiction between equality and efficiency: 'increases in the size of public sectors, expanding welfare state programs, lower income inequality or higher potentials for political and organizational penetration into markets . . . [are not] negatively associated with product and productivity growth' (Korpi, 1985a: 34). Indeed, as one observer summed up the evidence: 'a consensual political structure and practices of a corporatist mode of interest intermediation and conflict regulation leads to a more reasonable economic performance' (Keman, 1984: 166).

But just exactly what is meant by economic performance? Corporatist accommodation has been found to be clearly linked to high levels of employment (e.g. Cameron, 1984), but bringing in other measures blurs the picture. For example, in ranking Austria, France, Italy, Sweden, Switzerland, the UK, the US, and West Germany on the basis of their record in price stability, economic growth, and employment in the 1970s, Scharpf (1981: 7) found an 'extremely low degree of correspondence' between these three measures of economic performance.

The other axis of the correlation also raises questions. Are there other than subjective criteria, ultimately, for locating nations on a continuum from corporatist to pluralist? Here a general consensus seems to have developed, namely to stress the role and structure of organizations operating in the labour market: the trade unions, and the business interest or trade organizations. Cameron's fivefold classification scheme, which incorporates (1) the percentage of the labour force that is unionized, (2) the degree of centralization, (3) the importance of the peak labour organizations in collective bargaining, (4) the scope of collective bargaining, and (5) the extent of worker participation in management (Cameron, 1984), is perhaps the most widely recognized. (Not surprisingly, Sweden, Austria, and Norway easily topped the other OECD nations in their composite scores.)

Like other scales, this one serves as a shorthand for the more profound aspects of corporatist relations, not only in so far as labour–business–government relations are concerned, but also with regard to other characteristics of corporatist systems, notably the political strength of labour parties and the extent to which the economy is a small and open one (Muller, 1986). Cameron points out that the empirical result of applying his framework is nearly identical to that attained when one uses the more subjective methodology of Schmitter and his associates. In this he provides added grounds for concluding that economic co-operation between business and labour helps explain the capacity of certain more egalitarian societies to be economically efficient at least in so far as employment creation is concerned.

This simple corporatist contention, however, runs smack into a sophisticated restatement of neo-classical economic ideas based on a 'public-choice' analysis of organizational behaviour. A main tenet of public-choice theory is that regulations based on free co-operative behaviour are inherently unstable since actors come to learn that their interest is best served by 'free riding', that is, deriving benefits from the regulated restrictions on what others are allocated but then violating those restrictions themselves. Applying public-choice theory to interest group behaviour, Mancur Olson Jr. cogently argues that the existence of powerful institutionalized interest organizations will bring economic decline through 'institutional sclerosis', that is the forming of distributional coalitions in the form of combinations or cartels or through special-interest lobbies that shield members of these organizations from the exigencies of the market. The result is a decline in innovation, mobility, and, sooner or later, economic performance (Olson, 1982). Smaller countries, plus those that have not experienced the cleansing effect of military defeat, are especially susceptible to institutional sclerosis.

Applied to co-operative economic behaviour at the micro level, the logic goes as follows: 'Suppose we are talking about a labor union, the members of which earn wages that are in the aggregate one percent of the national income of the country in question. If they get one percent of the benefits of their action and bear the whole costs of their action, then it will pay them to try to make the society more efficient and prosperous only if . . . the cost–benefit ratio is better than a hundred to one.' Hence the conclusion:

Both cartelization and lobbying to get a larger percentage of the national output, will, in general, make the society less efficient and productive. . . . The special-interest group's members . . . get the whole of the increase in the size of their slice of the pie but they will bear only one percent of the losses from the shrinkage of the pie. It pays our hypothetical special-interest group to seek to redistribute income to its own members even if this reduces the national income by up to 100 times the amount redistributed. (Olson, 1983: 11–14.)

Yet despite the currency of the term 'Eurosclerosis', Olson recognizes the fact that in certain European countries 'cartelization' has not had the expected results. Responding to his critics, he points to the other side of his argument: 'suppose, by contrast, that an organization for collective action encompasses half of the income-earning capacity of a country. If that organization uses some of its resources to make the country in which its constituents live more efficient and prosperous, the constituents of the organization will get, on the average, one-half of the increase in the national income. Thus such an organization has some incentive to strive to make the country more prosperous' (Olson, 1986: 72).

Like the corporatists, Olson identifies Austria, Sweden, and Norway as countries with such 'encompassing' organizations. The experience in these countries thus becomes common ground for fruitful research to test the assertions of both practitioners and critics of corporatist analysis. Research in this vein has analysed the relationship between economic performance and the degree to which trade unions are encompassing organizations, correlating various measures of economic performance with the percentage of the potentially organizable in labour unions and the degree of centralization of trade-union structures (e.g. Lange and Garrett, 1985). This relationship is clearest, notes a leading researcher, when there are large, labour-oriented, social-democratic parties continuously in or near power able to play their part in implementing what he terms the 'neo-corporatist strategy for economic growth' (Paloheimo, 1986: 8). It is not the only path, however: the alternative 'laissez-faire strategy for economic growth' also appears to succeed, he finds, as Olson asserts it should, in countries with more right-wing parties in office and 'where there are weak and fragmented trade unions'

(Paloheimo, 1986: 8). This body of literature gives rise to the notion of a 'U-shaped curve' for economic growth on the one side of which is the corporatist model and on the other the neo-conservative one, each achieving respectable economic performance but through diametrically opposite means. And at the bottom of the curve are those societies caught in the middle, like Britain with its powerful but fragmented labour movement, structurally impeded from successfully implementing either strategy.

By pursuing the neo-corporatist strategy for economic growth, the social democratic system emerges not as a middle way but as a kind of polar opposite to a system based on the *laissez-faire* strategy. But does such a dual, 'U-shaped' approach reconcile both corporatist and public-choice approaches and thus meet Olson's objections? Only in the short term, he, in effect, responds, insisting that the encompassing interest organizations at the base of the functioning of the corporatist strategy are inherently unstable.

Branch organizations of an encompassing neo-corporatist business or labor organization have an incentive to push for the interest of their own branch, even when this is not in the interests of the members of the encompassing organization as a whole. . . . In the long run the members of these relatively encompassing parts of the neo-corporatist organization will suffer in comparison with the members of units that are less encompassing. . . . Subsets of members that would gain from monopolizing a particular market, or from special-interest legislation for that market, may be able, if 'selective incentives' can be found, to organize a caucus or lobby *within* a neo-corporatist organization to pressure it to serve the sectional interest at the expense of the encompassing interest. . . . In the very long run, how could a society prevent subsets of members of the neo-corporatist organization with a legal monopoly of representation from being controlled in large part by internal lobbies working on behalf of internal sub-groups? (Olson, 1986: 77-9.)

And in case anyone missed the implications of his argument, Olson concludes this essay by citing 'observers on the Swedish scene who point to events that would appear to be consistent with the theoretical logic I have just set out'. In the same year, in a long article, Olson recapitulated and restated his argument, directly challenging the corporatist analysts, concluding that 'the long-run dynamics of neo-corporatist organizations are likely to lead to anti-social developments' (1986a: 165). In the pages that follow, the opposing theoretical case is made—also with an eye on the contemporary Swedish scene. By extrapolating from our understanding of the role and functioning of the 'neo-corporatist organizations' in the Swedish social system we shall be attempting to complete the corporatist explanation of social democracy, by adding a necessary missing dimension.

Sweden thus again serves as a battleground for divergent analyses. But the battle here is not the broad ideological contest addressed in the Introduction. Even to one sceptical of the validity of public-choice abstract reasoning, Olson's critique serves a useful foil in that it places the debate on appropriate terrain. It does not degenerate into the 'new totalitarian' (Huntford, 1971) tautology which asserts in effect that only an enslaved people chooses to act in a co-operative and socially responsible manner. If the Swedish system is to degenerate, as Olson expects it will due to the inherent instability of encompassing organizations, it will be in the direction of less rather than more control. Unlike those who see in the very success of the Swedish approach an unacceptable new totalitarianism, Olson would not quarrel with our presumption, as stated in the Introduction, that if social democracy proves able to maintain levels of economic performance in the same range as the more successful competitive capitalist systems, then its egalitarian accomplishments, spelled out in later chapters, make it worth seeking to understand and, where possible, emulate.

In the Introduction we maintained that Swedish social-democratic institutions proved resilient under the most severe of economic tests. Substantiating this assertion in itself, however, does not disprove the contention that equality is doomed to founder on the shoals of inefficiency. Required is an analytical model of the economics of social democracy that explains the actions and strategies of the encompassing organizations whose continued acceptance of their role and ability to play it is at the core of the corporatist explanation.

Corporatist theory, reduced to its bare essentials, is based on the notion of a macroeconomic social contract in which labour keeps down money-wage increases and collaborates on industrial adjustment in return for a 'social wage' in the form of redistributive social and full-employment policies (e.g. Kuttner, 1984: 138–68; Marks, 1986). The additional burden that the social wage places on firms is more than balanced by pay-offs in the form of greater price stability, fewer work disruptions, and a greater openness to new technology. As one corporatist writer put it: 'Labour, interested in wages, working conditions, social security, and to a lesser extent, participatory democracy, is forced to take account of inflation, productivity, and the need for investment; employers, interested in profit, productivity, and investment are forced to take account of social policy' (Wilensky, 1976: 53).

The problem with such formulations is that they create the impression that everything is resolved within a small group at the highest 'macro' levels, neglecting the requisite supporting activities at the 'micro' level of day-to-day organizational life. Left at the macro level, the corporatist explanation seems simply to assume a basic social stability.[3] As long as prevailing conditions do not change, each actor can be expected to continue to act responsibly, in an accommodating fashion. However, if a destabilizing element is introduced which undermines the confidence in macro-level pay-offs—such as the government miscalculating trends in setting fiscal or monetary policies, as took place in Sweden in 1976—we are left uncertain as to why it is that actors should not take to pursuing their own immediate micro interests through, for instance, wildcat strikes and local deals ('wage drift') which would set in motion a spiral that would undermine confidence in the macro-level partnership.

Unless there are perceptible micro-level gains worth defending for employers and employees operating within the system of expectations, inevitably, it would seem, the relentless narrowing of perspectives by micro actors predicted by Olson would set in, and the complex network of encompassing organizations, agreements, institutions, and policies that are at the base of the workings of the system would not be

---

[3] Elster (1982) posed the question as one of incentives: corporatism easily reduces into a functionalism which simply presumes actors will act in the required manner because the system requires them to.

'robust' enough to withstand the strains. For the corporatist explanation to meet the challenge posed by this school of thought, it must be able to meet it on its own—micro-economic—ground. As Hedström (1986) points out, the missing link in the corporatist approach is the logic underlying the micro-level behaviour of organizations and their members.[4]

THE ECONOMIC COST OF THE COMPETITIVE MARKET

Let us recapitulate. The corporatist framework that has come to dominate writings in comparative political economy in Europe has proven fruitful in identifying key macro-level elements in the workings of social democracy and the resilience of the Swedish economy. But it has failed to explain that resilience fully since it lacks an adequate micro-level analytical framework. For that, we return to the more mundane concerns of economists by setting the workings of the solidaristic market economy against those of an economic system that conforms more closely to the classical economic model.

Classical economic analysis is built on the notion of a competitive market of independent suppliers competing among themselves to meet demand. For any given supplier, demand is necessarily uncertain since it depends on the decisions of a great many autonomous consumers. Regulations, taxes, and tariffs affect aggregate demand, but they leave fundamentally unaltered the uncertainty that confronts actual and potential suppliers of goods or services. The necessary information for market actors is provided by the price system to signal fluctuations in the demand for particular goods and services. The market rewards with increased revenues those firms best able to respond to those signals, and in Hobbesian fashion,

---

[4] Hedström suggests a conceptual approach that complements our own which is termed 'social exchange theory'. The 'system of interaction . . . has an incentive structure which resembles a "Prisoner's Dilemma". If unions and employer organizations in isolation develop their own optimal strategies, an undesired stalemate situation is likely to develop. In order to secure their own governmental position, state managers must circumvent this stalemate by transforming the political game into a co-operative one. They accomplish this by encouraging a centralized form of bargaining between unions, employer organizations and the state' (Hedström, 1986a: 21).

the classical competitive micro-economy punishes with failure those less able to do so. For markets to reach price levels that 'clear' all available products and services, firms must engage in a no-holds-barred price auction. There is no sharing of useful information; each firm uses whatever means at its disposal to get the upper hand. Moreover, the antagonism extends to relations within the firm. Like suppliers, employees are expendable if others prepared to work better or for less come along, since if one firm doesn't hire them, its competitor will.[5]

Uncertainty is the driving force, compelling actors to take risks. It requires only the rigorous enforcement of property laws to maintain this process and secure the economic blessings of a thriving free market. The only real threat comes from 'outside', political, interference in the form of state planning. The ideas of Smith, Ricardo, and their followers emerged as an attack on royal charters and other mercantilist controls. The bugbear of their twentieth-century heirs (e.g. Brennan and Buchanan, 1980) is socialist state planning.

As set against the inflexible Soviet-style command economy, in which demand is calculated by state planners, and producers are parcelled out their shares in the form of periodic quotas, the competitive market of neo-classical microeconomics wins the contest hands down (Sik, 1980). By distorting market signals, the command economy breeds hoarding, 'black' marketeering, bribery and graft, and plays into the hands of a 'nomenklatura', rewarding personal and political connections and inside information rather than efficiency. But we can conclude that the only route to efficient production and distribution is through the ravages of the competitive marketplace only if any systematic reduction of uncertainty necessarily implies direct state control over the economy. (Indeed, the reduction of uncertainty through central planning under the command economy is more apparent than real: economic decision making, despite being 'public', is carried out in a highly secretive environment in which officials at all levels hoard needed information.) Thus if these are the only

---

[5] Unions are necessarily presumed to be weak: the US, where the 80 per cent of the workforce that is unorganized check the power of the unionized fifth, is exemplary here.

choices available, we would have to accept the aggregate costs of investment errors, due to misinformation resulting from the uncertainty built into the competitive market system, as a necessary evil.

These costs are becoming more evident both to economic decision-makers and academic economists. If uncertainty is a fact of life even in the command economy, economic actors in a competitive system will go to great lengths to reduce it. Reducing uncertainty shrinks the 'information costs' of firms (see Okun, 1975). In a complex, ever-changing market, buyers and sellers have to invest time and effort to find the desired commodity or service at the best price. Long-term arrangements with suppliers and sub-contractors, as well as one's own employees[6] on the principle of trust, namely that both sides will incorporate changes in market conditions into the pricing of their product or service, reduce information costs. Generally speaking, the wider and fuller the access to reliable information among buyers and sellers of goods and labour, the lower the information costs, and the greater the overall efficiency. A similar line of reasoning explains the tendency of even non-unionized firms to retain existing employees rather than seeking 'cheaper' substitutes even in times of high unemployment. In today's technological world, where manufacturing and extraction are very capital-intensive, requiring highly specialized robots in production, and sophisticated computer-based instruments of control with highly trained operators, the costs of misallocating technological, human, and natural resources are immense.

Another applicable concept in this regard is that of transaction costs. For pedagogical purposes, we have in this chapter simplified the discussion of 'mainstream' economic thinking by limiting it to the neo-classical views of Adam Smith and his followers. In fact there is a respectable economic nationalist tradition associated with the use of tariffs, central banks, state regulation, and public enterprise to enhance economic growth which holds out a very positive view of the economic role of the state. Recently, the writings of the economic historian D. C. North have developed the theme that the state generally

[6] The successful Japanese, as a series of American best-sellers early in the 1980s revealed, are exemplary of such practices.

plays a productive rather than destructive role in the modern economy (North, 1981). In a recent essay, North points specifically to the kinds of costs that are reduced by properly functioning state institutions in modern economies. Economists, he notes, have still largely failed to incorporate this basic fact of economic life into their analysis.

The exchange process is not costless . . . the costs of transacting can be high, because there are both problems of being able to measure the attributes of what is being exchanged and problems of enforcement of the terms of exchange; and in consequence gains to be realized by engaging in cheating, shirking, opportunism, etc. . . . Resources devoted to transacting are large (although small per transaction) but the productivity associated with the gains from trade is even greater. . . . [For] individuals in highly complex interdependent situations [to] . . . be able to have confidence in their dealings with individuals of whom they have no personal knowledge . . . an ongoing exchange relationship is only possible as the result . . . of the existence of norms of behavior to constrain the parties in interaction (North 1985: 4–6).

The transaction costs entailed are directly proportional to the absence of norms constraining behaviour where uncertainty dominates economic relationships. In the competitive market economy of the neo-classical economists, each firm seeks to entice skilled workers and competent managers and technical experts away from its competitors and find cheaper unskilled workers (or machines), all in an effort to produce, market, and sell more. Precisely because such a climate breeds uncertainty at the micro level, especially in a complex society, producers are induced to seek out less 'classical' methods of competition to reduce risk by securing their market share through government contracts, special-interest legislation, subsidies, protective tariffs, and tax loopholes, not to mention the tendency to invest large proportions of revenues in short-term projects such as 'unfriendly' takeover bids of cash-rich corporations, real-estate speculation, or expensive advertising campaigns, instead of in long-term projects requiring scientific research and co-ordinated planning.[7]

   In such a situation, aggregate inefficiency is the likely

---

[7] Well over half of the money spent on advertising in the world is spent in the US.

outcome as firms are rewarded for, among other things, access to and use of 'inside information' and personal contacts, while constraining such practices raises enforcement (transaction) costs. As the stakes of failure and success rise, firms are motivated to attempt to improve their comparative position by keeping needed information from potential competitors (and thus the society at large) who then make errors in allocating resources to the advantage of the firm but at the expense of aggregate efficiency. Secrecy becomes pathological. As one student of information costs put it recently: 'our welfare, individual as well as collective, is much less than what it could be, unless we identify the invisible prisons in which the invisible hand of competition has locked a good deal of existing information (and actors holding it), and devise ways to get them out from there' (Keck, 1986: 26).

Just as the owners operate in a climate of fear of being outcompeted by rivals, so employees relate to real or potential co-workers within the firm. To look good in comparison to possible rivals, they hoard information, perhaps spread false rumours, even to the detriment of the efficient operation of their firm. Especially, as in the US, where competitive market systems provide comparatively little at the macro level in the way of a social net to 'catch' those who lose their jobs or their businesses—the additional taxation and bureaucracy entailed being viewed as unwarranted and costly outside interference— fear of failure on the labour or commodity market is especially intense. The effect of such a situation is well portrayed by Kuttner:

I recently interviewed a trade unionist from . . . General Electric. GE is a company which would just as soon be rid of unions. It has embarked on a program of rapid automation, and is shifting a good deal of human labour to its non-union plants in the South. My union friend . . . meticulously described how the union, in defense of the remaining jobs, systematically limits output. The union, he confessed, could probably improve productivity by 40 per cent without even trying. The GE situation is typical of industrial America (1984: 185).

One measurable transaction cost thus incurred is in unfair labour practice litigation. 'When the NLRA was passed, it was thought that unfair labour practices might wither away as unions and collective bargaining gained greater acceptability and as the statute clarified the rules of the game in labour–management relations. Instead, the number of unfair labour practice charges filed by unions, employers, and individual workers has doubled every decade since the late 1950s' (Flanagan, 1986: 4). Moreover, union-busting is no answer either to the insecure working environment. No greater productivity characterizes non-unionized than unionized plants in the US; the opposite is in fact probably the case (Carnoy *et al.*, 1983: 223).

Apart from its effect on the relationship among competing firms, and between firms and their employees, unnecessary uncertainty places additional costs upon firms in their interactions with those who provide them with needed services. Suppliers of services are typically in a state of insecurity, their customers providing them with a minimum of information for fear of that information getting into the wrong hands. One such service concerns written communications. Firms receive and send orders, bills, cheques, advertising circulars, and other written messages; the reliability and rapidity with which they are transmitted is crucial to their efficient operations. In the competitive market economy, in accordance with the dicta of neo-classical economics, courier companies spring up to take the lucrative business market away from the state-run mail service which is compelled to serve everyone down to the lonely rural-route dweller. The post office becomes less efficient: delivery vehicles sit idle, workers' time and energies are wasted: apathy sets in. The cost per unit of mail goes up, a cost paid in increased stamp rates, poorer service, and increased customer dissatisfaction: the classic vicious circle. Even aggregate productivity is affected by the decline in efficiency of those who must use the postal services as well as by the cost of compensating for lost post-office revenues.

If the only alternative to this situation is placing firms at the mercy of an undependable, inefficient postal service, then it might be termed a necessary evil. But that is not the case. The manner in which 'public' services are provided to 'private' industry distinguishes the solidaristic market economy. In the final section of this chapter we shall attempt to show, drawing examples from Sweden, that solidaristic market relations make economic sense since they bring down information and transaction costs to a significant degree. Furthermore, this effect is at least partially discernible to microeconomic actors in and through fostering a high level of confidence that they share with those with whom they transact both the required knowledge and appropriate norms and values to maximize the aggregate gains from their transaction. Understood in this manner, solidaristic economic relations operate at all levels, from the shop floor to that surrounding the implementation of government policies. Evidently, the solidaristic market economy is an 'ideal type' not fully corresponding with practice in Sweden from which we shall be drawing examples, just as is the case with the competitive market economy *vis-à-vis* the US from which we also drew examples.

THE SOLIDARISTIC MARKET ECONOMY

The solidaristic market economy associated with a social-democratic social system may be conceptualized as a system of economic relations that reduces uncertainty by channelling market competition to those spheres of activity where they are seen to contribute to aggregate productivity, while fostering relations of social solidarity in other spheres to complement that productivity. The first aspect of the application of this fundamental principle that naturally comes to mind is a guaranteed safety net to protect individuals from the 'excesses' of the market. A second aspect commonly associated with the economic policies of social democratic governments is the tendency to engage systematically in Keynesian-inspired efforts to stabilize aggregate demand through spending and taxing to smooth out the peaks and valleys of the business cycle. Yet these characteristics are not the most fundamental. Indeed the label 'interventionist' associated with these two aspects is more a hindrance than a help in getting at the essence of the solidaristic market economy. The term immediately raises the spectre of a command economy: state bureaucrats replacing market actors in investment decisions.

The fundamental question is of a different order: not who

makes the decisions, but what factors must they bring to bear in making them. If the context is one where immediate, narrow, short-term gain must be realized at all cost, then a market actor—even against his 'better' judgement—will make decisions in that framework. What distinguishes the solidaristic market economy is the larger context in which market decisions are made. As one long-time leading proponent and practitioner of Social Democratic economic policy in Sweden and at the OECD has repeatedly argued, the goal is not to weaken market forces but to create an appropriate environment for dynamic microeconomic market behaviour in competitive industries. It is no less than to induce the market to live up to the claims made for it and unleash its productive power to maximize human welfare (Rehn, 1984). In the schematic description below of the major characteristics of the solidaristic market economy—contrasted against those of the competitive market economy—Swedish experience serves as both inspiration and illustration. The analysis surrounding that description provides the shell of an explanatory framework to be filled in with the detailed, systematic discussion of each characteristic in the rest of the book which in turn will enable us to put the explanatory power of our analysis to the test.

As noted in the Introduction, the starting point is that a solidaristic market economy is, typically, a small and (therefore) open economy. Unimpeded foreign competition (outside of agricultural and defence-oriented production) makes it impossible to 'corner' the domestic market: like tariffs, subsidies to inefficient producers are excluded in principle and, with few exceptions, in practice. Consequently, there is noticeably less variation in working conditions, size, degree of technological development, etc. than under competitive capitalism, and a greater degree of industrial concentration.[8]

There is a cultural side to these characteristics—what we earlier termed the 'small country mentality': a widely shared understanding and consensus that continued prosperity depends on industry's being able to remain internationally competitive, a consensus expressed through the corporatist

___

[8] Fifty-seven per cent of workers in manufacturing are employed by Sweden's 40 largest manufacturing firms (Eliasson, 1986); 25 per cent by its five largest (SIND, 1987: 7).

actions and interrelations of organizations on the labour market. The evolution of Swedish values is traced in chapter 2, which emphasizes the contribution of its political parties. That exploration is broadened in chapter 3 to include the role of the major organizations and associations in what we termed the 'buffer zone'—the vital centre of social-democratic life. The wide scope of publicly oriented private activities of organizations in the buffer zone is seen to renew and reinforce those values complementary to the operations of the solidaristic market economy.

The solidity of these values is at the foundations of solidaristic market relationships and they are reinforced continuously by the experience of living out those relationships. Information and transaction costs are kept down since consumers and producers are able to rely on the system functioning as it should with no group taking a 'free ride' at the expense of another. They are assured that where the market is in force, it is only the market which rewards: that powerful organizations do not get preferential treatment due to inside information or connections, or the exercise of political pressure. In consequence, uncertainty is reduced not only on the labour market, but also in the commodity market itself. Secrecy prevails over the narrow area of design of marketable products, but collaboration on applied research and joint planning are the rule.[9]

Exchange of information through various formal and informal channels of communication reduces uncertainty. The revenues of Swedish corporations, like those of private citizens, are matters of public record. The organizational environment in which industry operates fosters a high level of informal communication. On the business side, the regular gatherings of trade associations provide forums where the various representatives meet regularly to share experiences. Similarly, on the labour side, joint organizations made up of representatives of different local branches meet regularly to compare their

---

[9] Sweden's world-famous institute of wood technology research is but one of several score collaborative research institutes (see chapter 6); on its board together sit representatives of the forestry industry, labour, and public agencies involved in the funding. Close co-operation between competing producers extends, for example, to a plan under way for Volvo and Saab to co-operate at fostering the modernization of their common suppliers.

experiences in adapting to new technology, redesigning the
working environment, and the like.

Moreover, the communication of information relevant to
firm decision-making takes place at the level of the wider
'corporatist' societal institutions through which representatives
of the interest organizations (dominated by those active in the
competitive sector of industry) are brought into relevant
aspects of decision-making in other sectors. Representatives of
labour and management sit on public boards investigating
state policies and making long-term administrative decisions in
such areas as retraining, research, education, communications,
transit, energy, environmental protection, health services, and
consumer information.

Consider again the role played by the post office in a
solidaristic as compared to a competitive market economy. As
stated in its latest (to 1989) three-year plan, the Swedish Post
Office is 'a market-oriented public utility . . . [conducting]
its operations so that business interests and the interests of
the national economy are both satisfied' (p. 2). To best serve
its clients, it needs money, and money is to be found
in profit-making enterprises. That means providing services
tailored to corporate needs as articulated at the national level
by representatives of industry on its board and users' council.
Among the services provided are the handling of companies'
internal mail and the delivery of their products. The Swedish
Post Office goes so far as to deliver the bread for a bakery
early in the morning in postal trucks that would otherwise be
sitting idle. Moreover, both individuals and firms draw
advantage from the Post Office's guarantee of overnight
delivery and the handling of bills through the 'postgiro'. The
Post Office is but one example; another closely related case is
that of the Swedish public telecommunications corporation,
Televerket, especially in its mutually beneficial collaboration
with Sweden's main telecommunications manufacturer, L. M.
Ericsson (Richardson, 1986).

In these illustrations we see the principle of complementarity
at work. *The solidaristic market economy enhances the operations of
the market by channelling them to those areas where competition has
the salutary effects claimed for it,* while concertation characterizes
the remaining sectors of the socioeconomic system, reducing

uncertainty and consequently eliminating the costs entailed by unnecessary risk. Under such conditions, another characteristic emerges: co-operative or non-profit forms of ownership and management abound in many fields of endeavour, especially in the service sector. As long as the operations of the market are facilitated by competitive energies being channelled into those activities where they respond to demand as efficiently as possible, then it matters little from the standpoint of the market whether the enterprises are owned by the shareholders, the workers, public authorities, or any combination thereof.

What does matter is the framework in which they operate: the macro-level economic arrangements based on encompassing agreements between centralized trade unions and employers' associations spelled out in the second part of chapter 3 and in chapter 4. The application of these agreements brings added flexibility by forcing uncompetitive producers out of business since they are inhibited from reducing wages, while firms are constrained from drawing skilled labour away from competitors by offering appreciably higher pay. Within the firms themselves, co-operation is encouraged by small pay differentials, and recourse to consultative mechanisms ensuring that employees are able to take part in informed decision-making, are protected against arbitrary dismissal, and benefit from work reorganization designed to make the best possible use of labour-enhancing devices.. The entire participation process (discussed in chapter 5) fosters a spirit of trust and thus informal communication among employees as well as between management and labour. Sharing the small country mentality, employees in the service sector, public and private, generally make some effort not to undercut private industry's competitiveness through inflationary wage settlements. Strikes and lockouts when they occur are widespread so that specific employers or groups of workers are not played off one against the other. Similarly, nation-wide environmental, safety, consumer, and worker-protection standards make it very difficult for firms to play off one region or industry against another or gain advantage from transferring costs to others.

Generous social support services that carry no stigma, as well as comprehensive training and retraining programmes, mobility support, and a sufficiently high and flexible level of employment in public works (described in chapters 5 and 7), enable those concerned to allow non-competitive firms to 'exit'. High taxes on private consumption, and income—but not on reinvested profits—pay for these services.

The macroeconomic benefits accruing to the successful application of these general principles take especially the form of reduced transaction costs. As pay-offs for respecting the norms surrounding economic relationships become clear, the costs of enforcing them—through tax inspectors and the like— are lowered, and the possibilities for the rational utilization of human and material resources enhanced. In following the principle that competitiveness is channelled toward industrial production and away from basic human services, information costs are reduced, since an informed, educated populace (discussed in chapter 6) means a significant reduction in uncertainty. Sweden achieves this notably through free public education at all levels, a major effort at adult education, publicly owned communications media, and heavy expenditures on libraries, museums, and popular culture. Overall, the system discourages spending on domestic mass advertising in favour of research and development.[10]

SOLIDARISTIC POLICY COMMITMENTS AND HUMAN NATURE

These then are the major aspects of solidaristic market relations in brief summary. To leave it here would be to imply that a solidaristic market economy automatically results from the existence of corporatist structures, which is not the case. Human choices make a difference: the operations of these structures must be supported by complementary policies based on appropriate commitments. The first of these is the attainment of full employment through measures designed for that purpose such as those discussed in chapters 3 to 5. The alternative 'Dutch' solution of seeking increased productivity, while effectively letting employment take care of itself and

---

[10] There are no radio or television commercials, and all but the most successful newspapers receive subsidies to lessen their dependence on advertising. (R and D spending in Sweden was at 2.5 per cent of GNP in 1987, a rise from 1.6 per cent in 1973, an exceptional record, according to the OECD—see chapter 6.)

providing a generous dole for the jobless, must be rejected. It risks giving rise to a significant category of people semi-permanently outside the labour market, the presence of which inevitably subjects institutions based on solidaristic relations to the irresistible strains foreseen by Mancur Olson.

The second policy commitment concerns the manner in which services are provided to citizens as described in chapter 7. The key principle is that they should not be marginal, that is residual, intended just for those unable to afford privately bought services; the services must rather be institutional, intended for everyone (Titmuss, 1974; Esping-Andersen and Korpi, 1987). As noted in the case of the Post Office, service delivery organizations are rendered inefficient if limited to serving those scorned by the marketplace. Similarly, the existence of an alternative network of 'élite' institutions in education, day care, training, health services, recreation, etc. places firms under irresistible pressure to make such services available, either through high pay or special arrangements, to their most highly prized staff. Such micro decisions bring macro results. For example, secondary pensions and sick benefits provided by employers, however efficient, serve to inhibit labour mobility as compared to nation-wide public plans in which all acquired benefits are fully transferable. As a general rule, the absence of universal guarantees places great strain on the underlying solidaristic market relationships, as well as inhibiting the necessary economic flexibility that fosters the movement of labour from 'sunset' to 'sunrise' industries (see chapter 4).

There is in these two policy prescriptions a presumption underlying the effective workings of the solidaristic market economy. The first is that people *want* to be productive, that is, to work. Evidently, no description of Swedish economic relations can ignore the inherited Lutheran work ethic. But attitude toward work is more than a matter of 'national character'. Sweden's most famous analyst of public opinion (and now editor of the Conservative daily, *Svenska Dagbladet*) Hans Zetterberg, surveyed attitudes toward the 'work ethic', in the US, the UK, Germany, Sweden, and Japan. As he concluded before his confrères in Montreal, 'Mainstream economists . . . talk about the price of labor and they treat wages as the one and only force driving us to work more or less hard. A very striking fact in our research, however, is that in most countries there is little immediate correlation between good pay and hard work. Majorities in every country report from their workplaces that there is little or no difference in pay between those who work hard and efficiently and those who don't. This came almost as a shock to the economists in our research teams' (Zetterberg, 1984: 4). Similarly, Ringen (1987: 10) cites a 1984 University of Michigan study which confirms that most people in all categories place the intrinsic value of work above its pecuniary rewards.

On a similar note, Robert Frank looked at the behaviour of real-estate and automobile salesmen in the US—the most competitive of occupations in the most competitive of societies—occupations requiring no teamwork and for which relative individual productivity is apparent for all to see. He found that pay differentials between the most productive and least productive among the salesmen were noticeably smaller than their difference in productivity. How did the companies manage to keep the most productive from demanding more or going elsewhere? The answer is that the productive salesmen want to be respected—but not resented—by their co-workers (Thurow, 1985). The main contention of the *In Search of Excellence* school of management (Peters and Waterman, 1982) follows similar lines. Characteristic of 'excellent' firms is not the diffidence of the Hobbesian competitive economy but rather a stimulating and rewarding working environment. Indeed, Sweden's very high labour participation rate testifies to a human desire to work once drudgery is no longer a significant factor and worker health and safety protection is secured (as elaborated in chapter 5).

To conclude, the characteristics of the solidaristic market economy presented in this chapter[11] appear to constitute the elements of a system of economic relations different in fundamental aspects from the two with which we are familiar. Though no real-life society can or does correspond exactly to the economic model described here, contemporary Sweden comes close enough to suit our purposes. Conversely, the case

[11] Another version of the argument in this chapter was published recently (Milner, 1987).

for arguing that Sweden's system of social-democratic economic relations is more than a felicitous mix of borrowed policies and favourable circumstances emerges from our conceptualization of the solidaristic market economy. Of course, our analysis is not necessarily likely to be publicly endorsed by Swedish business leaders. Owners of firms cannot but be aware of the fact that though success in business is respected in a solidaristic market economy, that respect does not legitimize business's claims to wider prerogatives as it does elsewhere. Olson's reasoning is helpful at explaining why, because they constitute a relatively small group, business leaders are more suspect with political power than representatives of a labour movement which, in Sweden, numbers a majority of adult citizens among its members. Concretely and ironically, this means that a labour government that is linked to a widely representative national labour movement can be relied upon to enforce market discipline better than ones dominated by 'bourgeois' parties more susceptible to particularistic pressures, such as that of Sweden in the late 1970s and early 1980s (Eliasson, 1984). Yet, labour spokespersons, too, are sometimes a little uncomfortable at admitting the truth of the above description since, in certain international circles, the notion that there is something shameful about labour collaborating to make enterprises more efficient is still quite alive.

The illustrations drawn from Swedish experience in this chapter will be fleshed out in detail in the pages to follow. We shall try throughout to keep in view the whole of which these details are part, to link each policy area to the workings of the solidaristic market and the values underlying it. In the Introduction we drew the connection between a social-democratic social system and small size and relative cultural homogeneity, an association reinforced by the analysis of solidaristic economic relations presented here. We also spoke of values, but only abstractly. In chapter 2 we turn again to values but concretely, set in the context of Sweden's particular path of historical development.

2

Values and Politics

The members of a society are linked together by structures: economic ones, organizing the production and distribution of needed commodities; and political ones, setting out responsibility for taking and carrying out decisions. Structures are arrangements of institutions: regularized relationships among individuals and organizations. But structures are but one side of the coin; societies are linked together by a culture, a common set of attitudes and beliefs about those relationships.

Ultimately, the question of whether structure or culture came first, or which is more important, is one of chicken and egg. They are separable only conceptually. In real life, institutions operate according to cultural values while values governing human relationships grow out of the content of the institutionalized relationships. Of course, since, at any given moment, institutions are more responsive to conscious democratic policy choices than are popular beliefs, political activists naturally look primarily toward structural change. Limiting one's perspective in this manner is short-sighted, however, since the degree to which the outcomes of structural changes live up to intentions depends on the extent to which the changes conform to underlying values.

If social democracy is not just a fine-sounding theory, or a felicitous mix of government policies, but an actual practicable social system, then it necessarily comprises *both* institutions and values. The importance of the fit between the two has already been stressed. It is why we look at a given society as an integrated whole rather than comparing partial aspects of several; and it is why this chapter, like the others, concentrates on the 'buffer zone' of participatory and voluntary activities, where, so to speak, institutions and values meet. It explains why, in the end, our prognosis is positive for social democracy in Sweden, but not necessarily elsewhere.

We have so far laid the theoretical groundwork in conceptualizing the main principles guiding economic activities in a social-democratic society. If we are right in contending that Sweden has managed to transcend the supposed contradiction between economic efficiency and social equality because of the fit between these principles and the workings of its social institutions, then the next step is to delve into the origins and evolution of its underlying values as a society. Just as we contend that the workings of its institutions complement and foster social democratic values, so its values must complement and foster social-democratic institutions.

The interrelationship, evidently, is a historical one: the institutions of one epoch shaping the values of the next, and vice versa. Moreover, a historical perspective allows us to distinguish the lasting from the ephemeral. Values especially are best understood in historical context, being less tangible than institutions. Only history separates the deep-seated belief from the passing fad. This chapter looks at the dominant values of Swedish society as they have evolved through emerging political structures and institutions into the social-democratic era. It combines elements of two divergent explanations of contemporary Swedish social democracy: one emphasizes Nordic values as they have developed over many centuries; the other stresses social-democratic principles and practices espoused in this century. Typically, Swedish observers sympathetic to the Social Democratic party are more likely to take this second tack, though not necessarily. The social critic Jan Lindhagen, a lifelong Social Democrat, is especially hard on what he sees as his party's failure to live up to its potential, a potential so great precisely because Sweden's traditional values are conducive to social democracy.

In the pages to follow we shall attempt to identify those conducive elements in traditional Swedish values. Then we shall examine how social-democratic principles and programmes guided the evolution of Sweden's institutions during the period of rapid modernization, most often complementing rather than counteracting traditional Swedish values. Our necessarily short treatment cannot hope to do justice to Swedish traditional values. Nevertheless, the wide agreement among scholars charts an accessible terrain for our synopsis.

Once allowances are made for ideologically rooted terminological differences, such agreement becomes quite apparent. Critical observers sometimes dismiss the very notion of
fundamental Swedish values, seeing instead a society whose
attitudes are shaped by social engineers to suit policy orientations. For their part, sympathetic observers regard a
certain malleability of institutions as a value in itself. Both
formulations get at the underlying truth. Swedish culture
has continually accommodated changing objective conditions
rather than demanding loyalty to inherited abstract principles.
But Swedes have not discarded traditional patterns of behaviour; they have rather found ways to bring them into
harmony with new conditions.

Indeed, as chapter 6 will make clear, this book is as much
about the culture of social democracy as it is about its
institutions. Culture matters: attitudes, beliefs, expectations
are not merely by-products of institutions; they are the living
expression of what is most important to—and about—a social
system.

Swedish reality is accessible, identifiable. There is little
mystery, no profound contradictions, in the secular, ra-
tionalistic character of the 8.4 million inhabitants of this
homogeneous and resource-rich nation. An aggressive military
power in the seventeenth century, Sweden has lived at peace
behind stable frontiers for 200 years. (Norway peacefully
gained independence in 1905, but the evolution of Norway
has been very similar to that of Sweden and their relationship
remains a close one. Much of what will be said of Sweden
applies in varying degrees to Norway.)

Industrialization and liberal democracy came rather late,
but the changes were rapid and far reaching. For example,
universal suffrage was attained in 1918, even though ten years
earlier only a very low 9.4 per cent of the people had the
right to vote. Moreover, change usually came peacefully,
through accommodation. Sweden never experienced anything
akin to the French Revolution. At decisive moments of
confrontation, for example in 1866 with the replacement of
the four-estate assembly by a bicameral legislature, or in 1919
with the institution of the eight-hour day, receding groups
gave up their privileges voluntarily, if not gracefully, and

ascending groups moderated their demands (Gustafsson, 1985).

Moreover, public policy debate is traditionally empirical, much more a marshalling of statistics than a summoning of abstract principles. When the Swedish parliament first discussed abolishing capital punishment early in the nineteenth century, proponents and opponents, even then, concentrated on comparative deterrence statistics rather than abstract principles of just retribution or right to life. Similarly, with a few notable exceptions that prove the rule, twentieth-century debates over welfare state policies have eschewed ideology for empirical investigation and practical argumentation. When the Social Democrats first entered the government in 1920, they translated their programmatic commitment to socialization into the setting up of a party commission that studied the empirical effects of different forms of ownership of enterprise at home and abroad (Tilton, 1987).

Venerable institutions are not abolished but rather transformed to suit the new age. This scrupulously egalitarian nation has a king, but a king who—since 1971—neither rules nor reigns, serving as official greeter and presenter of awards. Sweden is a devoutly secular society in which priests are paid officials, responsible for civil registers. They conduct marriages, funerals, and other such ceremonies, and the well-maintained churches serve primarily as concert halls. Traditional holidays and ceremonies are widely observed though their religious content has all but vanished.

Understandably, thus, the historical record is one of peaceful reconciliation of differences, a tendency to compromise rather than polarize often associated with the term 'lagom'. 'Lagom' translates as 'in moderation' or 'just right': something approximating 'the golden mean'. It is a condition to be sought, both in action and in personality. The origin of the term appears to lie in the word used for a jug of beer passed among drinking men. 'To drink more than one's due from the community jug is of course unforgivable, but drinking too little is equally unsociable; it means opting out of the common spirit' (Ruth, 1985: 53). Thus *lagom* implies moderation, but it also evokes a second fundamental aspect of Swedish values, a responsibility to participate in common activities.

If the first of Swedish values might be termed practical

moderation, this second might simply be referred to as public-spiritedness, 'the proper performance of public duties' (Tomasson, 1970: 277). In pre-democratic days, public-spiritedness went hand in hand with paternalism. Appropriate behaviour was taught and closely regulated by religious and political officials whose authority was based neither on title to land nor on the divine right of the king. Feudalism was never highly developed. Especially after the defeat of the Danish overlords early in the sixteenth century, the power of the nobility was checked by that of free peasants who, unlike in much of Europe, held title to most of the land in post-medieval Sweden. The nobility, in turn, jealously guarded its prerogatives against the Crown. Only for 40 years at the turn of the seventeenth century, in the heyday of its imperial conquests, did the Swedish regime approach absolute monarchy; the attempt to restore such a regime a century later failed altogether.

The role and character of the nobility was altered during this period, the majority of its members taking their places in the state administrative and military élite (Kesselman *et al.*, 1987: 456). Though sanctioned by a puritanical religion, the legitimacy of traditional authority lay primarily—quite early on—in its claim to rational administrative efficiency based on qualifications, training, and honesty. And, though centrally co-ordinated, authority tended to be neither distant nor impersonal. For a small population scattered over a large, northern territory, local allegiances were necessarily very strong. The rural villages, were, as a rule, governed by elected councils of free peasants, who, until enclosure in the nineteenth century, jointly farmed their separate strips of land co-operatively under the watchful guidance of Church authorities. Paternalism was even more pronounced in the *bruk*, the (iron) factory villages in which the physical and spiritual needs of the villagers were the responsibility, respectively, of the owner and the priest. Public-spiritedness, as well as hard work, was expected of all, and repaid with housing, schooling, and care in sickness and old age. As in the villages, work in the *bruk* was organized along patterns of co-operation or self-help (Heckscher, 1984:23).

With agricultural mechanization, the land-holding strips

became too small and scattered to support a family; enclosure was decreed—the most important such decree enacted in 1827—but its actual implementation was left up to the village councils. Though the ensuing adjustment, which consolidated the position of the class of small farmers and forest-plot owners, was indeed very painful—and many peasants, in the end, chose emigration to America—it also in fact served to strengthen local allegiances and self-government. Moreover, public responsibility led most local councils to put aside the land closest to the towns as community property, a decision that was to significantly affect urban development in this century.

Attitudes toward education illustrate the difference between a paternalistic and an egalitarian approach to human welfare. Class distinctions, though resented, were also still widely taken to be inherent in the natural order a hundred years ago. It was widely considered inappropriate for the son of a farmer or worker to aspire to any education beyond the most rudimentary. In contemporary, social-democratic Sweden, in contrast, any impediment whatsoever to the worker's children advancing in school as far as their abilities can take them is viewed as an unacceptable stain on the social fabric. Yet this passion for equity has profound roots, pre-dating the industrialization which made possible its realization. It is, as one writer put it, an echo of a yearning deep in the Nordic soul (Andersen, 1984: 111).

While this passion led some to America in search of a land where all could be equal, others acted to democratize institutions at home, beginning with education. The educational foundations for popular participation had in fact been laid in pre-industrial Sweden in which it was the responsibility of the local priest to ensure that every man and woman acquired basic reading skills. Hence, astoundingly, Sweden approached 100 per cent reading literacy in the seventeenth century (Fägerlind and Saha, 1983: 146). By 1850, elementary schools were to be found in every village and town; every Swede was taught to write as well as read. New ideas now spread far and wide. The Folk High Schools' movement made its way from Denmark in the latter half of the century, providing access to secondary-level education to talented and ambitious young workers and peasants.

To participate voluntarily and effectively, and to be disposed toward taking a constructive approach to resolving differences and accommodating to change, requires being informed. While reading material was originally tightly controlled by Church authorities, the passion for written knowledge apparent in the enormous consumption of books and newspapers (discussed in chapter 6) is long standing (Fägerlind and Saha, 1983). Thoroughly informed individuals can reasonably hope to arrive freely at a common ground on which to rationally and peacefully resolve differences. A recent study confirms 'Sweden . . . to rank highest among nations in a desire to resolve conflicts by peaceful methods' (Hofstede, 1985).

Our third value, equity, is not synonymous with mindless levelling as right-wing critics sometimes suppose. In its present guise, equity is in contradiction with the old trappings of authority—formal dress, formal titles, chauffeured limousines, etc.—it is not, however, in contradiction with differences in knowledge and respect for expertise; indeed, it presupposes them. Equity has been termed 'the most absolute of values in Sweden' (Tomasson, 1970: 287), linking democracy as a system of institutions and processes with the product of that system, that is social justice. Equity exerts a moral imperative on public authorities to act honourably and scrupulously fairly. Attempts by political leaders or, in fact, élites in any milieu, to exercise prerogatives often regarded elsewhere as excusable 'perks' are not tolerated in Sweden (Heckscher, 1984: 153–5). Indeed, this is a crucial aspect neglected by observers with perspectives drawn from administrative behaviour elsewhere. This 'realist' approach to administrative decision-making, by stressing subjective interests, in fact produces, at least in so far as Norway is concerned, 'a systematic underestimation of the impact of the concepts of equity and justice on the operation of the political system' (March and Olsen, 1976: 218).

Public-spiritedness through participation is not of the 'populist' variety with its 'charismatic' leaders and cathartic public events of great immediacy. It is manifested rather in the steady, undramatic, and unheralded activities that allow organizations to carry out their tasks over the long haul. Swedes are not, comparatively speaking, an overly sociable people, nor are they given to public displays. They seem to derive a sense of natural well-being and fulfilment alone in a natural setting, and derive much aesthetic pleasure through home decor and design (Hancock, 1972: 4). The chapter on political socialization in a standard English-language political science textbook on Swedish politics is, appropriately enough, entitled 'the co-operative individualist' (Hancock, 1972). It seems fair to conclude that Swedes act co-operatively because they feel it is the right thing to do more than to gain social approval. Of course, they likewise expect to be treated with appropriate respect by the relevant authorities.

A fourth fundamental value is thus respect for individual autonomy. It is an error to interpret practical moderation and public-spiritedness as something akin to uniformity. Acting responsibly toward the community through participating in its structures is an individual act, freely chosen. 'Public participation has never been conceived of as something to offset the indulgence characteristic of a more private, in-dividual world. Public and political participation for many centuries has been a sign of individual activity and well-being' (Allardt, 1984: 172).

Finally, no listing of fundamental values can ignore Lutheran Sweden's dogged attachment to the work ethic: work is still regarded as a good in and of itself, intrinsic to human virtue. The extremely high labour participation rate attests to this. Indeed, the work ethic is incorporated into the Swedish approach to the welfare state. In the 1930s, Sweden led the way in creating jobs through public works projects which, in order to eliminate any possible stigma attached to 'relief work', paid the going wage. Yet it was only in 1934 that the state began to make any contribution whatsoever to unemployment insurance, and only on the condition that the compensation paid out by the unemployment insurance societies be kept low. The fundamental principle then as today was that labour market support should take the form of work rather than cash (Wadensjö, 1980). 'One hardly has an identity in Sweden without an occupation' (Tomasson, 1970: 284).

CONFRONTATION AND CONSOLIDATION

Practical moderation, public-spiritedness, equity, individu-ality, and the work ethic: these are the values that observers time and again discern among Swedes (and Scandinavians generally)—values compatible with, if not integral to, social democracy. The roots of these values are in the *bruk* and villages of pre-industrial Sweden, a society starkly different from the Sweden of today. Well ahead of most nations in literacy, parochial support for the least fortunate, and local self-government, Sweden was backward by European standards in most other ways. Though the Swedish countryside is home to some of the first factories built, Sweden lagged in overall industrial development. It was a virtual economic backwater at the threshold of the twentieth century. The end of its imperial ambitions marked by the cession of Finland to Russia in 1809 meant, in the words of the national poet Tegnér, that greatness would have to be restored from within (Gustavsson, 1986: 17). Industrial development turned out to be that mechanism.

When it did come, change was very rapid, fundamentally altering long-standing economic and social relationships. How, then, did traditional values fare under changed circumstances? Cultural values governing behaviour toward others grow out of experience in regular and continuing—that is institutionized—relationships (Douglas and Wildavsky, 1983). If the institutions do not reinforce inherited values, then those values will gradually be replaced by others which fit. As a rule, industrialization and urbanization irrevocably changed both the institutions and cultural values of societies. Sweden underwent as profound and rapid a transformation as any comparable society, yet, in this crucial period, Swedish social democracy developed institutional forms that complemented and reinforced rather than undermined inherited values.

The particular conditions under which industrialization came to Sweden help explain this process. By 1870, the preconditions for industrial expansion were in place: a network of canals and railways to transport materials, modern banks and mortgage societies, vast forests that supplied the charcoal fuel, and a literate and quite skilled labour force. Employed as high state officials rather than living on property rents, the nobility was generally predisposed toward joining forces with the emerging industrialists (Laxer, forthcoming). New

technology and increased demand spurred on by war pre-
parations opened up development potential, especially in steel
and forest products. In 1870, 72 per cent of Swedes were
engaged in activities dependent on agriculture; by 1900 the
number had fallen to one-half, while the industrial workforce
had quadrupled. The value of manufactured goods increased
twentyfold between 1870 and 1914 (Tilton, 1974: 563). In
those years its economy grew faster than any other except
those of Japan and the US; by 1914 growing exports had
practically eliminated the trade deficit, and foreign debt
declined after peaking in 1910 (Gustavsson, 1986: 293). One
important effect of the rapidity of industrialization is that
trade unions developed along mainly industrial lines, which
meant greater unity within the labour movement than in
those nations where narrow craft unions set the trend.

Despite the rapid transformation, certain traditional relationships persisted, though taking new forms. Following the *bruk*
model, the new industries sprang up less in the port cities than
in the small countryside towns; moreover, they tended to be
small and paternalistic in their attitudes toward employees.
In addition, despite the advantages of plentiful forests and
other raw materials, Swedish industry diversified into various
areas of engineering-based manufacturing quite early on, its
industrialists unwilling to be dependent on resource extraction.
Swedish inventors led the way: Gustaf Pasch invented the
safety match, Gustaf de Laval the cream separator, Lars
Magnus Ericsson the table telephone, and Sven Winquist
perfected the ball-bearing—thus laying the foundations for
major Swedish industrial corporations: Swedish Match, Alfa-
Laval, L. M. Ericsson, and SKF. Still, it was only gradually,
early in this century, that the mercantilist and protectionist
attitudes that predominated in the second half of the last
century gave way. Many of the firms of this period operated
as local monopolies: steel production continued to be strictly
controlled, while in pulp and paper and other industries the
state encouraged cartels and producers' organizations to
co-ordinate efforts at production for export. Moreover, traditional Swedish values were ever present. One study of the
men who brought Sweden into the industrial era noted that
'most of these nineteenth-century figures were strongly imbued

with noneconomic values: an addiction to hard work that was not limited to the making of profits, the necessity of team play with their colleagues, and a strong compulsion to display civic spirit' (Gustavsson, 1986: 296–7).

The Swedish pattern of modernization was thus closer to the German pattern of cartels and direct state initiatives than to that preached by Adam Smith and pursued by his nineteenth-century English followers with its emphasis on competition based on individual interest. Rather than constituting a break with the traditional emphasis on administrative rationality and co-operation, the Swedish pattern of industrialization, on the whole, served to complement them. But the Swedish pattern only partly resembled that of Germany. One difference lay in the fact that the rich iron-ore deposits lay in the far North, far from the centres of population. Moreover, Swedish enterprises were relatively small and rural-based, and the role of the state was limited by the absence of direct military and colonial expenditures. State ownership was restricted to railways, canals, large forests, and hydropower installations (Tilton, 1974). Hence the dependence on central, urban authority that accompanies industrialization on the bureaucratic model was counterbalanced by the traditions of self-help and local involvement in decision-making.

While these factors spared Sweden from some of the worst ravages of class exploitation during early industrialization, Sweden was still very much a class-bound society, and inequality was on the increase. Substantial family background and connections were required to advance economically. Under the developing conditions, Sweden's traditional values made it especially congenial to another phenomenon that appeared in the latter part of the nineteenth century: the rapid spread of the popular movements. First came the temperance societies, some still active to this day, which were largely an outgrowth of the 'Free Churches' that broke from the established Lutheran Church. These soon proved especially significant, constituting the first nation-wide organizational network operating outside the structures of traditional authority.

One concrete result of the existence of this parallel organizational network was the establishment of a number of producers' and consumers' co-operatives, culminating in the foundation in 1899 and 1905 respectively of the national consumers' and producers' co-operatives discussed in later chapters. Another was the spread of the already-mentioned folk high schools, the first of which was founded in Sweden in 1868 and of which more than a hundred were established in the following decades. In these schools, the sons of workers and farmers were able to study economics, politics, philosophy, and literature (Heckscher, 1984: 37).

The various co-operatives and popular education associations were closely linked to a growing labour movement, the two major arms of which were the Trade Union Confederation (LO) and the Social Democratic Labour Party (SAP). Founded in 1889, the Social Democratic party antedated and engineered the founding of the LO in 1898. In the paragraphs to follow we examine the role of the labour movement in both changing and reinforcing underlying social values as it faced the process of modernization. We concentrate on the SAP, leaving specific discussion of its partners in the trade-union and co-operative movements to later chapters. Nevertheless we bear in mind throughout that the labour movement cannot be reduced to any single organization. For example, the first real strike in Sweden, in Sundsvall in 1879, was organized not by a trade union nor even a political party, but rather by the temperance and Free Church movements (AIC, undated: 4).

SWEDISH LABOUR IN POLITICS

While a programmatic link can be drawn between the Social Democratic party and the Marxism of the German labour movement with its emphasis on nationalization and class antagonism, in practice the Swedish labour movement soon adopted a pragmatic style more in keeping with inherited Swedish values. In contrast with their continental comrades, SAP leaders came predominantly from working-class families and were educated in the folk high schools, fitting poorly into any sort of cosmopolitan intelligentsia.

The original (1897) SAP programme was clearly inspired by the German Social Democrats' 1891 Erfurt programme, but, unlike the latter, it specified that socialization of the means of production was to be gradual and peaceful. Yet, from the outset, the programme proved irrelevant to the day-to-day concerns of the movement, which were focused on achievable reforms. This 'revisionism' associated with the party's first leader, Hjalmar Branting, was seldom contested right from the outset, and unchallenged after the war when the left of the SAP split off to form the Communist party. Branting had, in fact, served in Parliament first as a Liberal, and during its first two decades, the SAP's main priority was its joint campaign with the Liberals to extend the suffrage.

The democratization of the political system through universal suffrage coincided with the onset of the post-war era with its economic swings. The Liberals were reduced in numbers, giving way to the Social Democrats on one side and the Agrarians and Conservatives on the other. Having participated in several short-lived governments during the 1920s, in the 1930s the SAP was faced with the real possibility of forming a government. It both moderated and laid aside its programme to concentrate on instituting measures designed to overcome unemployment and establish a comprehensive system of social security. In return for farm subsidies, the SAP won Agrarian support and was able to form a government that, before the decade was over, had instituted unemployment insurance, paid holidays, maternity benefits, and improved old-age pensions. In setting up the welfare programmes, the Social Democrats were careful to stress the value of personal responsibility, taking pains to preserve and strengthen the work ethic.

This political moderation on the part of the labour movement should not be confused with what was taking place in the plants and mills. Strikes and lockouts abounded in this period, a few turning to nasty violence. Indeed, the violence had some impact on the SAP's outlook. Leaders concluded that the strikes and lockouts that had become almost endemic were counterproductive for the labour movement. Instead, the co-operation of the rapidly growing LO was enlisted in using political power to exercise labour's responsibility to promote the expansion of Swedish industry so as to allow for a rise in the standard of living of Swedish workers. In consequence, rather than Marxist, the economic policies of the Swedish governments in the 1930s (sometimes described as Keynesian before Keynes in providing state subsidies, loans, and relief work to stimulate the economy) were fiscally cautious, wary of fostering expansion through augmented aggregate demand. They usually resorted to monetarist responses to international revaluations.

Despite its official—though much watered-down—commitment to class struggle, SAP policy and philosophy came to articulate and embody the traditional values of moderation and compromise. A system of elections based on proportional representation, which made inter-party co-operation a virtual prerequisite for majority government, contributed to this evolution. But co-operation was more than tactical. Its most accomplished practitioner, the post-war SAP Prime Minister Tage Erlander (1946–69), saw himself as heir to a legacy traced back to the founding party leader Branting, whom Erlander described as a 'convinced reformist, not only for tactical reasons—because he wanted to cooperate with radicals of the bourgeoisie—but above all because gradual reforms had to take root in the broad masses of the people and be brought about by them' (AIC, undated: 5). Branting's successor, Per Albin Hansson (1925–46), had 'questioned the class struggle, arguing that the Social Democrats were a party of the people. Hansson personally put a premium on cooperation. He stressed a policy of cooperation and mutual understanding as a means of securing a better society' (Sainsbury, 1980: 33).

In his classic, and somewhat sarcastic, treatment of the evolution of the SAP up to the 1940s, Herbert Tingsten sums up its transformation: 'Socialization has been replaced by social welfare, class conflict by "the people's home", democracy as a tactical means by democracy as the highest principle, the total conquest of power by compromise, agreement and collaboration . . .' (Tingsten, 1973: 707). The fact that the Social Democrats' vision was rooted in traditional Swedish values is manifested in Hansson's celebrated theme of the 'people's home', characterized by, as he put it in 1928: 'equality, thoughtfulness, cooperation, helpfulness . . . a breaking down of all social and economic barriers which now divide citizens . . .' (cited in Heclo and Madsen, 1987: 157).

What then of nationalization? Experience in the 1920 election and again in the 'Cossack' election of 1928 had taught that when the party sought to bring nationalization into the election campaign it served only to strengthen support for its opponents (Sainsbury, 1980: 31). The party commission that had been set up to investigate the question in 1920 met continually until its dissolution in 1935. In conformity with Swedish values, the commission ignored ideology—the expropriation of the expropriators—and got down to the practical, economic problems associated with implementing nationalization measures. 'The upshot was that nationalization came to be increasingly viewed in terms of promoting a better performance of the economy. . . . After several reprieves, the commission . . . failed to deliver a final report containing concrete proposals' (Sainsbury, 1980: 29). Its one earlier concrete proposal for nationalization, that of a state shoe factory to compete with existing firms, had been rejected by the party executive in 1931 (Tilton, 1987: 151–2).

The major architect of Sweden's Keynesian economic policy was Ernst Wigforss, who served as finance minister from 1932 to 1949. Though not himself a professional economist, Wigforss was regarded by his colleagues as a leading member of the 'Stockholm school' of economists which included Gunnar Myrdal and the future Liberal party leader Bertil Ohlin, among others. The Stockholm school originated with the turn-of-the-century economist Knut Wicksell, who was among the first to contest classical economics' assumption of an inherent equilibrium between aggregate supply and demand. Following upon Wicksell's insight, Wigforss and his colleagues anticipated Keynes, contending that the cause of depression lay not in too high wages but in too low consumption. Consequently the state had a duty to stimulate demand through an expansive fiscal policy—in no small part in the form of welfare-state programmes. Thus treating economic and social utility as complementary rather than contradictory became the cornerstone of Swedish Social Democratic thinking, a line of reasoning most advanced in the work of Gunnar Myrdal, another leading figure in the SAP. Policies embodying this principle enabled Sweden to make significant economic gains during the 1930s and to consolidate them in the post-war era. Moreover, the role of the Stockholm school economists illustrates the value placed on public participation in Sweden. Myrdal, Wigforss, Ohlin, and the others not only saw no contradiction between their academic and political activities but, on the contrary, assumed it only appropriate to channel their talents and expertise toward shaping their nation's destinies.

The sweeping SAP election victory of 1936 attested to the widespread support for its policies, inciting the employers to take a more conciliatory attitude toward the party and the LO, a willingness that culminated in the 1938 Saltsjöbaden agreement discussed in the next chapter. Wigforss fostered this development, telling employers that 'the working-class movement [and] private capitalists should cooperate to achieve their common interest—increased efficiency in production [through] detailed discusssion . . . on methods for increasing capital formation, exploiting natural resources and new technology, promoting exports, and avoiding recessions' (Tilton, 1974: 509).

Yet for all his revisionism, Wigforss was animated by a profound striving for equality. The egalitarian aspirations awakened by the labour movement had to be renewed in each generation. He feared the SAP would be tempted to rest on past laurels, and would thus see the gains of the thirties eaten away by a 'business as usual' attitude imposed by the war. Accordingly, his major concern shifted in the 1940s to labour's taking advantage of post-war prosperity to advance its egalitarian agenda. The war had showed that, notwithstanding the conventional wisdom, people would pay high taxes and still work hard. Its end, he argued, was the moment to embark on a greater and wider programme of reform, one geared not to propping up a faltering capitalist economy, as in the 1930s, but to overcoming the injustices of an expanding one. A more equitable system of taxation and comprehensive economic planning were to be the means, but change could not come only at the top, it required the active participation of the working class in the organization of production. 'Only through conscious control of the economy for increased and efficient production can resources be exploited most effectively and material prosperity increased at the fastest possible pace' (Tilton, 1979: 513).

As with any mass democratic organization, SAP policy commitments often emerged as immediate responses to political or economic pressures, and not as the logical applications of an all-knowing programme, as those sympathetic to the SAP and some even less so (e.g. Heclo and Madsen, 1987) tend to see from hindsight. Still, by any reasonable yardstick, the ideas of Wigforss and his colleagues showed an impressive internal consistency. Though convinced that production under private ownership had to be controlled through co-ordinated public planning, they also understood that market-imposed discipline was needed to moderate inflation. And rising prices were no secondary matter. Oriented toward the policy perspectives of a nation with a small and increasingly open economy, the economists of the Stockholm school understood earlier than the Keynesians the havoc that inflation could wreak on the prospects for continued prosperity in a booming economy. It was the next generation of labour economists, notably Wigforss' young collaborator on the SAP's post-war programme, Gösta Rehn, that was to elaborate a far-reaching economic philosophy based on non-inflationary growth. (See chapter 4.) Finally, in calling for workers' participation in plant decision-making, Wigforss anticipated developments a generation later. In the 1970s Social Democrats took up his insistence that workers' needs as autonomous human beings, not merely as instruments of production, be taken into consideration in the organization and planning of production.

While the 1944 SAP general programme and the 27-point Post-war Programme of Swedish labour to which it gave rise were more moderate than earlier versions, they did make reference to nationalization as a matter of state policy. The programme was therefore interpreted and attacked by political opponents as evidence of SAP radicalization. As in 1928, the attack resulted in a loss of votes for the SAP whose share declined from 53.8 per cent in 1940, to 46.7 per cent in 1944. As post-war prosperity and the Cold War were taking hold in Western Europe and North America, the SAP's electoral programme was noticeably toned down and its 1948 vote stabilized at 46.1 per cent. It was able to retain control of the legislature, but only by a narrow margin.

The party's support solidified during the 1950s and early 1960s, which, like the 1930s, may be characterized as a period of moderate but significant practical reform. This time emphasis was placed on measures affecting labour and social security, such as secondary pensions, universal access to education, and housing subsidies. As we shall see, these various programmes constituted an integrated set of policies that placed the nation's prosperity on a firm long-term footing, and distributed the gains throughout the population in the form of guaranteed employment and decent living standards. This time, unlike in the thirties, the party's programme evolved to make it more congruent with the moderation of its government's policies (Sainsbury, 1980: 162). A further radicalization linked to the theme of industrial democracy took place in the 1970s and is discussed in chapter 5 below. As we shall see, even here moderation won out—as always. As a distinguished long-time political opponent of the SAP summed it up, the Social Democrats have known 'never to move too far ahead of public opinion' (Heckscher, 1984: 51).

PARTIES, PROGRAMMES AND POLITICS

The Social Democrats' evolutionary views themselves evolved in the context of a wider political debate in which the other political formations were the chief actors. We have seen how the SAP collaborated with the Liberals to consolidate parliamentary democracy in the first two decades of this century. First coming together as a party in 1895, the *laissez-faire* oriented Liberals in 1936 joined with the Prohibitionists, adopting the name the 'People's Party', and a programme termed 'social liberalism', based on the principle, as its contemporary slogan put it, of 'social responsibility without socialism'. Under their highly respected leader, the economist Bertil Ohlin, the People's Party emerged in the 1940s as an articulate exponent of progressive liberalism and second in popular support to the SAP. Liberals' support helped legitimize many of the social reforms of the SAP. At the same time, by constituting a viable electoral alternative, their presence in the political arena had a moderating effect on the SAP.

The SAP–Agrarian coalition that prevailed through most of the 1930s was reconstituted in 1951 with the entry of Agrarians into the SAP government. It was dissolved in 1957 when the Agrarian party's fortunes fell to their lowest since it first entered Parliament in 1917, a consequence of the party's narrow identification with a declining segment of the population. Its adoption of the name 'Centre', and the ability of its new generation of leaders, Gunnar Hedlund and, after 1971, Thorbjörn Fälldin, to intelligently articulate the widespread concern about the human cost of rapid modernization and rapid urban migration, led to a revival in its fortunes in the 1960s. This culminated in the successful campaign against nuclear energy which, in 1976, attracted enough voters to bring Fälldin to power as Prime Minister heading a bourgeois coalition that finally put an end to the SAP's stranglehold.[1] Even in power as, briefly, the leading constituent in the anti-SAP parliamentary bloc, Centre remained largely outside the left–right polarization, its appeal (beyond its rural base) based more on its expressing shared sentiments than on adherence to a programme for governing. This has left it with a public image of being well meaning but somewhat vague: in the words of its 1988 election manifesto: 'the Centre party is a non-socialist party but stands apart from the other non-socialist parties in Sweden'.

On the right, the different conservative groups first united in 1905 and their party is today officially known as the Moderate Unity Party or, simply, the Moderates. While the nineteenth century Conservatives' views were largely paternalist and opposed to democratization, their twentieth-century successors rapidly came to favour liberal democracy and *laissez-faire* capitalism. This latter doctrine placed them

---

[1] Some bourgeois cabinet members are reported to have confronted the raised bayonets of armed guards in trying to get into the palace for the customary royal reception through the wrong door; they had been out of power so long (Gustavsson, 1986: 303).

squarely in opposition to the views and policies of the labour movement, as well as increasingly outside the mainstream of Swedish societal values. The electoral successes and undeniable economic achievements of SAP policies, which had brought their employer allies to the table at Saltsjöbaden in 1938— and moved the Liberals to the left—forced the Conservatives gradually to reconcile themselves to the basic tenets of the welfare state—though never abandoning their commitment to the sanctity of private property. An influential role in this transformation was played by Gunnar Heckscher, the respected political scientist, writer, and diplomat, and party leader from 1961 to 1965. Though unsuccessful in winning the party entirely over to his moderate position during his tenure in office, his legacy was incorporated into the 1969 party programme and its chosen new name.

In the wake of the rising neo-conservative tide in the Western world during the late 1970s, identified with the political careers of Margaret Thatcher and Ronald Reagan, the Moderates of the 1980s—and especially the youth wing— began to espouse ideas reminiscent of their pre-war precursors. But recent developments seem to have turned back the neo-conservative tide. The Moderates were dealt a severe electoral setback in 1985 when they failed to lead the bourgeois bloc back to power and, even more unexpectedly, were almost replaced by the moribund Liberals as the leading non-socialist party. The result was widely interpreted as a rejection of the neo-conservative rhetoric, which the party itself attempted unsuccessfully to play down as the election neared. While the Moderates, under their new leader Karl Bildt, remain the largest party in the bourgeois bloc, both they and the Liberals, led by Bengt Westerberg, lost ground in the 1988 election. According to the official Moderate programme, the party 'rejects both socialist collectivism and the individualism of classical liberalism . . . [and] defends the principle of an economy that is both liberal and social'. It is fair to say, however, that it has stressed the liberal over the social in recent years, and in so doing, according to one study (Holmberg, 1988), has moved to the right of its electorate. The Moderates' loss of an additional 3 per cent of the vote in

1988 seems to reflect this, especially on the environmental issue.

The Left Party Communists (VPK), formerly the Communist Party, is, on the whole, a negligible force in Swedish politics though the SAP has relied on the passive support of the VPK legislators to retain a parliamentary majority. Independent of the Soviet bloc, the VPK is a mini version of the early SAP, combining an electoral and parliamentary stance clearly within the mainstream political consensus with a programme resounding in nineteenth-century Marxist rhetoric. Its supporters are increasingly made up of public-sector, white-collar workers whose ideology takes a more green than red hue. Indeed, according to the polls, the VPK in 1987–8 seemed in real danger of losing enough votes to the fledgling environmentalist party to slip below the crucial 4 per cent threshold and lose its seats in the Riksdag, possibly to the environmentalists—a turn of events that would have upset the delicate balance of parliamentary forces. Undoubtedly the VPK's strong showing of almost 6 per cent in the 1988 election reflects strategic voting by a number of SAP supporters to avoid such an eventuality.

Political debate in recent years has reflected the strains between business and labour over the issue of worker participation in industry which culminated in the battle over wage-earner funds. But despite the strains, the underlying values appear to have withstood the test, and, from the vantage-point of 1988, never seem to have been truly challenged. The role played by Olof Palme, who led the SAP from 1969 to his untimely death in 1986, seems to have been a factor. In his economic views, Palme was a moderate in the tradition of his predecessors, but his 'unSwedish' argumentative debating style and fiery public personality contributed to the heightened polarization that characterized his period in office. The style of his successor, Ingvar Carlsson, is more consensual and down-to-earth, more akin to that of Erlander and Hansson.

The tragic murder of Olof Palme served to underscore for observers and Swedes alike aspects of Swedish society far more lasting and far-reaching than the personality traits of its prime minister. It was perfectly natural for a Swedish prime minister to go to the cinema with members of his family, unaccompanied

by chauffeurs, bodyguards, etc., to stand in line, take his s
and walk home afterwards. The surprise foreigners showed at
this reminded older Swedes of how foreigners were jolted to
learn that Prime Minister Per-Albin Hansson's death of a
heart attack in 1946 had occurred on a street-car returning
home from a late evening meeting.

A more profound lesson was to be derived from the non-stop
stream of visitors who, for many months afterwards, came
silently to pay their respects to Olof Palme by laying a rose
at the grave or murder site. Especially noteworthy were the
many young people, who had increasingly been regarded
as apolitical if not conservative. While Swedes' immediate
reaction was one of grief and bewilderment at such an act
(especially as the murderers' identity, and hence motivation,
remained a mystery), it gradually gave way to a renewed
though unspoken determination to preserve what Palme had
accomplished and represented, a sentiment enhanced by the
widespread and moving tributes from abroad. Yet perhaps
most of all, Swedes were surprised to discover the depth of
emotional commitment within themselves towards preserving
the institutions and values of their society. It seems to this
writer that no one who witnessed these moving events could
have failed to be impressed by the strength of this commitment,
and, therefore, by the solidity of the underlying values set out
in this chapter.

The above has provided only a glimpse of the richness of
the process surrounding the evolution of Swedish values that
took place in and around the labour movement during this
century. The social-democratic commitment to equality gave
voice to yearnings deep in the Nordic character and, through
the development of appropriate structures and policies, wove
egalitarian relationships deep into the fabric of life in modern
Sweden. Not without impassioned debate, but indeed without
armed struggle, the insistence on equity was widened into the
pursuit of equality,[2] taking its place with practical moderation,
respect for the individual, work, and, of course, public-
spiritedness, forming what we are seeing to be an integrated

[2] An exhaustive study comparing equality in the US, Japan, and Sweden (Verba
et al., 1987) finds Sweden to be far more egalitarian both in reality and in the values
of its people than not only the US but even Japan.

whole. The political side of the process is aptly summarized by Heckscher: 'The idea of the "welfare state" became generally, if not universally, accepted . . . regardless of political affiliations. . . . Critics of social security proposals were apt time and again to lose ground in the next political election. . . . In the long run the new order came to be regarded as a natural characteristic of the Scandinavian way of life' (Heckscher, 1984: 51).

POLITICAL INSTITUTIONS

Over the last hundred years, debate among the political parties surrounding the democratization of institutions has played an important political-education function integrating inherited Swedish values with modernizing structures. The most important of these institutions were the representative bodies through which politics itself takes place. The earliest were local peasant assemblies, later transformed into parish councils, which go as far back as the tenth century; provincial assemblies with the power to select the king came into being at roughly the same time. In its struggle against hereditary royal power in the middle of the fifteenth century, the aristocracy joined with representatives of the three other estates (clergy, burghers, and peasants). In these meetings lie the origins of the Swedish national parliament which came to be known as the Riksdag in the next century. The Riksdag began to meet regularly in the seventeenth century, though its position remained weak, especially during the period of royal absolutism from 1672 to 1718. The influence of the Riksdag waxed and waned over the next century until a true constitutional monarchy was established under the constitution of 1809. This constitution remained in effect until 1971, though highly significant changes took place in the interim.

In 1866, the four-estate parliament was replaced by one with two chambers. At the same time the foundations for meaningful local government were reinforced through the establishment of the county (regional) councils. The two reforms were related since members of the lower chamber came to be selected by the county councils (and the municipal councils of the four largest cities). Because of restrictions as to eligibility for service in the lower chamber, the new constitution resulted in a sharing of power between the Conservatives, representing the nobility and bourgeoisie who dominated that chamber, and the farmers who controlled the upper house. Virtually all government ministers during this period were non-partisan, that is career civil servants usually from aristocratic backgrounds (Kesselman *et al.*, 1987: 458–9). Only in 1906, after the arrival of the Liberals and polarization over the extension of the suffrage, was the first partisan cabinet formed. The culmination to this period came in 1919 when universal adult suffrage was enacted.

A system of proportional representation was adopted at the time, in part to keep the growing SAP from winning an absolute majority of seats now that workers had the right to vote. Since then, proportional representation has been an integral fact of Swedish political life. The electoral system was rendered even more strictly proportional as a result of the new constitution which came into effect in 1971. Election to the new single chamber is on the basis of party lists in each of the 28 regional constituencies together accounting for 310 of the 350 seats. The remaining 40 come from a national list used to compensate for any regional underrepresentation of a given party. (After the 1973 election produced a 'hung' parliament, this number was changed to 39, and the total number of MPs to 349.)

A similar system was set up at the county and municipal levels, the only difference lying in the threshold for representation. To be represented in the Riksdag, a political party must win 4 per cent of the popular vote nationally (or 12 per cent in a county); for regional councils the threshold is 3 per cent, while no threshold exists at the municipal level. Elections are simultaneous at all three levels and fought by the same party organizations. Recognized parties are entitled to state subsidies to cover electoral and organizational expenses.

While the above rules appear to be mere technicalities, their existence is in fact closely related to the underlying values discussed above. The electoral system facilitates and encourages co-ordinated, organized participation, both within and among the political parties. This is due first of all to the use of large regional constituencies, rather than British-style, single-member constituencies which foster parochialism among representatives and voters alike. But the link is more profound and more subtle.

Almost one-quarter of adult Swedes are members of a political party (and well over half of those are members of the SAP).[3] The mass, participatory nature of the political parties, which operate through the same structures at each of the three levels (and in quasi-governmental bodies like school boards, and certain municipal-council subcommittees, the members of which are appointed—proportionally—by the parties at the municipal level), assures a high level of co-ordination throughout the political process. Moreover, legitimate groups, such as women and young people, are assured representation far more proportional to their importance than in the Anglo-American single-member plurality-based electoral systems. As a case in point, the 32 per cent of women elected to the Riksdag in 1985 was highest among democratic nations, next only to Norway (Sainsbury, 1985), and the proportion of women members of municipal and county councils is even higher.

Interparty co-ordination is part of a wider corporatist relationship among organizations noted previously and taken up in chapter 3 in which the decentralization of political power is discussed more fully. In practice, proportional representation means that national governments require the tacit if not active co-operation of two or more parties, while rules governing the formation of municipal executive councils make multi-party administrations the rule in Swedish local government. This state of affairs goes hand in hand with a spirit of compromise and moderation and an empirical approach to resolving differences.[4] In the Riksdag, seating is by region,

[3] According to The Swedish Election Guide of 1988, published jointly by the five political parties, membership figures stood as follows: SAP 1,200,000; Centre 210,000; Moderates 140,000; Liberals 46,000; VPK 14,000. Twelve per cent of voters surveyed after the 1985 election reported having attended at least one campaign meeting.

[4] In the parliamentary system of government, the legislature's refusal to adopt cabinet policy results in the fall of the government. This principle in fact places policy-making power clearly in the hands of the cabinet which is responsible for effecting compromises in the cabinet and the bureaucracy, and in investigative commissions and legislative committees, necessary to ensure the adoption of the legislation once it reaches the floor of Parliament.

not party; electoral documentation for visiting journalists prepared jointly by the five parties. No Swede seems to find these practices odd.

Voting patterns in Sweden are extremely stable by international standards, with the total left-bloc and bourgeois-bloc vote typically fluctuating by no more than a few percentage points between elections. In the 1988 election, the Environmentalist Party first entered Parliament, winning over 5 per cent of the vote: yet the combined SAP and VPK vote held firm to its 1985 total of just under 51 per cent. Indeed, in the seven elections of the 1970s and 1980s that total never fell below 47.5 per cent. Yet such stability is far from absolute. Significant fluctuations have characterized a number of recent regional and municipal elections, and the distribution of the national vote among the three bourgeois parties has been quite unstable for many years. Between 1973 and 1988, Moderate support varied from 14.3 to 23.6 per cent, support for the Liberals from 5.9 to 14.2 per cent, and Centre party support from 12.0 to 25.1 per cent. Moreover, polls show a gradual decline in class voting: the SAP received 79 per cent of blue-collar votes in 1960 compared to only 69 in 1985. A much larger proportion of voters today (39 per cent) state that they are undecided at the beginning of an election campaign and that they split their votes, voting one way locally and another nationally (SIP newsletter, 28 Apr. 1987).

Yet in its basic contours the political constellation established before the war is very much present. We have in this chapter traced the link between the ideals of social democracy in Sweden and the values inherited from its pre-industrial past. Practical moderation, public-spiritedness, equity, individuality, and work remain at the centre of the values that guide social relations in Sweden. But paternalism gave way to egalitarianism, responsibility for social well-being coming to be assumed by the mass of the people, not the élites, a responsibility borne pre-eminently by the labour movement in and outside government.

To the outsider, there is something perplexing in the workings of the political arm of the labour movement, the Social Democratic party. With a membership of close to one in four Swedish citizens, the SAP shows little of the spontaneity one might expect from a mass party. Political careers follow traditional patterns with few if any meteoric rises or falls. Wide participation in committees, working groups, study circles, etc. is the norm, but discussion of issues, though wide, is more often low-keyed than passionate. The operative word is 'responsible': political discussion is rarely treated lightly, for rhetorical ' purposes. Talk and action are not divorced from each other. At the triennial SAP congresses which mark the culmination of a year of internal policy discussions at lower levels, the resolutions from the local party organizations are accompanied by a statement of the party executive setting out its position pro or con. The leadership's position is most often that endorsed by the congress; but even if it is not, the congress's resolution can be expected to be incorporated into SAP government policy.

There is a certain irony that a movement born as the expression of class struggle and dedicated to radical change became the prime instrument of social reconciliation through which traditional values found expression, and that a fervently egalitarian labour movement consolidated as it transformed the traditional relationships of the *bruk* and village. Yet it is this very continuity in Swedish values that helps explain the resilience of the social system. Swedish values are, comparatively speaking, 'more integrative and harmonious . . . contain few internal conflicts and inconsistencies . . .' (Tomasson, 1970: 289–90). For, indeed, what is genuine and lasting social change if not the linking of the ideal and the practicable, the past and the present, underlying values and evolving institutions?

3

Organizations and Collective Bargaining

We have chosen to view social democracy as a social system, because a system denotes a series of separate phenomena in interdependent relationships: change in one of them causes changes in the others. If we understand that interrelationship, then we can make sense of the evolution and functioning of a given social institution and in turn apply our insight into that institution to explain the workings of the social system. In chapter 2 we looked at values and how, in their operations, interactions, and realizations, Swedish political parties expressed and advanced those values. We now extend that analysis to organizations outside the political arena.

The role played by the network of interest groups and voluntary organizations in the decision-making and policy-implementation process of a society like Sweden is best characterized by the French term 'concertation' (see Catherine and Gousset, 1965), which, following Goldthorpe (1984), I anglicize for the purpose of this book. As noted in chapter 1, there is wide agreement that Sweden is an exemplary 'corporatist democracy'. Corporatist democracies are 'characterized by the interplay of strongly organized, usually centralized interest groups, especially labour, employer, and professional associations with at least a centralized or moderately centralized government obliged by law or informal arrangement to consider their advice' (Wilensky, 1976: 53).

Wilensky, like others who write within the corporatist framework, focuses on the role of economic interest organizations in the setting and implementation of national policy. We too shall be looking later in this chapter at the interplay between encompassing organizations representing labour and management in and around the process of collective bargaining. But we shall first consider the role of and interrelations between organizations generally, on the understanding that the Swedish system of collective bargaining can only be understood in the context of this wider relationship. In chapter 1 we examined the logic of concertation at the level of microeconomic strategies and understandings. We begin here with the interplay between organizational activities at all levels and the social values of Swedish social democracy.

To conceptualize the range and impact of interest-group activities, we earlier introduced the notion of a buffer zone lying between those aspects of life subject to the exigencies of the marketplace, on the one side, and those under the aegis of the state bureaucracy, on the other. From this perspective, the traditional Swedish values of social responsibility, practical moderation, individuality, and work, combined with the democratic egalitarianism of this century, are complemented by the activities of representative groups in this buffer zone. These activities constitute a web of relationships governed by the fundamental values of the society. To the extent that these organizations function well, participation in them reinforces conformity to these values, as does the dissemination of information about these activities and their results. To put it simply: satisfactory experience or knowledge of organizational participation reinforces the values of public-spiritedness and practical moderation which in turn reinforces organizational participation.

The institutional essence of social democracy is expressed in the functioning and scope of the buffer zone. It is where both the narrow self-interestedness of the market and the mechanistic inefficiency of state-bureaucratic regulation are counteracted through concertation, the articulation and operationalization of a common interest and long-term perspective. We shall argue that in Sweden the buffer zone is especially wide due to the participation by representatives of unions, business, and other interest organizations on publicly-mandated boards, agencies, and commissions, and the provision of important services to the public by the interest organizations themselves. Before looking at these relationships, however, we need to know something about numbers.

Levels of participation in representative organizations in Sweden, as in elections (Eliassen, 1981), are comparatively very high (Heckscher, 1984). In fact, as suggested above, there is a clear link between electoral and organizational participation especially at the local level. 'The development of the local government system . . . involved large groups of citizens in the social decision-making system. . . . The polling at the general election of 1982 was 91.4 percent in the parliamentary election and 90 percent in the elections to municipal councils and county councils' (A. Gustafsson, 1986: 44–5).

The various interest groups have for a long time now included a very large number of the potentially organizable. As one American observer concluded upon surveying the development of Swedish interest organizations from 1950 to 1980: 'They have organized more members, become economically more sound, if not rich, taken on a greater number of tasks; come to be large organizational structures; and developed new organizational procedures to make goal attainment more effective. On the whole, these Swedish organizations show a degree of professionalization, scope of activity, and membership diversity quite unlike their counterparts in most countries' (Micheletti, 1984: 29). The rich literature on interest groups is unequivocal in supporting such a conclusion (e.g., A. Gustafsson, 1986: 36; Elvander, 1974).

While it is difficult to measure very precisely membership participation in voluntary organizations, the conclusion of a 1977 investigation that 80 per cent of adults are members of one or more organizations may even be a bit low. Broken down, the 1977 figures provide the following portrait: one-third of Swedes have only a single affiliation, most commonly in a trade union; slightly less than one-half have two or more memberships. These figures give Sweden an average of 1.63 organizational affiliations per adult, the highest rate of organizational density in the Western world (Pestoff, 1983). According to information distributed at the 1987 SAP congress, nine of ten Swedes belong to one or more of the 150,000 local associations, two-thirds of which are members of one of the 577 nation-wide federations.

The largest single category of affiliations is the trade unions with nearly one in two Swedes being members. At the end of

1986, the blue-collar LO (Swedish Trade Union Confederation) had approximately 2,275,000 members, the white-
collar TCO 1,230,000, and the university-trained professionals'
association, SACO/SR, 290,000 members. Largely due to
TCO's growth in recent years, these combined figures constituted an increase of well over one million since 1970.

Sports clubs are in second place with over 3 million members
(Rehn and Petersen, 1980: 54) in 39,000 clubs affiliated with
one of the 58 national federations in the Swedish Sports
Confederation; consumer co-operatives (KF and Konsum)
come third with just over 2 million members. Political parties,
including their affiliated youth movements and women's
associations, rank a close fourth, and the various charitable
organizations fifth. They are followed by the National Tenants'
Association with 600,000 members, many of whom are also
member/owners of one of the 350,000 flats in co-operatives
affiliated with the HSB (the National Tenants' Associations'
Savings and Building Societies Movement). Next come the
pensioners' associations, by far the largest of which is the
PRO (Pensioners' National Organization) with over 400,000
members, closely followed by the HCK, the confederation of
25 national organizations for the various disabled groups.
Mention should also be made of the LRF, the Federation of
Swedish farmers, which unites agricultural wholesalers' and
processors' as well as producers' organizations in what has been
described as 'the most encompassing of interest organizations in
Sweden' (Micheletti, 1987).

As the LRF illustrates, the importance and strength of
economic organizations is not merely a matter of numbers but
also of the capacity to co-ordinate resources. For employers
as for farmers, it is also a matter of proud tradition. The oldest
existing organization in Sweden is the Swedish Iron Masters'
Association (Järnkontoret), founded in 1741, while the Royal
Patriotic Society was founded in 1766 to promote the development of business. In 1846 the guilds were dissolved but
by 1864 restrictions on the formation of economic interest
organizations had been removed (Pestoff, 1987). In 1902 the
Swedish Federation of Employers (SAF) was established, while
the Swedish Federation of Industry (SI) was founded in 1910.
SAF today has over 42,000 members. One measure of the

wide role of the employers' organizations, next only to the trade unions, is to be found in the very large and influential organizational press. One study identified 1,021 such periodicals, but among which one-third of total circulation of 211 million was accounted for by business papers, a total just below that of the trade-union oriented publications (Pestoff, 1983).

Trade-union activities date back to the mid-nineteenth century. The oldest LO-affiliated union is the Typographers' Union, founded in 1846; the oldest TCO-affiliated union is the Swedish Engineer Officers' Association, founded in 1848, and the oldest SACO/SR-affiliated union is the Swedish Veterinary Union, founded in 1860. In 1880 the first local milk co-operative was founded. These dates signal the origins of these interest associations in the popular movements that arose in this period to challenge the old paternalist structures. Some of these movements are still in existence. The Workers' Temperance Society (established in 1896) with 50,000 members today and the Folk (people's) High Schools' movement continue to be active though within a narrower scope. The same is true, though less so, of the associations of the 650 people's halls and the 160 people's (amusement) parks which were set up early in this century to enable ordinary Swedes to get together for cultural and recreational purposes. Though part of the wider labour movement, the links of these groups to the SAP and LO tend to be informal rather than formal. The same is true of the Pensioners' Association, PRO, founded in 1941. An indirect link for several of them is the ABF, the Workers' Educational Association, to which we shall return.

After the LO and SAP, the co-operative movement is the most important constituent in the labour movement. Founded in 1899 by representatives of 40 local consumer co-operative societies, the Swedish Co-operative Union and Wholesale Society (KF) today has almost two million members and 90,000 employees, making it the third largest of Swedish enterprises. Its retail outlet, Konsum, accounts for approximately 15% of non-food and 20% of food of Swedish retail trade, and its subsidiaries produce many consumer items for sale and export. The initial aim of KF, that of providing otherwise unavailable low-cost goods to ordinary people, has largely given way to that of testing products and educating its members—and Swedish consumers generally—so that they get the best value and nutrition for their money.

With LO and TCO, KF plays a central role in Folksam, the co-operative insurance company set up before the First World War to enable Swedish workers who could not afford the premiums charged by the private companies to insure their homes. Folksam sells roughly one in five of Swedish insurance policies, a market share similar to that of OK (the Union of Oil and Gas Co-operative Societies) of the heating-oil and gasoline market. The federation of housing co-operatives (HSB), first organized nationally in 1923, builds some of its units through a construction company of its own. Other units are built by SR (Riksbyggen), the co-operative housing construction company of the building workers' trade unions. Together, HSB and SR account for 20 per cent of housing construction in Sweden. Mention should also be made of RESO, the co-operative travel bureau set up to provide low-cost holidays for Swedish workers, as well as a number of publishing houses. Finally, like the trade unions, the Swedish co-operative movement is extremely active internationally, through the International Co-operative Alliance.

Participation in organizations is in keeping with the norm of public-spiritedness; it is also an expression of self-help and practicality. The development of common interests naturally leads to the forming of associations to promote them. In accordance with Swedish values, promoting common interests means assuming responsibility for providing the requisite service, rather than waiting for the state bureaucracy to set up an agency or for the private market to take up the service as sufficiently profitable. It is in this synthesis of private interest and public service that the network of intermediate organizations constitutes a buffer zone at the centre of the Swedish social system. They are not, as in the pluralist conception, 'special interests' as opposed to common interests. Their activities are incorporated into the very institutional structure of society in a complementary relationship.

There are a number of dimensions to this relationship. First, incorporation is facilitated by the fact that organizational activities are concentrated at the local and regional (county) level and co-ordinated at the centre in a manner parallel to the operations of the administrative structures. Though Sweden is a unitary state, significant power is delegated to the regional and local levels of government. Municipalities are responsible not only for local services, but also health protection, welfare, and education. County councils are responsible for hospitalization and other forms of care. Over three-quarters of municipal expenditures go toward services mandated by parliamentary legislation (Kesselman *et al.*, 1987: 506). OECD figures reveal that, at 29 per cent, Sweden was just below the US and West Germany in the proportion of taxes collected at the regional and local levels, and well ahead of such countries as France and Britain, with 7 and 10 per cent respectively (Heidenheimer *et al.*, 1983: 286).

Moreover, much power is delegated to the various administrative agencies and their constituent bodies at regional and local levels, distinct from the formal structures of government. In fact, only 2,000 or so of the more than 250,000 public servants are directly employed by the ministries; the remainder are under the authority of regional or local governments or central state agencies (von Otter, 1980: 147). The non-partisan central ministries are engaged essentially in goal-setting and policy-making (Kesselman *et al.*, 1987: 498), their main task being to prepare bills to be presented to Parliament. The agencies, on the other hand, are mainly involved in administering and regulating the programmes within their legislative mandates. Because of this original form of delegation, Sweden is viewed as highly distinctive in its approach to administrative decentralization (Self, 1985: 197). The origins of the system date back to the sixteenth century when collegial boards controlled by aristocrat-administrators were established within the state bureaucracy. Collegial boards were maintained in modern times, only lay members replaced civil servants, thus in effect moving the agencies from the bureaucracy to the buffer zone.

An investigation in the late 1970s revealed that four of five central administrative agencies were governed by boards the majority of whose members were non-civil servants. Estimates had set the percentage at 64 in 1964 (Ruin, 1974) and 71 per cent in 1976 (Hadenius, 1976). One study of the members of

62 such boards found that roughly 40 per cent were members of parliament, while 36 per cent represented interest groups. Of these interest-group representatives, 40 per cent represented business, and 37 per cent were from the trade unions. Another study reported that, in 1980, LO and TCO were represented on approximately thirty central agencies, including the labour market board, the occupational safety board, the national board of education, and the immigration board. Other central agencies worth mentioning in the welfare area alone include the housing board, the social insurance board, and the board of health and social welfare. SAF and SACO/SR were each represented on roughly ten of these (Forsebäck, 1980: 115).

The quality of representation does not typically appear to be token in nature. The authoritative study on the TCO (Wheeler, 1975), for example, found that TCO representation on the National Board of Education allowed it to contribute significantly to programmes and policies some of which were later taken up in legislation. In fact, criticism of the boards has tended to come from the opposite side. Concern by some parliamentarians that lay membership of public agency boards creates unclear channels of political decision-making led to the setting up of an investigatory commission to study the question. Published in the autumn of 1985, the commission report called for minor changes but upheld the principle (SOU, 1985). The commission itself was, of course, composed of representatives from the political parties and appropriate representative bodies.

Indeed, such royal commissions have for a century constituted a second major original feature of Swedish political life; their part in the formulation of major legislation is largely at the expense of that of the central ministries. In 1884, the Riksdag appointed a famous commission to investigate the idea of social insurance. Its members included a provincial governor, the farmers' leader, several employer representatives, and even a worker (Sainsbury and Castles, 1987: 287). Today, an annual average of about 75 investigatory commissions is appointed, with life-spans of up to four years. Their size varies as well, from one-person investigations to panels of 15 members, with the appropriate secretariat attached. For example, a royal commission on the role of university teachers which reported in early 1980 included among its 13 members five members of parliament (one representative for each of the three bourgeois parties and two Social Democrats—the bourgeois parties formed a majority government at the time), and one representative from each of: LO, SACO/SR, TCO, and the two public employer organizations representing the associations of regional and local councils. The SFS (student union) representative was a non-voting member and resource person. These and many other groups also took part in the 'remiss' process subsequent to publication in which commission reports are submitted to interest groups and administrative agencies for comment. Hundreds of such comments are normally received by the responsible ministry. Once made public, they enter the parliamentary process, which normally entails further organizational input through committee hearings. The major groups expend great effort continually commenting both privately and in the news media on commission reports. Even minor groups are involved. An illustration brought to the attention of the author was of an association of users of community-garden allotments (a common phenomenon in urban centres) solicited to contribute a remiss commentary on the report of a royal commission on a major, and unrelated, political issue.

In the above, we can discern the emerging features of the buffer zone : the 'loosening of roles'.

Politicians work in central agencies; ex-politicians are appointed to high office within the administration. Civil servants themselves engage in politics and can simultaneously be MPs, as well as playing a key role in advising on the formulation of policy. The representatives of the large interest organizations are active in both politics, and in administration. Interest organizations concern themselves with questions far beyond their original areas of concern; they are represented in Parliament and in a number of central agencies. Researchers take part in politics and administration as they do to some extent even in the work of the interest organizations; politicians, administrators and representatives of interest organizations influence, for their part, the world of research . . . (Ruin, 1982: 163).

Individuals are encouraged to apply the experience acquired in their working life to voluntary activities within the buffer zone. Rather than raising fears of conflict of interest, such interactions are generally viewed positively as strengthening consensus and the sense of public responsibility. Union leaders, politicians, leading journalists, top civil servants, captains of industry, academic experts, managers of non-profit organizations, and local community leaders can work together, even interchange positions without risking denunciation for selling out.

One measure of the intensity of such interactions is provided in a study of the backgrounds of members of parliament in the years 1971 to 1979. Thirty-five per cent of MPs were members of LO; 29 per cent of TCO, and 16 per cent of SACO/SR, while 9 per cent had been members of employers' organizations. LO was overrepresented at 65 per cent among SAP deputies, while the latter two were best represented in the bourgeois parties. Forty per cent of Centre party MPs were members of LRF, the Federation of Swedish farmers (A. Gustafsson, 1986: 40).

Finally, just as administrative responsibilities have been transferred from the civil service to the buffer zone of public agencies with lay-dominated boards, many services elsewhere provided through the profit-oriented private sector are in Sweden offered and administered by these buffer zone agencies. In fact, in many cases, the interest organizations themselves are accorded public mandates—and public funds—to provide services to the public. In the chapters to follow we will look at examples of such concertation, on the labour market, in education and communications, and in social services.

If we leave out the sums allocated by the state to the unemployment insurance societies organized and run by the policy holders, the trade unions, and the Labour Market Board (AMS), an estimated 1.6 per cent of the total state budget is spent directly by Swedish organizations (Pestoff, 1983: 28). The largest single item is adult education, primarily through the adult education societies which annually provide courses of all kinds to 3 million persons (see chapter 6). The largest of these is the SAP-LO-affiliated ABF, second is the TBV, associated with TCO. The next three are each associated with one of the three bourgeois parties.

The second largest chunk of this money—over one billion kr. in 1983—goes to the various sports clubs and pays 45 per cent of the cost of the wide range of activities that account for the Swedes' legendary physical fitness. (A krona in 1988 exchanged for roughly one-seventh of a US dollar.) Next come agricultural price supports and regulations, a more conventional form of public goods managed by 'private' organizations. With the participation of public representatives, producers' co-operatives form price regulation associations in eight different areas of food production, which, in 1980–1, spent 566 million kr. to administer food subsidies valued at 3.4 billion kr. And in 1987 political parties at all levels received subsidies amounting to 110 million kr. (Gidlund, 1988).

Three other voluntary organizations providing services and benefiting from public funds merit singling out: that of the disabled, the HCK, which receives 50 million kr. in operating funds, the National Students' Organization which looks after student housing, recreation, and information, and the 300,000-strong Association of Touring Clubs (founded in 1886), which operates youth hostels, mountain chalets, and ski centres, clears mountain trails, and arranges travel plans. Of the many miscellaneous public administrative functions carried out in the buffer zone, a useful illustration is provided by traffic safety information. The National Road Safety Organization includes 26 local traffic safety associations, and about 70 national affiliates such as trade unions, women's groups, homeowners' associations, the police, military units, and even oil and insurance companies. In 1980–1, it spent 4.7 million kr. in public funds.

In some cases, the transformation of voluntary organizations into public agencies has altered their character from what it was early this century when they were dependent solely on their members for cash and support. Their activities have been increasingly integrated into the work of agencies, their advice sought, their services subsidized. In the process, the lines of demarcation between them have blurred. A recent in-depth survey of the 50,000 voluntary associations and popular groups concluded that members in voluntary organizations today 'divide their loyalties among several collectivities [whereas] before 1950, volunteer associations' membership developed solidarity along class and economic lines' (Engberg, 1986: 187).

Does such concertation mean the end of the 'golden age', the onset of a bureaucratization of Swedish society and its values? Such an eventuality is worrisome to Swedes whose point of reference is a pioneer past that can never be resurrected. Yet they neglect the fact that private organizations were enlisted into close co-operation with public authorities long ago—especially during the two world wars when they played a major role in the implementation of rationing (Pestoff, 1987). By any reasonable comparative standard, Swedish organizations are healthy and vibrant. As Swedish society has become more complex, it has entailed closer co-ordination and planning in decision-making. But shifts in power and responsibility between organizations and public institutions have been reciprocal rather than one-sided. Informed participation has not been sacrificed on the altar of administrative co-ordination. Union membership is a case in point. There is still no government certification of bargaining agents in Sweden, and closed shops are unknown. Yet, while elsewhere union membership is declining or at best stagnant, in Sweden it continues to grow. At an over 80 per cent rate of unionization, Sweden ranks highest in the world. Generally speaking, organizational membership shows no sign of declining; and organizational leaders have successfully managed to straddle the thin line between co-optation and social irrelevance.

An exhaustive study of the contribution of the various organizations to the development of policy in Norway concludes in words that are equally applicable to Sweden: 'the willingness of organized interests to become co-opted [is] influenced by a long tradition of political compromises and by the awareness of the importance of . . . the outcomes of decisions . . . and by a certain ability to adapt political institutions to new circumstances' (Olsen, 1983: 211).

In their ability to 'concert' efforts on public agencies and commissions and carry out public mandates to provide services, Swedish organizations manifest a spirit of accommodation opposite to the adversarial spirit of confrontation and polarization North Americans and Britons are accustomed to. As one American observer described it, 'In negotiations people often come to appreciate the perspectives and values of those with whom they are in conflict. Negotiations thus promote broad-mindedness and altruism in a way that adversary trials do not. By contrast when agreements are not reached on social conflicts . . . adversary trials do nothing to help develop bonds among opponents' (Kelman, 1981: 232). Nothing illustrates this difference better than the arena where it faces its greatest challenges, namely collective bargaining, and no area has proved more important to the development of Swedish social democracy.

COLLECTIVE BARGAINING: COMPROMISES HISTORIC AND OTHERWISE

From the above, one can discern what is in effect a tacit collective agreement among Swedish organizations. Sweden's approach to the more traditional form of collective agreements, which set wages and other working conditions in the labour market, must be placed within this wider context if it is to be understood. The scope of the collective bargaining process and its influence on the labour market is very wide in Sweden, its socioeconomic importance universally acknowledged. This is perfectly understandable, since labour accounts for the bulk of production and distribution costs in any given society, while its remuneration is what provides for the livelihood of the majority of the population in modern societies: a properly functioning labour market through appropriate mechanisms of collective bargaining is a *sine qua non* of social well-being. In Sweden, at least, where public attention seems to be constantly focused on collective bargaining, no one would suggest otherwise.

The stage for our consideration of the organization of, and organizations in, the labour market was set in the description in chapter 2 of the evolution of the labour movement early in this century. By the 1930s labour had substantially transformed itself from a network of organizations designed to defend workers from capitalist exploitation to a confident alternative source of national leadership. Its mission was to construct an efficient, caring society, a people's home. Farmers and businessmen were served notice of this mission and each, in turn, learned to accommodate to it. For the latter, accommodation lay in the collective-bargaining arena. The first step was the establishment of representative and centralized organizations potentially able to take a central place on each side of the bargaining table: the LO in 1896, and, in response, SAF in 1902. Initially labour conflicts intensified, but the organizational basis for avoiding them had been laid.

SAF is less well known than its union counterpart, but its role in the development of Sweden's system of collective bargaining is of equal importance. SAF's centralized structure is quite unique among employers' organizations. It is a condition of membership in SAF that each firm is also a member of the employers' (branch) association appropriate to its sphere of activity or sector. The 35 branches range from the Engineering Employers' Federation (VF) with 2,400 enterprises and 308,000 employees to the Swedish bakery and confectionery branch with 14,000 member firms employing an average of 12 workers. The association *and* the firm are members of SAF. Each firm pays to SAF and its own branch federation annual dues of approximately 0.4 per cent of its payroll. Each firm also contributes an indemnity used by SAF to compensate member firms which suffer losses from industrial conflict. Until somewhat watered down in 1982, SAF provisions forbade member branches and firms from ordering a lockout, or entering into a separate agreement beyond that negotiated centrally without the prior approval of the SAF executive board or general council.

For their part, the branches, as a rule, also hold tight rein on their members. These 35 employers' associations affiliated with SAF appoint delegates to its general assembly, general council, and board. The assembly has 430 delegates, each association having one delegate plus one more for every 3,000 persons of the 1.45 million employed in member firms. The 85 members of the general council are appointed by the branches. The board, which meets monthly, consists of the director general, the directors of the 17 major associations, and 13 members-at-large chosen by the assembly. Under the director general is a staff of 470 employees in four sections: collective bargaining, research, statistics, and public relations, the latter growing most rapidly in recent years. In this area especially, SAF works together with the Federation of Swedish

Industries (SI). Composed of 24 trade associations comprising 4,000 companies which, with rare exception, are also affiliated with SAF, SI brings together employers—including co-operative and state-owned firms—in their capacity as entrepreneurs to promote industrial development. It lobbies government on policies it sees affecting the growth and efficiency of industry, advises constituent firms and trade associations on these matters, and works to get these messages put before the public, leaving collective bargaining to SAF.

Largely through SAF and SI, Swedish business acts as partner in the elaboration and application of policy decisions. By one account, SAF nominated representatives to more than 200 central administrative agencies, councils, and other public or official boards, 6,000 representatives all told, in 1984. SAF was also represented on 10 *ad hoc* parliamentary committees and commented on proposals made by 132 parliamentary and other official committees, mainly concerning labour market policy or work environment matters, as well as general economic questions, social policy, and education. SI nominated 126 representatives to 83 central agencies and other official bodies in 1984. It was represented on 24 *ad hoc* parliamentary committees and prepared 50 remiss responses (Pestoff, 1986: 48).

SAF members employ just under half of the 2.6 million Swedes who work in the private sector. Not affiliated to SAF, but negotiating in concert with it, are the employers' organizations representing the banks, the newspapers, and the theatre companies with just under 100,000 employees between them. A comparable number of workers are employed by KF, Folksam, OK, and other co-operatives represented jointly by the Co-operative Labour Negotiation Organization (KFO). A separate organization, KAB, represents the various housing co-ops in negotiating with their 31,000 employees (Bengtsson *et al.*, 1985: 44).

The employers in the public sector are also centrally organized. Representing central agencies and state ministries is the National Collective Bargaining Office (SAV) which negotiates with 600,000 state employees; the Federation of County Councils (LTF) and the Swedish Association of Municipal Councils (SK) negotiate with cartels representing their 365,000 and 520,000 employees respectively. Finally, there are the government enterprises with 125,000 employees, whose association, SFO—though having no formal links with SAF—quite closely follows the contractual pattern set out by agreements between SAF and LO (and white-collar PTK), attempting to take into account both wage drift and differences in labour market conditions (Bengtsson *et al.*, 1985: 42).

The LO today comprises 25 national blue-collar unions; roughly two-thirds of its 2.2 million members are in the private sector. There are 1,800 regional organizations, themselves composed of 10,000 primary units, which, depending on the circumstances, are either factory 'clubs' or local branches comprising several clubs. The largest member union is the municipal workers' union with just over 600,000 members, an honour held until recently by the highly influential metal workers' union which now has 450,000 members. The highest body of LO is the congress which meets every five years to set policy. The congress is made up of 300 delegates from the member associations, plus the 130 members of the general council and the 15 members of the executive. The general council normally meets twice a year to oversee the activities of the executive, which meets weekly.

Like SAF, LO exercises considerable control over its constituent organizations when it comes to strikes and collective bargaining generally. If 3 per cent of LO membership are likely to be involved in a strike, approval of the LO executive is required. Member unions violating this provision risk losing 'the right to economic and moral support'. In cases of significant wage disputes, affiliates are required to inform the secretariat, which has the power to participate in the affiliate's contractual negotiations and, under normal circumstances, at a certain point to impose its proposals for agreement.

SAF and LO's wide membership and centralization of authority are the key to the success of the consensual Swedish approach to collective bargaining. They first reached wide agreement in 1938 specifically to forestall threatened legislation to protect third parties in labour market conflicts. But the goal was a wider one: to create a framework in which each recognized the legitimate goals of the other and developed the means for reconciling differences that arose. Though sometimes subject to differing interpretations in recent years, the doctrine of the 'freedom of the labour market' that emerged remains at the core of the Swedish collective bargaining system, subscribed to by labour as well as management. The parties are expected to assume for themselves responsibility for peace on the labour market and a wage structure compatible with balanced economic growth. An incomes policy in the form of wage and price controls is thus precluded, though, as we shall see, governments in the 1970s and 1980s have tried to influence contractual negotiations through linking them to fiscal reforms, prepared even to condition fiscal adjustments on the outcome of collective negotiations. In principle the government intervenes only indirectly as a mediator in labour conflicts. Moreover, like other courts, the Labour Court, which has the final appeal over interpretations of agreements or regulations, is not subject to government directives.

The main LO–SAF agreement of 1938 set out rules for conducting collective bargaining as well as guidelines for protecting workers from arbitrary dismissal, employers from irresponsible union action, and non-participants from suffering unreasonably from labour disputes. A set of rules was drawn up for avoiding conflicts in sectors that could constitute dangers to the well-being of the public. A central joint committee was created to elaborate these procedures and monitor their application, and to arbitrate in conflicts among affiliated organizations and members.

In 1941, LO's constitution was changed to enable it to reinforce its relationship with SAF and pave the way for a policy of equalizing benefits among wage-earners through centralized negotiations complemented by government labour market policies (described in chapter 4). When they proved successful, these policies provided sufficient incentive for specific groups of workers to forgo possible short-term gains for the longer-term advantages resulting from high growth and low inflation. The mechanisms came to be quite clearly set out: first a general agreement would be reached between SAF and LO followed by agreements within the parameters of the nation-wide contract at the branch and company level.

Centralized negotiations meant lower than maximal wage increases for workers in the most successful industrial sectors, but it also guaranteed that the increases won (and jobs created) would not be eaten away in an inflationary wage spiral set in motion by other workers attempting to catch up—especially public employees exploiting their strategic position in service delivery. With the power of decision over bargaining strategy lying with the widest possible units, it was difficult to play one group off against another. The instruments of industrial action had been placed by SAF and LO in the hands of their respective central executive boards and they made use of them. They alone could supply funds to compensate affiliates for losses due to strikes or lockouts. SAF could levy stiff fines on members who violated its by-laws and, more important, refuse them access to the insurance pool if faced with industrial action. On the union side, a dissatisfied section of the bargaining collective could break away by resigning from the LO federation—though this in itself is no easy matter. But even if successful it would likely prove pointless, since SAF would refuse to negotiate with the renegade group which would have to content itself with a 'tagged-on' agreement to that negotiated by the LO or one of its affiliates.

An LO–SAF agreement set the pattern in other areas of the labour market. The content was largely reproduced in the agreement signed by SAF and the largest white-collar association, the Swedish Union of Clerical and Technical Employees in Industry (SIF) in 1957. The SAF–LO model also played an important part when, in 1966, public employees were granted the right to bargain collectively and to strike. From at least this point on, LO was no longer in control; it now has to co-ordinate strategy with organizations representing white-collar workers and professionals. White-collar workers are members of a separate confederation, the TCO (the Central Organization of Salaried Employees) with its over one million members split roughly equally between public and private sector. Founded in 1944 through a fusion of two existing organizations, TCO, unlike LO, does not bargain directly for its members. Bargaining is carried out by TCO's twenty constituent federations usually in cartel with each other or with unions outside TCO. Eighty per cent of its members are concentrated in eight large federations of which SIF, TCO-S, and KTK—respectively representing white-collar employees in industry, national government, and local government—are the largest. The remainder are members of unions of nurses, police officers, teachers, journalists, armed forces officers, and others.

A third organization, SACO/SR (the Swedish Association of Professional Associations and National Federation of Government Officials), founded in 1947, now has roughly 250,000 members. There are 27 professional associations in SACO/SR. Members are university-trained professionals including physicians, dentists, architects, pharmacists, and certain categories of teachers.

SIF plus six smaller TCO federations together with the relevant SACO/SR associations and the union of foremen and supervisors (SALF) form PTK, the cartel of private-sector salaried employees. Thus, in the private sector, collective bargaining is conducted between SAF on one side and LO and PTK on the other. In the growing public-employee sector there are two cartels: negotiating with national employers (SAV) is a 525,000-member cartel made up of TCO-S, SF (LO), and 70,000 members of SACO/SR. The cartel for 900,000 employees at the regional and local level is composed of KTK (TCO), SKAF (LO), and SACO/SR.

As noted, government has come to play a significant informal role in collective bargaining, though stopping short of violating the principle of the freedom of the labour market. Alongside close LO–SAP co-operation, regular informal contacts between Prime Ministers Hansson and Erlander and their finance ministers and top businessmen were long well-known if unpublicized features of Swedish political life. As the government regularized these contacts after 1949, TCO joined LO and SAF as a participant. TCO was also invited to regular government–employer–union consultations over policy orientation between 1955 and 1962 which came to be known by their location as 'Harpsund democracy'. TCO made its début as a significant political actor in the supplementary-pension (ATP) debate of the mid-1950s (discussed in chapter 5). The role of the large labour market organizations in political decision-making became especially pronounced during the 1970s. A deadlocked parliament from 1973 to 1976, and an unstable economic situation, led to determined, if not highly successful, political initiatives to build consensus around proposed tax reforms. Most noteworthy among these were the Haga deliberations in 1974, 1975, and 1976.

The heart of the system lay in the LO–SAF partnership that flowered in the late fifties and early sixties, the 'historic compromise between labour and capital'. Among the features of the Swedish labour market underlying this compromise one observer identified industrial rather than craft unionism, centralization rather than fragmentation of collective bargaining power, exclusive bargaining rather than rivalry over the bargaining unit, and a basic willingness by both parties to approach problems analytically rather than polemically (Barbash, 1972: 39). This latter tendency is manifested in union–management collaboration in data collection. Following the lead of several of their respective constituent organizations, in 1970 LO and SAF agreed to collect statistical data together; their research departments continue to publish joint quarterly reports on wage trends.

The above mechanisms produced not only a series of collective agreements, but, more importantly, a number of principles for establishing their content. Industry-wide collective agreements were common as far back as 1905. Then in 1938 came a determined effort to concert action for stability and growth. Wartime pressures made it natural to negotiate centralized agreements on such matters as a combined wage and price freeze (with, at a later moment, an exception made for low-wage earners), creating a climate in which centralized negotiations seemed natural. The war over, and Sweden in relatively good shape, labour renewed its commitment to achieving long-term full employment. While, as we shall see in chapter 4, the economic principles underlying the realization of this goal were developed primarily within the labour movement, it was in fact SAF that now led the way toward establishment of one of the key mechanisms: centrally co-ordinated wage negotiations. As the LO reminds us continually, for example in the report of its executive to its 1986 congress, only a bargaining agent representing the largest combination of workers is in a position to see the 'big picture' and thus help avoid inflation. Smaller units, even large national unions, see their own pay situation as little related to inflation—and vice versa—and naturally seek the highest pay rises; others find out and try to catch up (LO News, Feb. 1986: 31). The same is true of the perspective of individual companies or industries as compared to those of employers as a whole.

Seeing that the labour movement in or near power had become a permanent feature of the Swedish social landscape, the SAF leadership had already concluded that centralized bargaining was necessary to stave off a worse evil—direct government intervention. SAF feared that a spiral of wage increases offered by employers forced to compete to attract skilled workers in short supply in the full-employment post-war economy would incite the labour-oriented government to bring in controls. Remaining doubts as to the SAP's new hegemony melted when, in 1960, having failed to reach an accord with SAF to bring in supplementary pensions, the party went to the people and won a popular mandate to do just that.

After shifting back and forth from centralized negotiations to more decentralized forms, in the early 1960s a centralized pattern of negotiations was firmly established. SAF–LO–PTK agreements were regularly signed without great tension, and the public and co-operative sectors followed suit. Of course, especially productive employers were able to find ways of rewarding their employees. But these additional rewards, called wage drift, were monitored jointly by SAF and LO, and, on the whole, kept sufficiently within limits to allow the system to operate smoothly.

The system functioned admirably for much of the 1960s. When it faltered temporarily, the unions and employers responded in unison, blaming inflation on political failure to act quickly enough in 1962, 1964–5, 1969, and 1973–4 to restrain demand once the economic stimulation policies to 'bridge over' the recession had taken effect. The overall results were nevertheless encouraging. During the 1960s, average inflation was kept to 3 per cent, unemployment to 1.5 per cent. Growth averaged 4 per cent, thereby making resources available for added social services and education programmes and massive construction of low-cost housing.

The newly created public-sector jobs made it possible for new groups, especially women, to enter the workforce. In 1965

women constituted 37 per cent of the workforce; by 1987 this
had risen to 47 per cent (AMS, 1987), giving Sweden the
Western world's highest labour participation rate. The new
arrivals added a complicating element to the negotiations
process. Initially the public-sector workers accepted the principle that applied to the private sector, namely of wage
leadership for the internationally competitive (K) sector of
the economy. SACO, however, demurred right from the
start, since application of the formula made it difficult for
professionals to counteract the effect of the reduction in pay
differentials—wage solidarity (see chapter 4)—that had been
built in. In later years, however, public-sector workers increasingly came to regard the system as unfair, feeling that
their added job security was not sufficient compensation for
the fact that they could not benefit from the wage drift of the
most productive K-sector industries.

   The debate centred on the application of the wage-setting
formula based on assuring a rate of return on capital in the
K sector high enough to induce continued investment. This
formula, borrowed from the Norwegians, and developed by
the leading economists of LO, SAF, and TCO, was known as
EFO (an acronym made from the names of the chief economists
of the three organizations). The EFO formula used figures for
productivity and external price growth to calculate the general
capacity of the competitive sector—that is, the sum total of
producers competing in foreign markets or against foreign
imports—to generate sufficient profits to stay competitive.
Through such analyses, the economists jointly drew what they
foresaw as the boundaries for wage increases between leaving
too much room for drift and leaving too little for investment,
thereby systematizing the data on which collective bargaining
was to be based. In fact, the EFO model as such was presented
only subsequent to the major wage developments of the 1960s.
Hence it had but a few years of application before being
superseded by world events.

   The first major problem over wage setting arose not in the
public sector, but in more traditional high-pay industrial
sectors where inflation was eroding the purchasing power of
workers relatively adversely affected by wage solidarity. A
major strike, in a nation where strikes had all but disappeared,

took place in a state-owned Northern iron mine in 1969-70. A total of 216 strikes were reported in 1970. All of these were illegal wildcat strikes, seeking to alter conditions in valid contracts still in effect. Though they expressed some sympathy for the workers' grievances, the central bodies did their best to end them quickly. In retrospect, it seems clear that LO and TCO launched a major offensive for industrial democracy in the 1970s in an effort to respond to the thrust of the wildcat movement in a way that did not challenge the nation-wide negotiating system.

As far as wage negotiations were concerned, the public-sector workers apparently came out best between 1970 and 1973 mainly because the government-employer sought to avert an impending police strike. Profits and thus wage drift remained low in this period, placing Sweden in a good comparative cost position when the first OPEC shock hit in 1973. However, in 1974 profits skyrocketed to their highest levels since the early fifties. And the government, lacking a parliamentary majority, and with only a three-year term of office to look forward to under the new constitution, failed to act to dampen demand by, as leading economists suggested, revaluing the Swedish currency.

Instead, it appealed for consensus on the labour market. For the first time, in 1974, through face-to-face negotiations at Haga Palace outside Stockholm, the government (along with the opposition parties) publicly entered the central wage negotiation process. They agreed on three measures: first, the politicians promised direct income tax decreases; second, LO, TCO, and SACO/SR agreed to integrate these tax decreases in their wage-demand calculations; and third, the state would replace its lost revenues by raising payroll taxes. SAF's consent for this third measure, according to its then chief economist, K. O. Faxén (the 'F' in EFO), was forced on it since an unholy alliance of the bourgeois parties and the Communists blocked the requisite significant rise in the MOMS or VAT (sales tax), an alternative measure for replacing the lost revenues which would have restrained consumption rather than raising production costs (Rydén and Bergström, 1982: 191).

As profits grew and prices remained high, Swedish workers

in 1975 won significant pay increases in a two-year settlement. Unfortunately, the recession that had hit all of Sweden's trading partners by 1976 led to a serious decline in demand for its goods just as increased wage costs and payroll charges led to their rising in price an average of 40 per cent over the two years (Martin, 1984: 294). Allowing this to happen has been termed by one observer 'a considered and competently executed strategic miscalculation' (Scharpf, 1981: 30), an assessment which, after the fact, is subscribed to by economic strategists on both the business and labour sides.

The hope had been to 'bridge over' the 1975 world recession through an expansion of demand (as recommended by the OECD but ignored by other member nations). However, the recession lasted longer than expected, and Sweden was priced out of a shrinking market just as international market conditions improved in 1977. The inexperienced and somewhat divided non-socialist government that took office in 1976 chose to preserve jobs in hard-hit sectors such as steel and shipbuilding through huge subsidies for continuing non-profit operations. This resulted in unprecedented budget deficits. It took two devaluations of the krona to bring down real wages and regain some of the cost competitiveness lost. The 'bourgeois' government was (barely) returned to power in 1979 on the strength of a partial economic recovery, but the problems caused by the second OPEC oil shock later that year placed new strains on the collective bargaining process and crisis again ensued.

The 1979 negotiations proved extremely difficult. SAF sought a wage freeze, while LO and PTK countered with varying Haga-like formulas tying restraint in wage demands to tax reductions which would benefit their members. Then progress in the private sector was pre-empted by a joint demand by the LO and TCO public-sector cartels (the 'gang of four' as they came to be known) for a 12 per cent wage increase, claiming this to be their just share of the 'available room for wage increases' under the EFO formula. LO and PTK thus found themselves forced to keep pace, with the result that total wage demands far exceeded the bounds of the EFO formula. Recriminations followed, each blaming the other; the public- and private-sector unions were more divided than ever before. Confrontation was imminent, and the mediation attempt by the Fälldin government, itself divided over the nuclear energy referendum, failed. As LO and SAF threatened strike and lockout action, the public-sector unions took the lead with rotating strikes. But a few days later, in response to selected work stoppages, SAF locked out 750,000 LO workers. The worst work stoppage since the 1920s had begun.

Evidently rattled, the government forced a settlement after ten days based on the mediation commission's recommendation of 7.3 per cent increases in the public sector and pressured SAF to accept 6.8 per cent for the private sector—an increase greater than LO had expected in the first place. In giving in, SAF's president denounced the bourgeois government for having undermined the bargaining system, and warned that it would have to pay the consequences. Indeed, had the government acted immediately and resolutely to resist public-sector demands, escalation might have been averted. With its roots in the labour movement, a Social-Democratic government might have been able to do just that. In any case, the SAP's return to power was hastened. The clearly inflationary settlement weakened Sweden's international economic position and with it the government's credibility. The final nail in the coffin was the very instability of the coalition. The Conservatives left the government in 1981, rejecting a tax reform package negotiated by their coalition partners with the Social Democrats that combined the lower marginal taxes for most employees they had sought with redistributive measures favouring the lowest paid (Haskell, 1987).

Once returned to power in 1982 and again in 1985, the Social Democrats found themselves faced with the challenge of restoring a collective bargaining system which had served as a mainstay of national economic and social progress. The obstacles were great. Though SAF finally signed a co-determination agreement with LO and PTK in 1982 in accordance with the 1976 MBL law, many, especially in the smaller companies, felt that business's legitimate role in the management of industry and in wage setting had been undermined by government actions in the negotiations and in adopting laws which infringed upon the prerogatives of

management recognized in 1938. These laws, discussed in
chapter 5, extended the rights of workers in enterprises and
created the wage-earner funds. The debate over these reforms,
especially the wage-earner funds, was extremely intense,
bringing to the surface differences between labour and management greater even than those over the supplementary
pensions in the 1950s.

Those members of SAF who wanted greater freedom to set
wage levels in their own sectors, most notably in the highly
successful engineering industry, capitalized on the resentment
and frustration, moving SAF toward a more decentralized
bargaining structure. In 1983 and 1984, in fact, the bulk of
negotiations were conducted by the different branch associations within SAF. Labour, however, though still somewhat
divided, was able to informally maintain wage-setting guidelines at the centre. This led to a protocol between SAF and
LO and PTK in 1985 to effectively centralize negotiations for
all but the engineering industry and its workers in LO-Metall.
In 1986, despite some grumblings due to tensions between the
most productive private-industry workers in LO-Metall on
one side, and white-collar public-sector employees, LO in fact
was able to have its way in the form of a co-ordinated
centralized settlement extending even to the engineering
industry. Public-sector workers this time waited until LO and
PTK had settled. A settlement with the 'gang of four' was
reached in the autumn, but only after an unpopular two-week
strike that disrupted a number of important services.

It would evidently be false to assert that the system has
now returned to normal, if by normal we mean the situation
in the 1960s. Even under the most favourable circumstances,
the 4 per cent annual economic growth of the 1960s will
not return. A significant role for government in collective
bargaining through its budgetary powers is here to stay.
Moreover, the scars of the crises and divisions of the latter
1970s have not yet fully healed. Still the trend toward
decentralization of collective bargaining has been reversed;
SAF is playing a more significant role, setting guidelines for
employers in wage settlements and, as in the case of a fine of
1 million kr. levied on the baking industry employers in late
1987, enforcing them when challenged. Late in 1987, the SAP

finance minister K.-O. Feldt and SAF virtually joined forces
to keep down wage increases. The finance bill accompanying
the 1988-9 draft budget emphatically drew conclusions based
on alternative outcomes to the ongoing bargaining. There was
an encouraging economic forecast based on remaining within
the government's target of less than a 4 per cent wage increase
(SAF offered 3 per cent), and a bleak one based on the 7 per
cent rise the unions would settle for. Indeed, the same line of
argument was imitated (initiated?) in SAF's public information
campaign. After a short series of symbolic strikes and lockouts,
LO and SAF managed to reach agreement on a new contract.
Once wage drift was calculated, however, the settlement was
found to amount to an increase of 6 per cent. The additional
increase was largely due to the ability of SIF and other
white-collar groups to weaken the hold of their bargaining
cartel, PTK, and win local concessions.

It is tempting to see in this situation an erosion of economic
institutions and a breakdown of consensus; such a conclusion
would be rash. Swedes, remembering two-and-a-half decades
when things worked smoothly and predictably, are troubled
by a decade in which consensus needs to be frequently
renegotiated. Not being used to continuing tensions, they tend
to see breakdown where, in fact, constructive solutions exist.
The long-run implications of this state of affairs are left to
later chapters but, before seeing the problem from that
perspective, we should remind ourselves that with 2 per cent
unemployment and the resulting sectorial and regional labour
shortages, wage pressures naturally build up, especially when
profit levels, by Swedish standards, are fairly high. Sweden's
problems are largely the result of having achieved enviable
success in the crucial areas of employment and economic
adjustment. In the next chapter we look at the microeconomic
strategies underlying this success.

For the time being, it appears reasonable to conclude
that labour market collaboration is sufficiently strong and
well-ingrained for it to prove resilient enough to withstand
the pressure. The LO, the institution at the centre of the
process described, will have to manœuvre carefully between
its private- and public-sector workers. Yet before wagering on
its likely failure, one should note that, as one rather critical

observer pointed out, 'the consensus between members and elected leaders stands out internationally as a highly re-markable trait of the Swedish labour movement' (Lewin, 1977: 3). Consider the issue of the collective affiliation of LO branches to the SAP, a provision which, though it provides for individuals opting out if they choose, has long been criticized for not respecting minority rights (e.g. Lewin, 1977). In 1986 the LO leadership opted to end the practice. Though not endorsed by the LO congress, the practice will be ended as of 1991 as a result of a decision by the SAP. Such sensitivity to public concerns would seem to bode well for the future of the labour movement—a question addressed in the concluding chapter. In the meantime, we turn to the other mainstays of the economics of Swedish social democracy.

4

Equality and Mobility on the Swedish Labour Market

Having first traced the evolution of Swedish social values to the present era, we continue our survey of the workings of the social system, that complex interweaving of institutions, policies, and relationships that puts these ideals into operation. Bearing in mind our initial caveat, that no single policy or institution is synonymous with Swedish social democracy and the spirit and practice of concertation that makes it work, we turn to what is commonly regarded as the most original aspect of Swedish political economy: its labour market and wage-setting policy. In chapter 3 we set the stage for discussing the content of wage settlements by describing their context, the pattern of centralized collective bargaining.

How can something as mundane as manpower allocation and wage setting be at the centre of social-democratic policy-making in Sweden? Part of the answer lies in the absolutely central place of work in Swedish values. For a distinctly non-religious society, the right to work is practically a gospel. Labour market policy entails influencing the allocation of economic activities in time and space to meet the supply of labour, or, more simply, getting people (through training, information, mobility allowances, etc.) to jobs, and getting jobs to people. Labour market policy is not social welfare, a means of keeping the unemployed off the streets and out of trouble. The rationale is first of all economic. Full employment brings an increase in the output of goods and services by making otherwise idle human resources productive. High unemployment means less output and greater dependency, thus increased cost in the form of income transfers. But the logic does not end there. Even if affordable, income transfers cannot replace employment for people able to work. Work is part of living a normal life, even—especially—for those otherwise handicapped. Thus human well-being is inseparable from the functioning of the labour market. Full employment is at the core of social-welfare policy, 'the practical means of breathing life into a widely shared equalitarian philosophy' (Ginsburg, 1983: 122).

Previous chapters drew attention to the web of the interrelations of representative organizations. Sweden's distinctive form of collective bargaining was perceived to have developed within a favourable institutional framework and, in turn, contributed to the shaping of those institutions. Government's role in the system of collective bargaining was largely that of a catalyst to enhance collaboration by rendering it effective. Only in those relatively few instances where agreement was not possible did government directly intervene. At the height of the labour–management partnership, disagreement centred on one issue: collective capital formation through the supplementary pension plan and—somewhat later—the controversial wage-earner funds. In chapter 5, we discuss this fourth element of Swedish microeconomic practice. Having dealt with the first, centralized collective bargaining, we turn in this chapter to the other two elements of Sweden's unique system of business–labour concertation: active labour market programmes and wage solidarity.

THE REHN–MEIDNER MODEL

State involvement in the labour market was accepted early in Sweden. At the beginning of this century there were already local public labour exchanges in existence; these began to be centrally co-ordinated and to receive state subsidies in 1906, and were made universal in the 1930s. In the 1920s vocational training programmes for the unemployed were introduced, and in the 1930s public relief work of various kinds came to take on great-importance, with workers in these programmes paid at regular market wages. Since the only other choice was very low cash support payments, the great majority of the unemployed were directed toward work. In normal Keynesian fashion, such 'active' labour market programmes were phased out when the war brought full employment (Wadensjö, 1980).

Yet Swedish economic policy-making with regard to the labour market soon came to surpass, and largely reject, the Keynesian form of stabilization policy. The new approach was associated primarily with the LO economists Gösta Rehn and Rudolf Meidner, coming later to be known as the 'Rehn model'. Influenced by the writings of the Stockholm school, but, as trade unionists, very much aware of the practical realities in which labour decisions are made, Rehn and Meidner were the main authors of a seminal 1951 LO document entitled 'Trade Unions and Full Employment', which placed on the labour movement's agenda ideas they and their colleagues in the LO research department had been advancing for several years.

Conditions favoured the new approach. LO's partnership with SAF, cemented in the 1938 Saltsjöbaden agreement, was put to the test after the war. The predictions of renewed depression which coloured the thinking behind the SAP's controversial 'post-war programme' proved unfounded. Instead came post-war prosperity, from which Sweden was in a particularly advantageous position to benefit. The LO economists were concerned that prosperity be a means to-ward—rather than a threat to—long-term full employment. Ignored by economic planners elsewhere, this threat was perceived as fundamental; and it was to be countered by applying the 'spirit of Saltsjöbaden' to the new situation. To maintain Sweden's economic position a number of practical measures were needed to foster the rationalization of the economy through new technology and changed working conditions. The unions, evidently, had a vital role to play in this process:

The Swedish trade union movement considers that one of its main tasks is to support and promote a development leading to greater efficiency in industry. Yet, this should not be at the expense of workers in the way of speeded-up work, or unhealthy work conditions. . . . [Instead] rationalization of the economy of private firms can be promoted by work concentration and large scale production, mechanization, standardization of products and means of production; and also rational day to day management and continuous flow of output. Of all these measures, the introduction of labour saving machinery always played, in the long run, the most important part as regards increasing efficiency. . . . The organization of a firm, and cooperation between the individuals working there, are both of paramount importance as regards the efficiency of work and rate of continuous rationalization (LO, 1951: 23-4).

For trade unionists in 1951, these were far-sighted ideas indeed. Yet the LO researchers took their economic implications even further. They understood that the stimulative policies that had succeeded in the 1930s would inevitably lead to inflation under the new conditions. While concern about inflation is very common today, even in some labour circles, in 1951 economic strategists on all sides effectively ignored the problem, assuming Keynesian countercyclical policies could be brought in to head off inflation if and when the need arose. Rehn contended that even if government had the wisdom and political support to take macroeconomic action to slow down the economy at exactly the right moment, external factors would necessarily be brought to bear upon the cost of products in an export–import oriented 'open' economy, setting in motion an inflationary dynamic that would, sooner or later, undermine full employment. This was unacceptable.

If the duties of the trade union movement were merely to endeavour to preserve and increase the wage-earners' share of the total national income, it could very well accept a continuous decrease in the value of money. . . . [This] however would hamper total productivity, and thus the increase in the standard of living and real wages of the wage-earners. In the long run, a continuous rise in prices would also lead to such complications both within the country and in foreign trade that full employment could no longer be maintained (LO, 1951: 82).

Instead, labour's strategy for full employment had to be one of non-inflationary growth based on *selective* labour market policies.

Any measures aiming at preserving the level of employment wherever it may be threatened, should be applied as locally as possible as opposed to any general increase of effective demand, which only could restore the inflationary pressure again. On this basis they should, on the one hand, consist in public works, subsidies to individual firms and the placing of State orders with firms and in localities, where, otherwise, unemployment would arise. On the other hand they should consist in encouraging the voluntary transfer of labour to firms, trades, and localities where the prospects of expansion are favourable. Much greater importance than hitherto should be attached to incentives to labour to transfer to places where it is most needed (LO, 1951: 92–3).

As unionists, Rehn and Meidner knew very well that appealing for trade-union wage restraint to hold down inflation, as economic growth led to high profits and labour shortages, was ultimately self-defeating. Anti-inflationary mechanisms had to be built into the very process of growth and employment creation. High demand pressure *per se* can simply lead to price and cost inflation with little increase in productivity. 'The condition for stable full employment is, therefore, that profit prospects should not be too good for individual firms, as this leads to inflationary wage and price increases' (LO, 1951: 92). Under the standard economic policy framework, nowadays termed accommodationist, inefficient industries and enterprises tend to survive inflationary conditions, while efficient industries see steep rises in profits but find few incentives and fewer opportunities for significantly increasing employment. With scant inducement to improve productivity, efforts on both sides go primarily into raising wages and prices.

The usual Keynesian non-selective fiscal stimuli to encourage employment by raising general demand were therefore ruled out. Rather than expanding demand, in a productive economy governments would normally have to restrain it by taxing consumption. Fiscal restraint had to be constantly exercised to keep profit levels—and thus wage increases—sufficiently low. With low profits, less competitive enterprises would be left to their own devices and laid-off workers would be channelled to more productive jobs through 'active' labour market policies: occupational retraining, relocation programmes and selective employment-creation measures. In this way, they argued, productivity could be increased through modernization and full employment could be achieved and maintained. These programmes were primarily the responsibility of the government. But the unions, the bulk of which were affiliated with LO at this time, had a crucial part to play. For non-inflationary expansion policy to work, the fastest growing firms had to be checked from bidding up wages. If wages were set on a firm-by-firm—or even, as was then the tradition in Sweden, industry-by-industry—basis, an inflationary wage-price spiral would inevitably set in. Required instead was a mechanism for jointly determining the division of revenues (value added) between wages and profits that would allow the largest wage share compatible with Swedish industry's remaining competitive internationally. As a corollary, it was understood that private industry left to itself could not provide full employment. Selective job-creation and restructuring-promotion policies would have to be pursued. Before turning to these, however, we should first look at the content and consequences of the wage demands thus arrived at.

WAGE SOLIDARITY AND ITS CONSEQUENCES

According to Rehn and his collaborators, wage differentials based on relative labour demand—the norm in free-market economic thinking—as opposed to those based on differences in the skill requirements of jobs, were inefficient means of transferring labour. Due to market 'imperfections', reaction to altered wage differentials is quite slow, especially if there is no pool of unemployed workers to draw upon. To attract new workers in a reasonably short period of time, rapidly expanding industries must increase wages for all their workers. And in high-employment situations, and/or where there are strong unions, large wage increases for certain groups spur compensatory demands from others. The inevitable result is an inflationary rise in prices (Meidner and Öhman, 1972).

The extraordinary means chosen by the trade unions to put these ideas into practice was wage solidarity. LO industrial workers had seen their position deteriorate in comparison to those employed servicing the sheltered home market during the years of depression between the wars, and the war years showed that solidarity was possible. Rehn and Meidner's analysis provided a clear and logical economic argument for the objective of income equalization. There were two aspects to wage solidarity: nation-wide rates of general wage increases, and special increases for low-wage earners to narrow differentials. For the purposes of collective bargaining all of Swedish manufacturing was one unit. Firms were to be forced, irrespective of their earning power, to pay an equivalent wage. And the effect was as expected. Those which had been kept alive by low wages faced irresistible pressure to rationalize operations or close. Laid-off workers were retrained and redeployed through specially designed labour market programmes into the competitive firms and industries where their services were needed.

Solidarity wage policy is at the same time an instrument of economic efficiency and an expression of the egalitarian goals of Swedish social democracy. Successful firms prospered, while wage differentials narrowed further as low-wage industries became scarce. The new generation witnessed a significant lessening of income gaps. For example, the difference between average wages in the industries with the highest and lowest average wage level was narrowed to only 13 per cent by 1976 as against 30 per cent in 1960 and significantly more before the war. An important consequence of the narrowing of the gap between and within branches was a parallel narrowing of wage differentials between the sexes (Forsebäck, 1980: 80–1).

Taxes have also contributed to the levelling brought on by wage solidarity. In 1939 a Swedish cabinet minister or high-level administrator brought home eight times the after-tax income of a blue-collar worker (Rehn, 1984: 141); the ratio is now just over 2 to 1. While the achievement of conditions of equality is a matter of some pride to labour, the real pay-off to the rank and file was the resulting continued economic growth which meant higher average wages, improved working conditions, and full employment. As a result of the successful application of these policies, until well into the 1970s, productivity in Sweden kept pace with the other industrialized nations, an impressive feat since Sweden's starting level was higher than that of Europe and Japan which were embarked upon post-war reconstruction. Returning to the principle of wage solidarity after a decade of practising it, the LO at its 1971 congress categorically rejected inequalities in wages based on differences in profitability, reaffirming its commitment to wage solidarity and, especially, to raising the pay of low-wage workers (Forsebäck, 1980).

Full employment without general profit inflation was thus found to be quite compatible with the principles of the free-market system. But genuinely competitive conditions turned out not to be automatic: they needed to be fostered to ensure that the market reacted properly. In a proper market, changes in market demand lead to corresponding shifts in the allocation of production resources through changes in relative prices. Inefficient firms lose ground and release resources to expanding industries and modernizing firms. Increasing productivity results from such a transfer of labour and capital to industries with expanding markets. Resulting rises in revenues allow for wage increases and increased expenditures on programmes to foster employment for those displaced from, as well as those entering, the labour market (Rehn and Lundberg, 1963).

As a consequence, programmes to foster the employment of displaced and newly arriving workers needed to be 'active', since wage differentials could not be used to stimulate needed adjustment. The LO strategists persuaded their partners in government to make direct and generous compensation available to the worker willing to change his or her job in conformity with the economy's changing labour requirements. Assuring the existence of an appropriate labour market to complement the industrial restructuring engendered by technological developments and stimulated by wage solidarity required active intervention for improving information and retraining programmes, paying part of the real costs of relocation, and providing decent income during retraining periods.

The skeleton institutional structures were already in existence in the labour exchanges and unemployment commissions of the 1930s which had been consolidated in 1940 into a National Labour Market Commission in order to respond to changes in labour allocation caused by the war. After a brief period of neglect, the government in the mid-1950s decided to place renewed emphasis on labour market programmes to complement wage solidarity. At the centre of the new structure was the AMS, the National Labour Market Board, which had been reconstituted in 1948 as a tripartite body and which, with the appointment of Bertil Ohlsson as its chairman in 1957, was poised to play the major role assigned to it. New policies were developed, existing programmes strengthened, expenditures multiplied. All were co-ordinated through one organizational network with the necessary financial and political support from the government as well as appropriate links with labour and business. Affected most of all, the textile workers, after some soul-searching, chose to retrain for better employment elsewhere rather than to preserve their declining and underpaid industry.

While controversial at the time, few today view the results with anything but pride. 'One of the most important social priorities is to create conditions of full employment. . . . In the short term, unemployment must be countered with special measures including labour market training and relief work.' This quote, taken from a recent party brochure, goes on: 'the Centre party stands for an active labour market policy of this nature'. The Centre party, it should be noted, is part of the bourgeois opposition, and was quite critical of these policies in the 1960s.

Business by and large accommodated itself to this labour movement initiative. Regular business–labour consultation had long been established, with the government playing an important but discreet role. Despite the difficulties that many of its members encountered in adjusting to the effects of wage solidarity, SAF could not deny its positive results at the aggregate level. Moreover, the other alternative, from SAF's perspective, could only be worse: either an inflationary wage–price spiral, or more direct involvement by an SAP government with the political wind in its sails. As noted above, it was at SAF's initiative that the wage-setting policies came to be co-ordinated through a system of centralized collective bargaining.

For a number of years, the system delivered the predicted results to the general satisfaction of those concerned. Under relentless pressure, stagnating sectors of the economy released labour to expanding industries. The pressure was exacerbated by the gradual shifts (mainly through tax deferrals) from direct taxation on net corporate profits to indirect forms such as payroll taxes, which foster competitiveness through 'expansion of the fittest', as compared to the former which cushion inefficiency by rewarding low profits with low taxes. By applying these quite original programmes, Sweden achieved full employment, well-controlled inflation, and solid economic growth. Continued growth made possible the financing of the various state programmes associated with the welfare state, including the active labour market policies themselves. The latter added flexibility, for example enabling the training and hiring of tens of thousands of additional construction workers after 1965 to build one million dwellings in a decade (see chapter 7), and their direction toward employment elsewhere at the culmination of the programme.

We should not, however, exaggerate the existing consensus behind the measures. We know that the proposals in the 1951 LO report were initially rejected by the finance minister and accepted with little enthusiasm by the LO Congress despite the endorsement of its president, Axel Strand. It took the inflation induced by the Korean War to give credence to the argument that action had to be taken to lay a permanent basis for economic growth. From its official acceptance by the SAP in 1955 until the years following the first oil shock in 1973, the Rehn–Meidner approach guided Swedish economic policy, and undoubtedly contributed substantially toward making Sweden a model of stable growth and full employment.

Swedish export-oriented industry was the engine. Under continuing pressure to modernize in order to pay good wages and stay competitive, it was assured union collaboration in efforts to do so. The fact that average labour costs were lower than they would have been had they bargained separately with their employees put expanding manufacturing companies at the forefront of technological development into an excellent position to absorb the workers released by the unsuccessful firms. And so they did, their efforts complemented by state programmes that underwrote and co-ordinated retraining and promoted geographical mobility. Though it itself was never expected to generate sufficient employment for the generation of workers entering the job market and especially the many women seeking work for the first time, Swedish export-oriented manufacturing did as expected: for many years it generated the needed revenues to permit the public and para-public sector to take up the slack.

Public consumption and investment complemented that of the private sector. Inevitably, however, the growth of the public sector, sheltered as it was from foreign competition, made it harder to determine an appropriate wage–profit share of economic growth, which ultimately gave rise to a more difficult and uncertain phase in collective bargaining discussed at the end of the last chapter.

As we noted, by the time the EFO formula had been established and agreed to, new conditions had emerged to put its applicability into doubt. The proliferation of service jobs created a serious problem in the application of the formula to determine the available room for wage increases, which, in the formula, was determined by changes in two major factors, international price developments, and productivity. Productivity was measured in large part by the performance of the competitive manufacturing sector, where rationalization was more rapid and complete than in the growing service sector. Looking back, we can see that something was amiss in setting the major wage and fringe benefit increase in the years 1973 to 1976. Since then, though the EFO formula was never abandoned, its application has been limited. Attempts to modify it to make it applicable to new conditions continue. The most recent effort in this vein, which has been termed the FOS report (the TCO economist replacing Edgren is named Spånt), was made public in 1988. Reaction was mixed, labour suspicious of its argument that since it is far more difficult than originally supposed to affect price setting in the competitive sector, more emphasis than ever had to be placed on norm-guided wage setting—a piece of advice evidently taken to heart by finance minister Feldt.[1]

As a highly internationalized economy with few trade barriers, Sweden was highly sensitive to developments in the world economy, and was to suffer the economic shocks of the 1970s. If the government had acted in timely fashion to slow

---

[1] One point in the report especially worth noting in light of our analysis is the stress on values: 'A lot depends on the values and norms developed by economic actors. . . . "Adequate values and norms" are among the premises of growth' (Faxén *et al.*, 1988).

down the economy and keep profits from shooting upwards by, say, raising the value of the krona (and thus lowering the cost of imported consumer goods), it might have been possible to avert some of the problems which began in 1975-6 when wages and payroll taxes—the latter a result of the Haga agreements—rose too quickly. Sweden, already beset with weak and inexperienced governments, was rendered especially vulnerable during the recession of the late seventies. The ensuing problems, however, did not undermine wage solidarity, and the active labour market policies remained at the core of Swedish policy-making. Full employment remained sacrosanct. In fact, labour market expenditures rose significantly as a proportion of government spending during these early years of bourgeois rule, settling back since to the level of a decade earlier. Before turning directly to these programmes, some concluding remarks about the economic analysis underlying the 'model' are in order.

THE MODEL REVISITED

Gösta Rehn is characteristically modest in taking credit for the 'model' that carries his name. Moreover, he insists that the model can be said to have been fully in operation only between 1958 and 1965. Only during that time was the government able (and willing) to act quickly to dampen inflation when it threatened—in 1960-1—counting on the selective programmes of the AMS to keep everyone working rather than—as in every boom since—responding too late and thus sharpening the next recession and placing added pressure on active labour market programmes. Still, looking back over thirty years' experience, Rehn is persuaded that the Swedish approach to unemployment proved itself under strain in recent years, providing a pertinent lesson to Western economists (Rehn, 1985), an argument summarized in the paragraphs below.

Unlike that of Sweden, most Western governments did little until recently to prevent price rises, calling upon unions to practise self-restraint whenever inflation started getting out of hand. But, outside of Austria, such a policy has invariably proven self-defeating. Union leaders, if they want to stay union leaders, can only make concessions in return for something tangible they can bring their members. It was inevitable that, when prices shot up after the first oil shock in 1973, unionized workers would insist on cost-of-living adjustment clauses to catch up, and inflation would skyrocket. Since unemployment also shot up, the standard Keynesian solutions which traded off inflation for employment were rendered problematic.

One approach saw governments turn to simple monetarist solutions, dampening expansion (in fact causing recession) by clamping down on the money supply through high interest rates. The theory was that inflation would first be overcome as a large pool of unemployed workers drove down wages; then, low wages would spur employment up to earlier levels. And indeed, helped by the decline in oil prices, years of painful recession finally checked inflation, but painfully little decline in unemployment ensued. Rehn explains this result as follows:

Unemployment is gradually being concentrated among those who have the least influence over wages (not to talk about prices) i.e. the handicapped, the old, the young and inexperienced, women with unstable connections to the labour market, people in underdeveloped areas. When they have been squeezed out in great numbers and employment is permitted to grow again, shortages will soon develop among the most attractive groups—able-bodied males in prime age brackets. Thus the reappearing risk of inflation makes governments or central banks inclined to give the screw of restraint another turn—again creating more unemployment (Rehn, 1983: 3).

He notes further that the fight against inflation entails cost increases per unit of output, through high rates of interest, low utilization of capacity, and taxes to finance at least some income for the unemployed (see Bellan, 1986: 55-7). This tends to increase prices despite restrained demand. Moreover, in highly concentrated product markets, lowered demand often does not lead to lowered prices, but rather to increased prices, in order for company managers to show satisfactory profits when sales volumes are low. In consequence, the monetarist battle against inflation was winnable but only at great cost, particularly to those least able to pay. Yet if the right wing's response was unacceptable, at least it had one. Some left-wing governments—France's, for one—loath to resort to unemployment-creating measures, chose a second alternative, to return to traditional expansionist policies. Profits, prices, and, soon, wages rose. The balance-of-payments situation deteriorated precipitously, and expansion had to be abandoned.

Sweden's response to the new situation came thus to be known as the 'third way', and was based on its unique experience with active labour market programmes and wage solidarity policy in the pre-oil-shock days. The immediate context was especially unfavourable. The bourgeois parties and, after 1982, the SAP found themselves at the helm of a small country highly dependent on trade with countries now willing to tolerate a high rate of unemployment to keep prices down. Yet, with the exception of the right wing of the Conservative (Moderate) party, no groups advocated remaining competitive by emulating Sweden's major trading partners and fighting inflation through unemployment. Taking this third way required skilful piloting. As Meidner put it: 'The appropriate balance was needed between contractive and expansive policies by supporting exports through currency depreciations, by limiting profits and yet stimulating investments, and by counteracting the pressures for wage increases above productivity growth through active labour market policies capable of improving the functioning of the labour market and attacking, in a selective and non-inflationary way, weak points in the economy (Meidner, 1985: 2–3).

As in past critical situations, the first step was to depreciate the currency. In response to out-of-line Swedish wage costs after 1976, the bourgeois parties had already reduced the krona in 1978 and again, by 10 per cent, in 1981. Upon taking office, the Social Democrats brought it down another 16 per cent. The harder task lay ahead, however, to ensure that the increased profits a lower currency would bring would not be dissipated in a spiral of rising wages and prices but instead find their way into increasing investment and jobs. Labour was prevailed upon to accept a loss in purchasing power on this assurance. Living up to the government's side of the deal meant, in part, taxing 'excess corporate profits' to be invested for collective purposes through the controversial wage-earner funds discussed in chapter 5.[2] It also entailed streamlining the entire gamut of active labour market programmes, giving them a far more pivotal place in the constellation of economic policies.

The adaptability of the Swedish system to new conditions—despite continuing uncertainty and tensions—is what makes it a 'model' to be studied and possibly emulated. Though originally designed to complement a rapid-growth, full-employment economy, the active labour market programmes were adapted to the exigencies of a period of slow growth and—elsewhere—high unemployment. This entailed reorienting existing programmes, instituting a series of new ones, and making changes in organization and mandate. Programmes had to be designed to improve prospects for company profits so that they would hire unemployed workers. But these had to be selective so that they resulted in increased output to brake the increase in prices rather than simply enlarging the profit share of GNP and in turn forcing up wages beyond those justified by rises in average productivity. These considerations underlay changes to the active labour market policy. Yet despite the changed context, the fundamental operative principles—to which we now turn our attention—were maintained.

THE ACTIVE LABOUR MARKET POLICY

The various programmes that comprise an active labour market policy are linked by one goal: getting people to productive work and productive work to people. Rather than Keynesian macroeconomic stimulation policies with their built-in inflationary effects, the engine of growth is the rising aggregate productivity engendered by low average profit margins and wage solidarity complemented by selective stimulation. The targets are geographically or occupationally defined categories among actual or potential workers. The

---

[2] One sympathetic observer has recently argued that the devaluations should have been at least partially avoided since they placed too much pressure on the unions to hold down wages, thus violating a central tenet of the Rehn–Meidner formula (Fraser, 1987).

economic objective served by thus getting them their fair share of jobs and benefits is the elimination of the incentive on their part to block the process of centralized negotiation based on wage solidarity.

Particular circumstances dictate the mix of labour market programmes used. These are normally classified as being either demand- or supply-oriented. Programmes directed at demand for labour themselves provide employment, or, more commonly, serve as incentives to firms to invest in appropriate industries and regions and employ difficult-to-hire workers. Those aimed at labour supply affect the availability of appropriately trained workers to meet specific demand.

The first set of demand-oriented labour market policies were those designed to temporarily affect the ebb and flow of private capital investment, making capital available during periods of slowdown. The earliest among these programmes was the investment reserve funds. Guided by the Stockholm school economists, the Social-Democrat-led government of the thirties sought to lessen the impact of fluctuations in the business cycle on employment. Companies were induced by tax advantages to withhold potentially inflationary expenditures during boom periods so as to be in a position to make them after the boom subsided and thus help avert recessions. They could set aside up to 50 per cent of pre-tax profits, half of which had to be deposited with the Bank of Sweden—an original role for a central bank—in investment reserve funds, which remained exempt from taxes if later invested during a declared economic slump in projects registered with the labour market authorities. Similar advantages were later made available to firms which invested in depressed regions.

On the labour market there operated a network of public institutions mandated to administer these and other labour market programmes. They were organized in the thirties on the principle that unions and employers were better equipped than state bureaucrats to institute employment programmes. From the beginning, employees of these labour market boards operated outside regular civil-service lines. The labour market boards were specifically excluded from the usual criteria applied to civil-servant hiring. The emphasis was on 'street-level bureaucrats'; educational qualifications mattered little since the necessary training would come with the job (Jangenäs, 1985). What counted was their experience in industry, usually from within the region, often as shop stewards, ombudsmen, or the like.

The present system really came into its own when the labour movement embraced the Rehn–Meidner approach in the mid-1950s. Today there are some 300 employment service offices and 90 employability centres. Above them are 24 regional boards, and at the top is the National Labour Market Board (AMS). The principle of lay representation on boards of public agencies was extended furthest on the AMS. Membership is predominated by employer and union organizations. Three of the 15 members of the AMS are from LO, two from TCO, one from SACO/SR, three from SAF; there is also a farmers' representative and a woman (usually named by LO), as well as the director general and deputy director general and two non-voting employee representatives. Members in 1986 included the chairpersons of TCO and SACO/SR, as well as the directors of the Metal Trades Employers' Association and the Construction Industry Employers' Association and the vice president of SAF.

The structure of the local and regional boards is parallel as far as union and business representation is concerned, while the public representatives are elected local officials. In 1986-7 the AMS administered a budget of 23.1 billion kr., almost 6 per cent of state expenditures, to provide services to 890,000 job-seekers with a total staff of 10,000. The primary task of the boards is to maintain constant contact with the firms, both labour and management, in their milieux, thus keeping informed of upcoming economic decisions and actions that affect employment within their jurisdiction (Jangenäs, 1985). The boards receive appropriate information on expected expansions, technological transformations, lay-offs, new investments, government projects, and the number and qualifications of school graduates. The information is compiled and monitored at the national level, and informs decisions concerning the application of the various programmes and the expenditures thereupon. The AMS reports via the Ministry of Labour to Parliament, which adopts its budget. Demands made by AMS, which represents labour and business working together at the highest level, are difficult for a government of whatever stripe to ignore.

A second category of demand-oriented labour market measures are public works projects which the county (regional) labour market boards are mandated to put into effect as they monitor economic conditions. Like the investment reserve funds, these projects are designed to counteract economic slowdowns. Municipalities and other employers apply to the boards for grants to fund employment-producing projects, and central government programmes are tailored accordingly. For example, during the 1971-3 recession, the government subsidy for the construction of sewage-treatment plants was temporarily raised from 25 to 75 per cent of cost, while grants to industry to prevent water and air pollution and reduce noise pollution rose from 25 to 50 per cent of cost. The economic downturns of the mid and late seventies prompted companies to take advantage of another such programme, stockpiling grants of 20 per cent of inventory increases. These programmes are estimated to have saved 25,000 jobs in 1975 and 1976, but were later phased out, having been criticized for subsidizing non-viable operations.

Traditional public works ('relief work') projects, paid at the same rates of pay as on the open market but lasting for limited periods, are still used to a limited extent to deal with local or sectorial 'islands of unemployment'. These projects are carefully regulated by the labour market boards to keep them free of any hint of political favouritism. Municipalities and counties are first given grants to cover planning costs and the plans for suitable public works projects are then filed with the county labour market boards. These are then collected and consolidated by the AMS. The board funds projects in light of local employment needs. With the plans all prepared, the projects are ready to be set into motion quickly, while labour and management representatives on the boards screen their activities to ensure that they do not distort the workings of the regular labour market. Ongoing projects go from traditional ones such as road construction, to more environmentally oriented ones such as reforestation, which became popular in the 1960s, to the dispensing of special services for the elderly, pre-school children, etc.

Job-seekers with less than 50 days left in insurance benefits get priority for public works jobs, as do young people entering the labour market. In 1986–7, an average of 17,600 Swedes, less than 50 per cent of the 1984 average, were employed in relief work: more than one-third were under the age of 25; 43 per cent were women. Since October 1983 workers on unemployment insurance with less than 50 days to go before the expiry of their unemployment benefits automatically become entitled to relief work. Altogether, these jobs accounted for 10 per cent of total AMS expenditures.

The various measures designed to secure employment for the handicapped are also normally classified as demand-oriented labour market programmes. These consist of specialized 'sheltered workshops' shielded from the profitability requirements of the market, and of subsidies paid to employers who hire handicapped persons. The subsidies cover a large proportion of labour costs for the first year (pay is always equivalent to that of other workers doing the same work) and decline gradually afterwards. In 1986–7, roughly 69,500 such jobs existed, of which 40 per cent were sheltered. A grant is available to cover 90 per cent of costs of up to 960 hours of wages in cases where the employee requires intensive preparation as well as the required modifications to the workstation. There are, also general subsidies to employers to pay people who assist the disabled and to purchase working aids and motorized vehicles (beyond the living aids provided through the social service network as described in chapter 7), as well as grants to older or occupationally handicapped people who wish to operate their own businesses.

While these expensive programmes which comprised 19 per cent of the AMS budget in 1986–7, are only part of what Sweden spends on the disabled, they are at the core of both Swedish attitudes toward the disabled and toward work: virtually no expense is too great when it comes to giving everyone a chance to work. Only meaningful work affords the opportunity to gain the self-respect that comes from contributing productively to the community. From a different perspective it is often much cheaper to place the disabled in institutions or on the dole than to provide the wherewithal to work. But any saving here would be made at the cost of the social solidarity that lies at the base of Swedish social policy and, as we have insisted, the effective workings of the solidaristic market economy.

With the lengthy recession of the latter 1970s came other demand-oriented 'bail-out' measures, most of which have now been phased out. Companies resisting pressure to lay off employees were eligible to receive subsidies of up to 20 per cent of production costs. A series of employment premiums for maintaining employment in designated regions and for groups in low demand (young and elderly workers, women) were also introduced. Employers could get 55 per cent of labour costs for the first five months if they arranged training for redundant workers instead of dismissing them. Adjustment grants were made available during the recession to lessen the impact of lay-offs and dismissals. Conditional upon its being informed in advance of impending lay-offs, the AMS was authorized to furnish 75 per cent of wage costs over a maximum of 6 months to allow the firm to stay in operation longer so as to give the AMS time to set up the necessary programmes to help the workers to adjust. With the SAP's return to power and the upturn in the economy, these programmes were phased out except in so far as they targeted designated regions. The regional thrust first came as a response to an effective campaign by the Centre party during the late sixties attacking AMS policies for depopulating the North, its name derided as standing for 'All Move Southward' (Wadensjö, 1980).

In 1984 two important new programmes were initiated after a number of pilot projects proved successful. Recruitment subsidies to private and public employers of up to 50 per cent of total wage costs for six months were introduced, with the aim of facilitating recruitment of hard-core unemployed and of the 10 per cent of young people who leave school at the age of 16. In 1986–7, 18,000 persons were placed by the employment service bureaux under this programme. In the same year, the bureaux were given responsibility for assigning out-of-school and out-of-work 18–19-year-olds to 'youth teams'. Municipal authorities were required by law to set up these teams, which provided a minimum of four hours a day at regular hourly wages for eligible young people. During

1986-7, an average of 21,400 persons were assigned to the youth teams. Of the young people who finished this programme, 51 per cent found jobs that same year on the open market. Together the recruitment subsidies and youth teams accounted for 11 per cent of the AMS budget.

Necessary as they are, these demand-oriented programmes have generally been viewed as complementary to the series of programmes affecting the supply of labour. Before turning to them we should touch upon the more traditional, intermediate function of the employment service. Linking the demand for labour with its supply is the transmission of relevant timely information to those seeking work or training and those seeking to hire them. In all employment centres across the country, every job vacancy is listed and described in detail on a computerized listing system with hands-on terminals. Relevant information is supplied to employment bureau personnel, who visit employers one afternoon each week, carrying with them lists and qualifications of available job-seekers. After a successful pilot project to test the idea in several regions was completed in 1976, a system of compulsory notification by employers of job openings with the employment service was instituted nation-wide. With rare exception, jobs lasting more than ten days must now be listed with AMS, though employers remain free to hire anyone, whether referred by the employment service or not, and to recruit by newspaper ads, personal contacts, etc. There is now, as a result, one comprehensive source of information relative to labour supply and demand.

The efficacy of the system is illustrated by the fact that the 890,000 job-seekers that in 1986-7 used the services of the employment bureaux is greater than the average number of vacancies reported that year. Understandably, therefore, though employers' representatives objected to compulsory notification on principle, they came to admit that the system functions well in practice (Ginsburg, 1983). We have already noted that co-operation of business and labour on the AMS is the best example of the concertation that is a key feature of the solidaristic market economy. We see in the universal listing system a manifestation of the workings of a second key principle identified in chapter 1. Important supplementary services to industry, such as those concerning labour supply, better complement the functioning of the competitive market in the productive sector when provided through the buffer zone, that is, outside the competitive-market sector through public agencies operating in concertation with business and labour.

Programmes affecting the supply of labour provide various forms of training or promote geographical mobility to assist workers who are unemployed or in danger of losing their jobs due to an impending plant closure or relocation. Workers whose prospects of getting a job in their locality are very low are eligible for relocation grants for family moving and travel expenses and an allowance for maintaining two households for as long as nine months. (Alternatively, though infrequently, the employment service buys the old house for resale.) In 1986-7, 33,000 job-seekers benefited from some form of assistance to mobility, the majority of whom were young people entering the labour market. Just under 2 per cent of AMS expenditures were for relocation.

Much greater emphasis is placed on occupational than on geographical mobility; indeed, as full employment was approached in 1987, moving allowances were retricted to designated regions. The carefully kept AMS statistics reveal a growing tendency for job vacancies to stipulate specific education or experience requirements. For 1986-7, 75 per cent of all reported vacancies carried such stipulations, adding a new urgency to the various training programmes which are at the heart of the active labour market policies. Starting in 1986, a new and separate organization took responsibility for employment training which up to then had been a combined undertaking of the AMS and the National Board of Education. The new National Labour Market Training Service, AMU, is independent of the AMS; it receives no direct government moneys but sells its services to AMS as well as directly to employers.

Vocational training is provided at special AMI centres and on the job. Apart from on-site vocational rehabilitation for the handicapped, there are four situations that qualify for state grants for in-house training: workers seeking to advance by moving to jobs where there is a shortage of skilled personnel, workers whose jobs are being transformed by technological change, workers threatened with probable lay-off, and workers belonging to the underrepresented sex in sex-typed jobs. In total 23,000 persons took advantage of one of these programmes in 1986-7.

The largest numbers in this category were job-seekers taking training courses given or supervised by the AMU (see the discussion of adult education in chapter 6), which in 1986-7 averaged 34,000, among whom were a disproportionate number of recently arrived immigrants. In addition, thousands of handicapped were registered at any given time in one of 31 employability institutes with special resources (AMI-S). Apart from free tuition and course materials, trainees receive a taxable stipend, indexed to the inflation rate and based on their eligibilty for unemployment benefits, which ranges from a minimum of one-half to a maximum of slightly over two-thirds of the average industrial wage. Persons ineligible for, or having exhausted, regular unemployment benefits receive the minimum. Young people under 20 without dependants, who are not entitled to regular unemployment benefits, receive a smaller amount, about a quarter the average wage. While the number of people in labour market training fluctuates somewhat, at any given time it tends to comprise around one-third of those not employed. Excluding the programmes directed at the handicapped, roughly 21 per cent of all AMS expenditures go to labour market training.

The AMS is also responsible for the monitoring of unemployment insurance benefits paid out by the unemployment insurance societies as well as the payment of direct cash benefits to those out of work not covered by the societies. The insurance societies are closely linked to the unions who initially created them. All unionized employees are members and others may choose to join. Eligible unemployed workers can receive up to 92 per cent of their former income, up to the maximum stated above, for up to 60 weeks. The cash assistance programme was established in 1974 for those not eligible and, like the unemployment insurance benefits, is funded by general state revenues as well as the social security contributions of employers and the self-employed. New entrants into the labour market qualify if they have been actively seeking work through the AMS for at least 3 months. The maximum for cash assistance is roughly 35 per cent of that for unemployment insurance, and lasts a maximum of 30 weeks, though for those over 55 it can be extended right up to retirement age.

In 1986–7, 31 per cent of total labour market expenditures were directed toward unemployment insurance or cash assistance payments. Overall, demand-oriented programmes including recruitment subsidies, public works, subsidies for hiring the disabled, and youth teams accounted for the largest part, 40 per cent; and supply-oriented programmes covering training, vocational rehabilitation, and relocation accounted for 19 per cent. The remaining 9 per cent went toward information and administration. Thus, while, at 3 per cent of GNP, Sweden's overall labour market expenditure is probably the highest among nations, more distinctive still is the relatively insignificant proportion of that amount that goes into cash payments to enable the unemployed to subsist (despite the level of such payments being very generous by comparative standards), and the large proportion going into programmes putting them to work.

In fact, as unemployment fell to 2 per cent in 1987, cash payments to the unemployed as well as the number of persons employed in public-works and youth-team projects declined. Yet AMS–AMU programmatic expenditures have not diminished markedly. The issue is not bureaucratic inflexibility, it is rather labour market flexibility. While the debate over whether the Swedish labour market will ultimately prove too rigid compared to ones with higher unemployment and weaker unions still rages (Bosworth and Rivlin, 1986)—and will be taken up in the concluding chapter—these expenditures lend credence to the optimistic view. In a period of full employment, AMS programmes concentrate on vocational rehabilitation for the hard-to-employ—the physically, mentally, and emotionally handicapped, new immigrants, inhabitants of depressed regions—and on putting those presently employed in jobs soon to become redundant due to new technology or cheap imports into a position to move toward those for which there is a shortage of skilled labour. The principle is that one must take advantage of the highs in the business cycle to put oneself in a strong position for the next low.

The means for doing so are the active labour market policy, wage solidarity, and centralized collective bargaining, three of the four cornerstones of the Rehn–Meidner model. The fourth is not general demand stimulation. Overall fiscal–monetary restraint through sales and payroll taxes is used to keep gross profit margins low enough for employers to effectively resist inflationary money wage demands. It bears repeating that this approach was developed by the Swedish labour movement itself in the 1950s, in marked contrast with the short-sighted attitude of much of labour elsewhere. Of course, keeping average profit margins down through restraint ultimately meant that governments would have to provide for additional capital from other sources to guarantee a volume of capital accumulation appropriate for the required long-run rate of investment. This is thus the fourth element which remains to be considered: the creation and investment of collective savings. As we shall see in the chapter that follows, the form this has taken has made the question especially controversial in recent years.

5

Investment Capital and Industrial Democracy

The rapid modernization of Swedish industry that followed upon the implementation of the Rehn–Meidner model created a demand for large amounts of investment capital. Some of this capital was generated internally in the form of self-financed reinvestment by the most successful companies. Such self-financing could not supply all the required investment capital however. An obvious first source of supplementary investment capital lay in Sweden's high level of household savings. The extraordinary growth that took place during the 1950s seemed to indicate that private savings were sufficient to fill the gap; in fact, the problem remained beneath the surface.

From the start, the LO economists looked to sources of collective investment to supplement self-financing and private borrowing. They had insisted that the profits of the successful firms favoured by the wage solidarity system should not be allowed to grow so great that employees of these firms were impelled to seek remuneration beyond solidarity wages. In the long term, keeping average profits down would mean a general shortage of investment capital. Moreover, the high levels of personal taxation required to pay the cost of the active labour market programmes accompanying wage solidarity and, especially, complementary social and income-security policies, meant that, even for the high-saving Swedes, household savings could not take up the slack (Heckscher, 1984: 116). Other public sources would have to be found. But the very notion of collective capital triggered a negative response on the bourgeois side: industrial investment was supposed to be a task left to market actors; the very nature of public bureaucracies, it was assumed, made them ill-suited for the task.

The need for sources of supplemental capital to make up for declining aggregate corporate profits due to wage solidarity dovetailed with LO's objective of winning supplemental pensions for blue-collar workers. Most white-collar and professional employees benefited from private pension schemes which supplemented the basic flat-rate state pension established in 1947. In keeping with the logic underlying wage solidarity, the LO wanted a universal, public, rather than pay-as-you-go, solution to avoid tying supplemental pension benefits to the profitability of particular enterprises, thus creating divisions among workers.[1] A long public debate took place spanning three royal commissions, a referendum, and a dissolution of parliament before it was settled. In 1959, following in large part the unanimous recommendations of the third royal commission, the government presented its plan for setting up the ATP: it consisted of three separate co-managed public pension funds which would be restricted in their influence on capital markets. Business was not entirely mollified, but the unexpectedly strong showing of the Social Democrats in the 1960 elections underlined the popularity of the plans and forced the opposition parties to reconcile themselves to the ATP (Heckscher, 1984: 117).

The three funds were constituted of employer and employee contributions, one from the public sector, one from the private sector, and the third from small business and the self-employed: each was to be administered by a board dominated by labour and management from the sector. The funds could lend directly only to the public sector. Thus, while part of the vast capital rapidly accumulated by the ATP funds found its way into private-sector activities through indirect, non-equity financing, the bulk went into public-sector projects. By far the largest investment was in housing, paving the way for the comprehensive modernization of Sweden's housing stock in the next decade.

As profit margins began to decline late in the 1960s, it became apparent that self-financing was falling well short of required levels of investment. Pressure mounted to open ATP funds more directly to private investment and to create other sources of collective capital. To facilitate the investment of

[1] The comparative defensiveness and fragmentation of Danish trade unions is not unrelated to the fact that, unlike their Swedish counterparts, they did not win universal public supplemental pensions.

ATP funds, a state investment bank as well as a number of intermediate credit institutions, such as the Business Credit Corporation and the Export Credit Corporation, were established in the late sixties. By the 1970s, ten such institutions served the credit needs of private business (Pontussen, 1984). In addition, certain of the labour market programmes described in chapter 4 provided a source of capital in the form of tax benefits or subsidies.

In its 1970 Long-Term Economic Survey, the Ministry of Finance estimated the profit share to be declining annually at an average of 1.2 per cent and predicted a shortage of investment capital (Martin, 1984: 268). The survey noted that collective savings through the ATP funds had increased to offset a good part of the decline in private investment; but it cautioned that these investments came largely in the form of loans, thus increasing the debt–equity ratio which, if unimpeded, would dampen corporate spending because of the high debt levels.

The obvious solution was to turn the ATP funds into a source of equity capital. The LO had first made such a demand in 1966, and at its following congress in 1971 reaffirmed its position using the Long-Term Survey to buttress its case. Action was not long in coming. However, rather than altering the mandate of the three ATP funds, the government created a fourth fund, towards which additional employers' and income-earners' contributions were directed, its board composed after changes later in the decade of five union representatives, three business representatives, and two from both central and local government. By 1982 the fourth ATP fund had built its base capital into assets with a market value of 4 billion kr., making it the fourth largest single owner of shares listed on the Stockholm exchange, though accounting still for less than 1 per cent of the total assets of the ATP funds. As in the case of the first three funds, SAF and the bourgeois parties' initial opposition to the fourth fund gave way as they came to see it play a generally useful role. It was the non-socialist government that in 1979 increased the fund's size and scope, though limiting it to 10 per cent equity in any one company.

There is substantial similarity between the fourth ATP fund

and the employee investment funds, commonly known as the wage-earner funds, introduced in 1983. Both were inspired at least in part by the situation observed in 1971 by the LO; both sought to build equity capital for investment in industry; and both, though opposed by business, proved useful to companies seeking capital. Yet there the similarity ends. Unlike the ATP funds, no consensus formed behind the wage-earner funds (henceforth referred to as the WEF). Indeed, the WEF were more than a means of building equity for investment in industry. They also constituted one of a number of initiatives to strengthen the position of labour *vis-à-vis* that of capital, many of which found their way into a series of laws discussed later in this chapter. Moreover, the original conception of the WEF, the Meidner plan, as it was known, went beyond these other initiatives which sought to strengthen the position of the employees within clearly defined limits. The proposed funds had an open-endedness as to just how far the transfer of ownership would go.

To come to grips with the at times emotional debate over this issue, we must go back to the climate at the end of the 1960s. Two forces were at work 'radicalizing' the Swedish labour movement. One was international: the end of the 'end of ideology', the rediscovery of Marxism by young intellectuals on the left and their influence on the Swedish labour movement. The other was largely the result of wage solidarity in practice. Wage differentials collapsed between skilled blue-collar workers in mining and manufacturing, on one side, and the new white-collar service workers, mainly public sector and often women, on the other. At the same time the most efficient manufacturing companies were earning record profits.

The combination of intellectual radicalism and discontent on the shop floor made for an explosive mixture. Industrial democracy became the cry at once to articulate and restrain the demands that grew out of this turmoil. Employers were unprepared for this new initiative on the part of labour, especially the trade unions' insistence that legislation be used to strengthen the position of workers in enterprise above and beyond agreements signed by the parties. For them, the whole idea constituted a violation of the principle of the freedom of the labour market. When the LO called for the establishment

of the WEF in 1976, it was, for many employers, the final
straw; a line had been crossed.

The idea, in fact, was not a new one. Ernst Wigforss had
called for industrial democracy in the 1940s and 'branch
funds' had been suggested in previous Congress reports. Yet
nothing concrete came of the idea until the 1971 LO Congress
mandated its executive to study the idea. Its former research
director Rudolf Meidner was named to lead an investigation
guided by three objectives: (1) to complement the lessening
of wage differentials based on the principle of solidarity, (2)
to counteract the concentration of wealth which stems from
industrial self-financing, and (3) to increase the influence of
employees over the economy. The report, made public in
1975, was overwhelmingly endorsed by the LO Congress a
year later. It called for setting up employee investment funds
dominated by the unions and financed by a 20 per cent surtax
on corporate pre-tax profits to be paid partly in money and
partly in shares into the funds, the proceeds of the funds to
be invested in Swedish companies through the purchase of
shares. Voting rights for these shares were to be exercised by
the company's employees.

The far-reaching character of the report itself, the rapidity
with which the LO Congress rallied to it, and the almost
apocalyptic language used by some in promoting it came as
an unexpected shock to many at the time, and fed the fears
of an already apprehensive business community. *LO-Tidningen*,
official journal of the confederation, proclaimed that capital
was finally to come under democratic control—with the unions
acting for the people. One chart suggested that the trade
unions would win majority interest in profitable companies
within 20 to 30 years (Lyon, 1985). SAP leaders, like some
within the LO itself, were caught off guard; the best the party
could do was delay taking any sort of stand (Åsard, 1986:
383). Even Rudolf Meidner, who had expected long discussion rather than immediate adoption of the plan, came to
exclude himself from the debate over it.

Once the campaign reached such rhetorical heights, support for the idea from outside the labour movement was precluded. Yet, ironically, it was not the SAP which initially promoted the idea of profit sharing. In the 1960s labour was lukewarm to the idea; the 1920s LO position ruling out any labour responsibility for management still carried some weight. It was the Liberal and Centre parties (as well as the Communists) who put forward a number of such proposals to encourage employee participation in company decision-making. The Conservatives too endorsed the idea in 1968. With the wildcat strikes of 1970 to spur them on, the labour leaders reversed their position. The Meidner plan followed, and before leaving office in 1976 the Social Democrats with the support of the Liberals set up a commission to look into profit sharing through employee-controlled investment funds. 'People's capitalism' was also in vogue in business circles. The Conservative minister of finance in the new non-socialist coalition government in 1978 introduced a scheme of incentives for employees buying shares in their companies. But as the rhetoric mounted on both sides of the Meidner plan, the opposition parties joined business in rejecting the idea of 'central' funds in which investors have no individual ownership rights. These they declaimed had more to do with altering power relationships than encouraging savings. By the same token, the LO could hardly support profit sharing at the firm level which would inevitably bring wage levels—or rather rates of wage drift—incompatible with wage solidarity.

The investigatory commission, composed of representatives from labour, management, and the political parties, proved unable to arrive at a consensus. The chairman at first used his position to delay any decision, awaiting SAP's committing itself on the issue, something it proved unable to do prior to the 1979 election. In the spring of 1977, SAP and LO had set up a joint working group to develop a common 'saleable' position. The following year the group presented a revised plan proposing a set of 24 development funds financed by a payroll tax paid by employers and specifically designed to increase collective capital formation. However, the ruling councils of neither the LO nor SAF endorsed the proposal in its entirety. Since the commission had not yet handed in its report, the issue was largely kept out of the 1979 election in which the non-socialists managed to retain their majority. However the lost time proved important. According to one close observer, the Liberals by this point were too closely associated with the SAP over such questions as nuclear energy to suit many of their supporters, and thus were no longer in a position—as they had been earlier—to negotiate a compromise on the specific form profit sharing would take, and thus head off the confrontation that followed (Åsard, 1986).

A third LO/SAP proposal was submitted for adoption at the union and party congresses of 1981. The plan set out the guidelines for the scheme finally enacted two years later. The following principles were recognized as fundamental: (1) the funds would be constituted from compulsory contributions in the form of levies on payrolls and profits (but not in the form of stock issues) on larger high-profit companies; (2) accumulated capital would be used to promote the growth of the economy through the purchase of shares; (3) the funds would be collectively owned and administered in a partially decentralized fashion and (4) they would take a businesslike approach, investing only in companies likely to yield at least an average return.

While there were important elements of continuity in the actual proposals, the tone had changed significantly since 1976. The underlying spirit surrounding specific application of the above principles was one of flexibility. The need to be open to discussion with other parties on all practical aspects was explicitly recognized in the report, which stated: 'The congresses [of LO and SAP] furthermore give the party executive, in cooperation with the trade union movement, a large leeway for decision making as concerns the technical shaping and the timing of actions for the establishment of the Funds. Openness must be shown in these matters, and other opinions shall be taken into consideration.'

These last two sentences constituted an unofficial invitation to a divided TCO to collaborate more closely with LO on the issue, and a signal for the leadership to introduce modifications leading to compromise with the employers' organizations in anticipation of the likely imminent return to power of the SAP. It was, however, too late. The representatives of business were unimpressed, dismissing the new proposals and flexible posture as public-relations efforts to calm public opinion. With the SAP returned to office in 1982, a renewed public battle loomed. In September of 1983, in anticipation of legislation expected before the end of year, the Federation of Swedish Industries (SI) issued a long and well-publicized statement on the wage-earner funds, which included the following:

All the claims that have been made to the effect that collective wage-earner funds would promote industrial growth, especially by providing a flow of venture capital, or by exercising a moderating influence on wage demands, have on closer examination shown themselves to be untenable. All that remains is the fact that the point at issue is a proposal to transfer in stages a considerable part of private industry and commerce into collective ownership by means of an increase in taxation—over and above the record level that we are already burdened by in this country. . . .

The Federation is prepared to view favourably various forms of ownership, provided they are permitted to compete in a free and unfettered manner on the Swedish and international markets. On the other hand, a process of socialization, albeit implemented in gradual stages . . . leads to a sharp deterioration in industrial efficiency and growth that will cause severe economic problems in any country that embarks on such a hazardous path. . . . The Federation of Swedish Industries categorically rejects any plan for the introduction of collective wage-earner funds in Sweden (SI, 1983: 6–7).

The strong language in this document and the even stronger language displayed on placards at the anti-WEF marches of the following month, if justified by the initial plan and the rhetoric surrounding it, seem out of proportion in 1983. Business appeared, for one thing, rather insensitive to the evolution of the context surrounding application of the plans. A crucial new factor was now at play. Labour had agreed to hold down wage demands and not attempt to recover all the purchasing power lost in the 16 per cent devaluation introduced by the SAP on its return to power. If the new growth were not to be dissipated by inflation, the resulting high profits (which business could hardly have failed to notice) could not simply be paid out in dividends and wage drift. The WEF constituted a concession in return for labour's wage restraint by diverting a small but symbolically significant share of profits away from dividends and wage drift and toward potential job-producing investment.

While business's representatives remained highly sceptical of labour's conversion to regarding the wage-earner funds as merely a 'means of capital formation like the ATP funds, a change had indeed taken place. The radical seventies had given way to the practical eighties and prominent social democrats were saying publicly what a few had been saying privately a few years earlier: the government could have achieved the desired goal by simply widening the fourth ATP pension fund without embarking on a symbolic battle over free enterprise. The TCO leadership's embarrassing failure to rally its membership behind the plan was perhaps the most significant practical consequence of that strategic mis-calculation (Micheletti, 1985). The Swedish labour movement has been taken to task on this score even by some of its friends. For example, in an article published by the Socialist International to which the SAP belongs, Peter Glotz, general secretary of the West German SDP, condemned the 'reckless radicalism of the proposal put forward by the unions . . . without any prior consultation of the Social Democratic Party [which only] served to strengthen and unite the Swedish right-wing parties. . . . The watchword must be: co-determination and co-ownership, not trench warfare!' (Glotz, 1985).

In keeping with the Meidner plan, the 1983 law set up employee investment funds financed out of corporate profits, to invest in Swedish companies through the purchase of shares, half the voting rights for which would be held by the firm's employees. But important safeguards were added to ensure that the 'confiscatory' aspect be eliminated. Five regionally based funds run by 9-member (of which 5 are union rep-resentatives) government-appointed boards were set up. The smaller part of the financing is drawn from a 20 per cent tax on the profits of larger firms above a certain threshold, and the rest from a 0.2 per cent additional payroll levy. The funds stop receiving further moneys in 1990 at which point it is estimated they will own between 5 and 10 per cent of publicly held shares of Swedish corporations for a value of 15 billion kr.

They must show a minimum 3 per cent return on their investment, and no fund can own more than 8 per cent of the shares of any given firm. (The theoretical maximum of shares of any one firm they could together own is thus 40 per cent.) The plan was put into effect early in 1984 but SAF and its affiliates refused to have private-business representatives take the seats to which they were entitled on the boards, while the non-socialist parties, led by the resurgent Conservatives, vowed to abolish the WEF if elected in 1985.

In Paris with the OECD until the mid-seventies, Gösta Rehn kept out of the WEF battle. He did, however, write a useful and balanced analysis for the EEC in 1983, in which, among other things, he asked the reader to look at the issue from the perspective of the LO: that of a trade-union federation operating democratically within a free-market system, yet negotiating wages that withheld expected rewards from workers in the most profitable firms in the long-term interests of all the workers. Rehn asked critics of the funds to 'consider the real dilemma of the Trade Unions: how to get acceptance among the rank and file members for a non-inflationary wage policy under full employment'. The fight was a manifestation of a fundamental choice to be taken between 'two alternative policies for managing the economy in Western societies: to brake the wage–price race by letting high unemployment reduce the bargaining power of workers *or* to create psychological and social preconditions for a non-inflationary incomes policy under a full employment that is created with other means than generalized high profits' (Rehn, 1983: 30). The second choice, when successful, he notes, places unions in an especially weak position since workers no longer see unions as necessary to defend their jobs.

Rehn adds that Olof Palme unsuccessfully tried to make this point to the business community in an effort to win some measure of sympathy from them before the law was passed: 'Some guarantee to the workers for a share in the increase of wealth had to be worked out. They [the businessmen] would be wiser cooperating positively in the endeavours to solve the problem in a constructive way. The congresses had given him rather wide margins for negotiations about "the forms and the timing" of the reforms for this purpose' (Rehn, 1983: 31).

The response was an unSwedish 'no'. In the words of the SAF president, Kurt Nicolin of ASEA, business was not going to bargain over its own existence.

Not only the employers were reticent about the funds. Polls revealed that the majority of the population remained opposed to the idea through the 1985 election. Nevertheless, an even larger majority, evidently, did not view them as sufficiently threatening to vote against the SAP, preferring to take a wait-and-see approach. Despite the protestations of business and its political allies, the public perception was that no irremediable harm would follow implementation of the modified plans. Partly for electoral reasons, but also partly because their views had considerably evolved since the mid-seventies, SAP and LO leaders had little to say about the WEF in the 1985 campaign, treating them as one measure among others. Labour leaders had come to learn that the majority of their own members were lukewarm to the plan, since they understood that some of the profits accumulated in the funds might otherwise have been used to raise their salaries.

The Moderates were unable to make the funds a major issue of the 1985 campaign and suffered badly in the results, losing much ground to the more middle-of-the-road Liberals. Since then the issue has receded but no formal reconciliation has taken place. Business leaders admit that the amounts of money concerned are trivial compared, say, to those accumulated by the ATP funds. It is, they say, the principle they cannot accept, that public bodies know how to invest better than businessmen. But such symbolic arguments carry little weight in Sweden, neither on the right nor on the left. The present attitude of the union leaders toward the funds, characterized recently by Rudolf Meidner as 'a faint shadow of the original idea' (Meidner, 1987: 10), can be summed up as 'the proof of the pudding is in the eating'. It is probably closer to Swedish mainstream public opinion than the ideological opposition of SAF and the Conservatives. Indeed, it may be SAF and SI that are further from their base at this point: as union representatives like to point out, whatever the official position, there has proven to be no shortage of firms seeking WEF investment in their operations, nor have the employers been able to point to any instance of the funds engaging in 'unfriendly' takeovers or otherwise using their powers improperly.[2] A poll conducted a few months prior to the 1988 election is revealing on this score. While only 18 of the 100 top executives surveyed favoured an SAP government, 39 believed the party to be better for business than the opposition (*Inside Sweden*, June 1988).

A useful contrast can be drawn between the wage-earner funds and the comparatively unheralded 'renewal funds' which also serve to channel a part of the profits of the most successful firms. The legislation had the effect of freezing 10 per cent of all 1985 company profits exceeding 500,000 kr. in non-interest-bearing accounts in the National Bank which, if used within five years for research and development and/or employee education and retraining in a manner agreed to by the local unions, are exempt from corporate taxation. As of this writing, tripartite consultations continue concerning use of the large sums accumulated in these funds. The 1986 OECD examiners, cited elsewhere, added a contribution to these discussions in their report.

A remarkable potential resource exists in the Renewal Funds. . . . Some Skr. 5 to 8,000 million will be available for use after July 1 of the present year. . . . It is felt that it is a once-only opportunity to achieve something big, and that any choice made will lead to difficulties because the total accumulated is in the same order of magnitude as total annual industrial R&D expenditure for Sweden. Spent over five years, it would enable industry to increase its R&D expenditure at a compound rate of about 15% more per year than it does today (OECD, 1986: 21).

The renewal funds, to which we return in our consideration of R and D policy in chapter 6, were not warmly greeted by business—but there was none of the hostility generated by the WEF either.

---

[2] In 1988 SAF published its critical analysis of the funds' performance, entitled 'Trade Union Funds in Sweden' (by Leif Widen); this contained little in the way of specific criticisms. The LO's defence of the funds, 'Three Years with Employee Investment Funds: An Evaluation', published in the same year, is equally general, suggesting that the major achievement of the funds was their contribution to the fine performance of the Swedish economy.

INDUSTRIAL DEMOCRACY AND JOB REDESIGN

As initially conceived, the wage-earner funds had sought to reconcile wage solidarity with newly emerging demands of various kinds for greater industrial democracy. The funds were one of a series of initiatives seeking to give workers greater control, to achieve co-determination in the workplace. Indeed, industrial democracy was viewed as one aspect, though a key one, of the wider goal, participatory democracy in every sphere of life.

Industrial democracy in Sweden took the form of both legislation and labour-management agreements. The relationship was two-way. The various laws served to enshrine practices that were becoming more common and, at the same time, left concrete implementation to be carried out through agreements between business and labour. The debate over legislative reforms is thus inseparable from ongoing developments in job design and workplace reorganization.

Dissatisfied with progress in negotiating workers' rights and concerned about wildcat strikes, LO and TCO turned to the government for action in the early 1970s; the question was, naturally enough, given over to a commission for investigation. Chaired by the former TCO president Walter Åman, the committee was mandated to propose amendments to the labour code to foster greater equality between employees and employers in the workplace. A series of laws were adopted following the commission's recommendations which came to be known as the Åman laws, the most important of which was MBL, the law on co-determination.

Consultative works' councils in each enterprise of more than 50 employees were negotiated by LO and SAF in 1946. In 1973, trade unions were given the right to appoint two representatives to the boards of companies with more than 100 employees, extended to companies with more than 25 employees under MBL in 1976. Once adopted, MBL became the centrepiece of a comprehensive reform strengthening the role of workers in the firm through information and participation. Unlike the case of the WEF, business accommodated itself to these laws and participated in their development and application despite serious misgivings about the erosion of management prerogatives.

The MBL law strengthened the position of the employees' representatives with regard to the scheduling of board meetings, the dissemination of information prior to them, and the right to speak and vote at meetings and participate in board committees. Two complementary laws were adopted in 1974: the law on the status of shop stewards, which guaranteed union representatives paid leave and freedom of access throughout the plant to fulfil their trade-union duties; and the Security of Employment act which permitted dismissal only for 'valid reason' and established mandatory provisions regarding notice. In 1975 a new law gave employees the right to the time off work required to pursue an education. In the same year, an agreement was reached on internal consultation mechanisms applying to corporations with 50 or more employees. The agreement ensured appropriate training in economics and business administration for employee board members, and the right to examine all relevant information about the firm's plans and performance and to engage a consultant at the companies' expense (Eiger, 1983). The unions accordingly instituted intensive three-week training programmes for employee board members.

These various laws were for the most part integrated into the MBL act adopted in the light of the Åman commission's final recommendations. Other important measures were adopted: (1) the range of issues subject to collective bargaining was substantially broadened; (2) employers were forbidden to make any decisions or take any actions prejudicial to the outcome of negotiations on all matters subject to co-determination; and (3) in disputes involving conflicting interpretation of non-salary-related aspects of collective agreements, the interpretation of the union came to prevail unless management chose to take it to the labour tribunals. Application of these provisions and those concerning job safety discussed below could easily bring economic chaos, but not in Sweden: the trade unions exercised their new prerogatives responsibly—as promised and expected.

MBL set out a framework for the negotiation of a detailed

co-determination agreement between the parties. Such agreements were reached in 1979 with employers in the state-owned companies (SFO) and the co-operatives (KFO) and, in 1980, with public-sector employers at the three levels. In the latter case, it was agreed that employee representatives would be excluded from participation in decisions of a political nature which were to be exercised only by popularly elected members, with special boards to arbitrate in cases of disagreement as to what was 'political'. After hard bargaining, in 1982 LO and the cartel of white-collar workers in private industry, PTK, signed an implementation agreement on co-determination with SAF. The agreement stipulated that as a rule one-third of board members were to be named by the workers, and laid out the modalities for consultation and information distribution concerning plans to reorganize the workplace and introduce new technologies. The matter-of-fact tone and language of the agreement belies an affirmation of two fundamental interconnected goals: making companies more efficient, and, getting workers more involved: 'the parties wish to state their common opinion that the development of efficiency and participation in the company will involve the better use of the expertise and skills and the experience of the employees.' The following quotes reflect the convergence in the approach taken by the parties. The first is from SAF's introductory brochure, the second from the manual used by LO in its three-week training programme especially designed for worker representatives on company boards.

Any individual who wishes to develop should be able to do so. The building blocks are knowledge, motivation, and confidence in the future, while personal capabilities and attitudes represent each individual's starting point. This is where employers have a major responsibility to develop tasks so that the competence and commitment of their personnel can be put to good use. This is the way we can bring together efficiency and job satisfaction and enable people to enjoy their work (SAF, undated: 5).

A democratic work organization and a good work environment which the employees like are not enough. If the company fails to keep pace with technological advances, or persists in manufacturing an obsolete product, it will fail. If the trade unions are to succeed in achieving genuine co-determination in matters that affect our daily work, we must also become involved in management issues (LO, 1986: 32).

MBL was followed by a series of complementary laws, some of them at the initiative of the non-socialists who took power at the end of 1976. In 1977, the minimum annual paid vacation period was extended to five weeks. In 1978, the law on parental leave was amended guaranteeing parents the right to share a 12-month paid leave for a newborn child (see chapter 7) and, subsequently, in the case of parents of children under 8, to reduce their working day to six hours. In 1980, a law was introduced requiring employers to take positive measures to overcome sex discrimination in employment. Laws were enacted in 1982 to reinforce protection of the privacy of the employee's personal files and regulate overtime work.

A comprehensive law to safeguard workers' health and safety, amending the existing 1949 law, was passed in 1974 and substantially revised in 1978. In 1974 work-environment improvement grants were instituted and made available to modernizing firms conditional upon the presence of union-appointed 'safety stewards' to review the introduction of new technology with regard to the health and safety of workers. The law also set up a tripartite work-environment fund to finance research and development in this area. In 1976, SAF, LO, and TCO signed a work-environment agreement, the provisions of which were then incorporated into the 1978 Act. Safety stewards were made mandatory in all places of employment, the larger firms were required to establish parity safety committees and provide them with the information, on-site access, and time off needed to carry out their duties. One duty of these 'safety delegates' is to order the immediate stoppage of dangerous operations. Money is provided by the state to the Joint (SAF, LO, TCO) Industrial Safety Council first set up in 1942, to train the safety delegates through a programme that funds the tripartite National Board of Occupational Safety and Health established under the act. Among the tasks of the Board, which now employs more than 750 persons (Pestoff, 1987), are the testing and certification of industrial equipment and the monitoring of the accessibility of medical and nursing services in places of employment.

The existence of a flexible institutional structure regulating employee involvement in these and other areas of corporate decision-making has in fact tended to make it easier for corporations to adjust to changing conditions due to new technology. In 1983 the OECD found that Sweden had more than twice as many robots per worker in manufacturing as Japan, and six times as many as Germany and the US (Bäckström, 1988: 245). 'One of four working Swedes currently uses a computer at work. . . . Five years ago the total was half as large' (Lundh, 1986: 2). A study by the Swedish Industrial Board (SIND) at the end of 1987 revealed that 60 per cent of Swedish manufacturing companies use computers in production and micro-electronics in their products, placing Sweden ahead of Britain and France and on a par with West Germany. The position of workers in the workplace has been improved in the process: 'microprocessors and other new technologies would allow many unhealthy and badly paid jobs in the production, distribution and office sectors to be done mechanically' (Thomas, 1986: 183). The trade unions have been closely involved with computerization projects at every stage, especially that of educating the workers to allow them to be directly involved. For example, a detailed guide was prepared in 1982 by the TCO and its affiliated adult education society, TBV, in co-operation with the publicly supported Swedish Centre for the Study of Working Life (Arbetslivcentrum) for use in study circles by employees confronted with the issue. Indeed the renewal funds discussed above were proposed by LO from just this perspective.

In the spring of 1984 the idea of creating some form of educational funds within companies . . . was raised within the LO. . . . The purpose was twofold. A fund financed by the companies' own profits would, together with other measures, contribute to easing future bargaining rounds . . . by means of partly ploughing back and utilizing individual companies' good profits, largely gained as a result of the government's successful economic stabilization policy. . . . At the same time particularly desirable causes, such as software-type investments in the in-service training of staff would be encouraged. . . . [By] sharpening occupation skills . . . the employee would be better equipped . . . [for] more interesting and meaningful tasks of work. The degree of security of employment and work satisfaction would

increase and . . . a raised level of knowledge on the part of the staff
would mean higher productivity, better competitiveness and probably
still higher yields from operative capital for the individual company
(LO, 1985: 27).

In addition, the involvement of labour in industrial
decision-making made it possible to make needed—if unwelcome—adjustments due to the constraints of tightened
international competition in vital industries such as shipyards
(Jones, 1976: 109) and steel (Burton, 1980). One 'typical' case
was described at length in a SAF publication, which, early
on, depicts the frictions brought on by MBL as temporary,
having given way to an agreement that 'enjoys the full support
of the employer and union organizations'.

The project . . . lasted for three years, between 1980–1983. At the
start of the project, the company had 2,700 employees . . . in a
town . . . with 15,000 inhabitants. . . . The personnel cutbacks
during the period totalled 800 made necessary principally by the
closure of the steel production units. . . . The company and the local
union organizations agreed that the personnel cutbacks should if
possible be implemented without declaring redundancies. . . . all
employees were to be given direct and open information by all the
company and union representatives. . . .
Agreement was reached on which positions and persons were
redundant before the action programme was put into effect.
Management and union executives were involved in both the
planning and the implementation. . . . A very extensive internal
training programme was . . . carried out. . . . All salaried personnel
above 58 years of age were invited to take voluntary retirement on
the same conditions as applied to retirement at the normal age. . . .
150 salaried personnel and 210 workers took advantage of these
offers. . . . 25 employees . . . were given personal and financial help
to set up their own companies. . . . Of the total personnel cutback
of 800 during this period, fewer than one-tenth were declared
redundant (Myrdal and Schiller, 1987: 6–11).

Clearly the aims of the SAF–LO–PTK agreement are being
attained. As in the case of the WEF in operation, there has
not been any real shift in ultimate power over the future of
firms, which remains in the hands of employers—nor, despite
fears to the contrary, was there ever really intended to be.
Given the breadth of the laws on worker participation in

plant decisions and the importance of co-operatives, observers are often surprised to find that Sweden has produced very little in the way of 'autogestion', that is, worker-owned or worker-run corporations. That fact comes as no surprise here. Worker ownership, like public or private ownership, is largely of theoretical interest, 'never a central aim of Scandinavian social democracy' (Thomas, 1986: 183). Swedish workers are primarily concerned with the practical purposes to which ownership is put. These practical purposes have been served by participation as distinguished from ownership. It is hard to see how it could be otherwise. Profit sharing within the firm is discouraged as running counter to wage solidarity; and the universal acceptance of the fact that firms must operate within the constraints of virtually unfettered international competition sets limits on the kinds of decisions that can be reached. Union representatives are more concerned with making sure that management is doing its job than with attempting to replace it.

Though business never officially welcomed the MBL and its sister laws, large enterprises often led the way toward co-determination. A recent survey of management opinion in 450 Swedish firms found 70 per cent (95 per cent of those in the largest companies) regarded worker participation in a positive light. The more significant the union role, the greater the satisfaction with it. 'Those who deny union participation a positive role . . . gain little support from the assessments made by company managements when they appreciate something they are most familiar with—the conditions of their own companies' (Berggren, 1986: 107). The same survey found that many union representatives feel employee influence to be insufficient since it usually begins too late in the decision-making process to be truly effective. They were generally positively disposed to participation, but they wanted the position of employee representatives reinforced.

Rather than concerning themselves with the question of ownership of the means of production, Swedish workers' organizations have focused on altering the means of production themselves in their form and organization. Transformations have indeed occurred, with far-reaching consequences in the working environment. Sweden's largest corporation, Volvo, is world famous for its achievements in the area of job redesign, though it is by no means alone. Many industries dramatically changed during this period. Significant examples include building materials (Euroc), insurance (Skandia), and ship-building (Kockums), (Foy and Gadon, 1976). In 1972, SAF and LO jointly set up the Rationalization Council to look into means of humanizing the work environment to achieve greater involvement and efficiency for an increasingly educated workforce. It was changes in the automobile industry, how-ever—and understandably so—that most caught the public imagination at home and abroad. Saab-Scania made sig-nificant changes, replacing line assembly by team assembly at its motor assembly plant in Södertälje and its auto plant in Trollhätten. The results were excellent. At Trollhätten, annual turnover declined from 53 to 14 per cent, enabling Saab to recover its outlay on retooling in two-and-a-half years (Logue, 1981). Indeed, synergy has developed between job improve-ment and technological advance and, in many cases, good business. Of the many examples that illustrate this, the report cited below from a January 1987 report of the Swedish Inter-national Press Bureau (SIP) is chosen because of the con-nection to Saab.

An effective paint removal method which is also free from unhealthy emissions has been developed by Sweden's industrial gas corporation, AGA. . . . The method is particularly applicable for the automobile industry, it is claimed, and Saab has been one of the co-developers. . . . The paint applicators to be cleaned are placed in a tailor-made rig and transported on a conveyor-belt to a cryogenic container filled with liquid nitrogen. . . . After a few minutes the tools have become very cold and the many layers of paint brittle enough to be blasted away with a shot-blast machine to which they are automatically transported. . . . The whole work-cycle only takes a few minutes. . . . Apart from being efficient, the new paint removal method is also healthier than conventional paint-strippers, which discharge contaminated solvents, watersludge, fumes and ashes.

Saab, while very successful, is dwarfed by Volvo which alone accounts for over 6 per cent of manufacturing employment in Sweden and 12 per cent of exports. Volvo's range of activities now spans everything from energy to food production. Still, 60 per cent of its employees make cars and trucks. The immediate motivation for humanizing their work came in the late sixties when the 'blue-collar blues' hit Sweden especially hard. Absenteeism and turnover rose sharply among the younger and more educated workers who now operated the assembly lines. Volvo's new top management decided to confront the problem with a complete and integrated strategy. The first order of business was to secure the co-operation of the unions.

After wide discussion, it was agreed that the best way to proceed was to build a totally transformed work structure into the design of the five new plants slated for opening. The number of plants involved is indicative of the first principle of the new design, namely that they were to be small: the maximum was 600 employees. The most famous was at Kalmar in the south-east, which opened in 1971, and has served as a model since. Here, as at Saab-Trollhättan, the traditional assembly line was eliminated. Vehicles are produced by work-assembly teams of 15–20 workers using specially designed mobile auto carriers. The workers assemble practically the entire car in a work cycle lasting roughly 30 minutes, replacing the cycle of 2 minutes or less on the traditional assembly line. The work team also takes care of ancillary tasks such as maintaining machinery, ordering materials (Engström and Levinson, 1982), scheduling time off and vacation periods, even on-the-job training and recruitment (Rationalization Council, 1976). At the Tuve truck plant opened in 1978, the position of supervisor–inspector is rotated each week to a different work-team member. The Uddevalla plant, opened in 1988, takes the Kalmar model into every aspect of car-building, representing, thus, a complete break with the old assembly-line procedures. In practical everyday aspects of working life, job redesign has placed important decisions in the hands of workers on the shop floor.

Volvo management has for many years been known for its exemplary relationship with its workers, taking pride in having signed a co-determination agreement in 1971 with its employees, long before being required to do so under MBL. At the top, a 20-member works council, composed of the 11 top trade-union officials and 9 senior executives, meets four times yearly, and between meetings co-determination decisions are made by the seven-member[3] works committee which meets regularly. The Volvo agreement stresses the need for decentralization and participation to achieve efficiency, going on to stipulate that such participation should occur 'before any choice of production strategies, adoption of new systems of production and investment and personnel matters associated with them are made' (Auer, 1985: 6). 'Quality circles' are part of everyday life on the shop floor at Volvo. And every two years Volvo conducts a detailed survey of attitudes and opinions of seven thousand of its employees, the results of which are seen by both management and the unions and form the basis of group discussions in which all 70,000 employees participate.

In these ways Volvo has managed to flatten the managerial pyramid drastically, limiting the number of supervisory personnel, and cutting staff at its headquarters from 1,800 to 100 persons. The president of Volvo, Pehr Gyllenhammar, insists that others could learn from Volvo that 'humanization of work and efficiency . . . in today's society are inseparable' (cited in Jonsson, 1980: 3). Volvo has published several issues of an English language magazine, *Ergo*, on production technology and quality of working life (QWL). Articles in its first issue, November 1985, describe various innovations in different plants inspired by the Kalmar model, in use of technology, job design, and labour–management relations. In his preface to the issue, Gyllenhammar applauds Sweden's low unemployment, which makes it 'rather natural for people and unions to see technological change and development as something positive because it has brought prosperity and few disasters. . . . In the United Kingdom technological changes or demands for increased productivity have often implied firing people, while in France the government-backed auto industry has said it needs to lay off 75,000 workers to survive which everyone knows will hurt mainly blue-collar workers. . . . In these circumstances I would feel hostile as a union official not only toward management but also toward change.'

In fact, new developments in robotization of production and computerization of design and production planning are

---

[3] It is composed of the four top labour leaders—two blue collar, one white collar, one professional—plus the company president and two vice presidents.

writing a new chapter in Volvo's history, as evidenced by changes at its huge Torslanda plant near Göteborg, the base of Volvo's operations. Built in the early sixties for 8,000 workers when bigger still seemed better, Torslanda was modified to incorporate many of the redesign features, including team assembly at the final stages and job rotation throughout. At the completion of the ongoing rebuilding and restructuring of Torslanda early in the 1990s, neither assembly lines of men and women, nor teams of workers, but rather robots and computers will be doing the bulk of the assembly work. As the plant becomes quieter, cleaner, and more orderly, the stratification that forms the basis of industrial organization is being undermined. At Volvo, all workers are all referred to as 'bilbyggare' (carbuilders). For Gyllenhammar, distinctions between blue and white collar and between skilled and unskilled labour, as between supervision, quality control, and production, are increasingly irrelevant in the automobile industry (Gyllenhammar, 1977).

In North America these distinctions remain anything but meaningless, but in Sweden a significant transformation of relations within the working environment is indeed taking place. Volvo has undoubtedly made significant progress at combining humanization of the work environment with efficient production. This success serves as an expression of—but also a challenge to—the Swedish model of concertation. It has fostered an extremely decentralized form of co-operation not entirely compatible with the centralized partnership of the solidaristic market economy. For example, Volvo's success (its growth averaged 12 per cent annually from 1973 to 1985) has led it to negotiate an arrangement whereby workers receive bonuses in the form of profit shares and incentive pay which can amount to as much as 5 per cent of wages. These premiums are infrequently mentioned and left out of formal wage-drift calculations, a state of affairs that will force changes such as the new legal requirement that subjects profit shares to the same payroll charges as wages.[4]

Will the slice that the WEF and renewal funds take out of these profit margins resolve the problem by keeping such

[4] It is interesting to note that the largest shareholder of Volvo is the fourth ATP fund.

wage drift within limits without creating deep divisions and resentments within the labour movement? One aspect of a potential solution lies in the possible reduction of the working day. Volvo's transmission component plant at Köping, which employs a large number of women, decided in 1974 to change the working day from two shifts of nine hours to three shifts of six. Approximately one million Swedes, 85 per cent of whom are women, take advantage of the right to work less than eight hours per day without any loss of benefits (Bäckström, 1984: 14). The position of the Swedish trade unions is that while a gradual reduction of working hours on a voluntary basis can be desirable on non-economic grounds, in the aggregate such a reduction cannot be expected to make more jobs available since demand will be reduced correspondingly (Bäckström, 1984). The LO has instead cautiously supported a call articulated notably by Gösta Rehn (Rehn, 1985), for a 'flexi-life' approach to work. The idea is for employees to use non-working periods in their lives in as flexible a manner as possible, as shorter work weeks, study periods, early retirement, sabbatical leaves, etc. Underlying this proposal, as in the Swedish approach to job redesign and industrial democracy generally, are the dual goals of maximum individual control over working life and optimal aggregate efficiency as a society.

DECENTRALIZATION AND PARTICIPATORY DEMOCRACY

Industrial democracy thus proved to be more than a rhetorical rallying cry of the 1970s, it was concretely embodied in significant Swedish innovations in job redesign, co-determination, and profit sharing. It paralleled a movement outside the work world for greater decentralization or, more generally, participatory democracy. The underlying attitudes were similar to those that gave rise to the spread of environmentalist and anti-nuclear energy sentiments. We have already noted how the widespread concern in the latter 1960s that rapid modernization was depopulating rural areas led to an increased emphasis on regional development to bring jobs to people instead of people to jobs. Labour market programmes designed to foster regional development were described in chapter 4. The application of these and other programmes such as regional (county) development funds, and the promotion of regional 'growth poles', takes place through the concertation of local and state authorities and relevant interest organizations. In the case of the growth poles, for example, the National Industrial Board (SIND), and the 24 county councils co-operate closely with the research community, as described in the coming chapter.

The discussion of decentralization does not end there. Municipalities were especially affected by the push for participatory democracy. We saw in chapter 3 how municipalities have traditionally played a more significant role than one might expect in a homogeneous society like Sweden. One further aspect of this lies in the election by local councils of the lay judges who sit with the professional judges on local (district) courts. Most important is finances: the average municipality in Sweden today receives a flat rate of 30 per cent tax upon incomes, of which one-third goes to the county councils. (The remaining income tax, which is progressive, that is, the rate increases with income level, goes to the central government, some of which returns to the poorer municipalities as equalization grants.) With these moneys come responsibilities over just those services citizens are most directly affected by and where expenditures have grown most rapidly (municipal income tax was only 15 per cent in the 1950s).

In the 1970s Swedes came increasingly to be suspicious of regulations and plans from the centre which placed constraints on local and regional governments when it came to exercising responsibilities within their jurisdictions. Was it necessary to sacrifice local innovation and participation due to the exigencies of rules and regulations intended to ensure equal standards of service for all?

Such questioning reflected the fact that municipal boundaries were altered radically in a short space of time. There were 2,500 municipalities in 1952. A first reform that year reduced the number to just over 1,000, and a second, begun in 1964, had, by 1983, reduced the number to the present 284. The main assumptions underlying the second amalgamation was that municipalities could be entrusted with more extensive tasks and greater autonomy if they were large enough—with at least 8,000 residents—to have command of appropriate economic and administrative resources. Critics contended, however, that the amalgamation created too wide a gap between elected representatives—reduced in number from 200,000 in 1952 to 70,000 in the 1980s—and the public, a gap filled by unelected public employees (Gustafsson, 1983). Starting in 1980, a number of municipalities began to take advantage of a law enabling them to decentralize powers to indirectly elected sub-municipal or district councils. The most interesting developments along these lines are probably to be found in the mid-sized south-central cities of Örebrö and Eskiltuna (Amnå, 1985).

The SAP government has, by and large, encouraged these initiatives and responded with a number of measures to meet the criticisms at the prompting of certain leaders within the labour movement. One leading exponent of decentralist ideas is Lars Engqvist, editor of *Arbetet*, the most prestigious Social Democratic newspaper. Engqvist looks to a resurgence of voluntary organizations as a counterbalance to the tendency 'to let the state take over much of what had previously been done by the popular movements, from libraries to health insurance. . . . We must reestablish some sort of balance between the tasks that can really only be performed by the state, and the activity, the personal commitment, that finds its expression in the various branches of the popular movements' (The Swedish Labour Movement, undated: 7). Before he succeeded Olof Palme, Ingvar Carlsson was another SAP leader associated with this tendency. As a cabinet minister he was instrumental in setting up a pilot project in which ten municipalities were delegated far wider jurisdiction in setting policy and spending money.

A second front has been opened in government services themselves, at the initiative of the minister responsible for public administration, Bo Holmberg, to weed out formalistic behaviour and bureaucratic attitudes. One method was a measure that, as of 1 July 1986, put to the 'guillotine' every regulation not specifically justified by the relevant agency or department. The new 1987 public-administration law requires officials at every level to treat citizens fairly in a clear and understandable language, and places the burden of proof on the public agency in cases of alleged unfair treatment.

The third and most delicate area concerns 'freedom of choice'. Part of it lies within the public service, including decentralization of municipal power, more delegation of services to voluntary organizations as Enqvist contends, and greater involvement by users in—and in selecting—schools, social institutions, etc. However, the labour government has been reluctant to extend the principle of freedom of choice to allowing privately owned companies to compete with public agencies in providing such services, for reasons taken up in chapter 7. Indeed, there is a delicate line between decentralization and creating a situation where residents of a given locality are deprived of basic guarantees Swedes have come to expect. Some warn of the danger of Conservative-dominated municipalities in the southern part of the country creating bastions of inequality.

These are the kinds of questions that the very success of Sweden's social-democratic system has raised for which the answers lie not in grand theory but in experimentation and compromise. The same kind of situation was noted earlier with regard to the danger of Volvo's employees 'desolidarizing' themselves from the wider labour movement due to the extraordinary labour–management climate there. The centralist-decentralist tension for the time being seems on balance a healthy phenomenon. The different initiatives seem to be meeting with at least some measure of success since the clamour for decentralization has subsided. They have become part of a complex scene composed of numerous and varied democratizing innovations. As we have noted, not all managed to win the desirable measure of consensus; some, notably the WEF, left scars that have not fully healed. Yet by and large, when it comes to political decentralization, as with collective capital formation, industrial democracy and labour market planning, the overall assessment applies: Swedish policy initiatives have proven successful because they have managed to weave together the combined goals of social justice and economic productivity. This is true in what is normally regarded as the economic domain, on which we have concentrated these last three chapters, and in the social domain to which we are moving.

6

The Dissemination of Knowledge

We return from the realm of economic policy to that of values and culture, more specifically to what we term the dissemination of knowledge. Yet there is no dichotomy: the rule for understanding the Swedish social system remains that of complementarity between culture and institutions. Certain aspects of the dissemination of knowledge covered in this chapter—research and development in particular—are directly related to economic well-being. But the link extends beyond R and D to the system of education, the world of mass communications, and the entire range of cultural activities. In this chapter as in previous ones, we focus on the part primarily to shed light on the whole, to set Sweden's approach to the dissemination of knowledge in communications, education, and culture in the context of the relationships and values of the solidaristic market economy.

An illustration from the previous chapter's discussion serves as a useful transition. It concerns the retention after the war of some kind of indirect (consumption) tax (now called VAT). LO was opposed to such taxes in principle as inherently anti-egalitarian; the SAP had promised the tax would go when the war ended. But the economists in LO's research department had a different idea. We have seen how their 'supply-side' analysis led them to reject growth driven by general demand stimulation as inflationary. In this, they were in fact expressing traditional Swedish values that rejected economic progress based merely on increased consumption: especially in a small open economy, real increases in wealth are created in producing—not consuming—more and better. From a position supported by profound societal values, the LO economists set themselves against prevailing conventional wisdom, arguing that it was both desirable and possible to tax consumption rather than merely production and still achieve egalitarian redistribution—through wage solidarity and social welfare programmes. In the end, they prevailed, managing to sway informed public opinion within and outside the labour movement to the logic of their position despite the fact that it went directly against labour-movement orthodoxy—able to argue their position, as Rehn likes to remind his listeners, without constraint from their trade-union employers.

The key expression in the above illustration is 'informed public opinion'. The various major policies depicted in this book emerged from informed public discussion through existing channels of democratic organization and mass communications made possible because of Sweden's approach to the dissemination of knowledge. The fundamental principle underlying this approach, in the media as well as cultural and educational institutions, is to make readily accessible to everyone the knowledge required to live full, rich lives as members of their community and as human beings. While policy makers in comparable societies no doubt voice this same ambition, its attainment, we shall see, is woven into the very fabric of Swedish institutions. The overriding goal of all of these, from television and radio, to museums and libraries, to adult study circles, is to provide knowledge of interest and use to the population as a whole and make it readily accessible. Some of the mechanisms of dissemination are formal and state-run, others are informal and private; most fall somewhere in between, in what we called the buffer zone.

The underlying rationale is humanitarian, but also economic: an informed public is a rationally efficient one. The costs of disseminating knowledge to achieve this goal in this way are great, but, to use the language introduced in chapter 1, so are the long-term savings in information and transaction costs. Because the link between knowledge and productivity in a modern competitive economy is recognized, no contradiction is perceived to exist between equality of access to knowledge, on the one hand, and the training of experts in necessarily specialized areas, on the other. In fact, despite the transformation of societal institutions that has taken place in this century, there is still great respect for expertise in Sweden. But expertise is one thing, and general knowledge and cultural development another. The solidaristic market economy requires a deeply informed population of producers and consumers. With respect to the use of the media, the accessibility of libraries and cultural resources of all kinds, and the availability and content of continuing education, the kind of general knowledge possessed by the university-trained expert and the blue- or white-collar worker is of the same order. 'There is not a gulf between what we might call general values and the values held by intellectuals' (Tomasson, 1970: 289-90).

In the larger Western societies there tends to be little overlap between mass culture and that of the élite. The fruits of knowledge, even more than the fruits of work, are distributed very unequally. For modern Sweden, narrowing differentials in access to knowledge has been at least as important as narrowing differentials in access to wealth. Of course, in knowledge as in income, differences remain, and egalitarian aspirations are never fully realized. But, though such a hypothesis does not lend itself to easy empirical verification, it will be contended here that Sweden's approach to the dissemination of knowledge has attained a unique measure of success. Comparatively speaking, ordinary Swedes are in an enviable position when it comes to knowing the things worth knowing about the world in which they live and work.

To return to the theme on which this chapter began, the key to Swedish popular culture is that it is not consumption oriented. Swedish mass culture is not a consumer culture, not oriented to the passive acquisition and consumption of commodities. Commodities are important, for quality of production, for aesthetic value, and for individual and collective use: these are matters of discussion and informed choice, and not mere passive consumption. Ideas and things are not located within two separate cultures, one for the intellectual élite, the other for the mass; they are interconnected aspects of what is basically a single cultural universe. This phenomenon is no accident; it is the result of conscious policy choices— some institutional, some less formal—surrounding the dissemination of knowledge guided by fundamental underlying values. We begin with the most formal aspect, the system of education.

THE SYSTEM OF EDUCATION

With the exception of its films, Sweden is not especially well known internationally for its cultural output, its educational institutions, or its mass media. There is no Swedish name among world pace-setters like Harvard, Eton, La Scala, *Le Monde*, *Der Spiegel*, or the BBC World Service. This is hardly surprising for a nation of 8 million speaking a language understandable only to a minuscule fraction of the earth's population, but it does caution us against searching for élite institutions as a source of what is original about education and culture in Sweden. (This caveat does not apply to research institutes where, most notably in the case of the Karolinska Institute for Medical Research in Stockholm, Swedish institutions are indeed 'world class'.) Rather, we must look at the overall system as an integrated whole.

Despite its impressive early attainment of universal literacy, Sweden entered the modern era with an élitist system of education and culture. The popular movements of the late nineteenth century and the labour movement early in this one established a system of alternative popular institutions, notably folk (people's) high schools, parks (performing centres), and libraries. With the consolidation of the labour movement's political power after the war, a systematic reconstitution of mainstream institutions came on to the public agenda: education was high on the list.

In the 1930s Swedish education was typically European, élitist in the Germanic tradition. At the age of 11, children were carefully streamed; the minority able to demonstrate mastery of classical subjects was permitted to advance educationally and take its rightful position in the professions and state service. Apprenticeship in a manual or clerical skill lay at the end of the other stream. Despite the important contribution of the folk high schools in providing a channel through which talented young men from working-class and peasant families might attain positions of responsibility, the odds were very much in favour of the élite.

The call for sweeping educational reforms in the 1920s and 1930s was resonant and widespread, but it was a call not only for fairness but also for efficiency. According to Gunnar and

Alva Myrdal, among others, Sweden was losing out by no. educating and training all its citizens so that they could advance as far as their talents and ambitions would take them, something that would take comprehensive reform. The reforms instituted in the 1930s and, especially, by successive SAP-led administrations after the war, sought nothing less than to remove all economic barriers to education. These included elimination of tuition fees, introduction of stipends and cheap loans for secondary and higher education, ending of streaming by 'comprehensivizing' elementary and secondary education, significant investment in adult education, and the institution of policies designed to enhance the educational potential of targeted groups such as immigrants, the handicapped, and women in fields of study traditionally dominated by men.

Similar reforms have been slower in coming in most comparable European nations (Heidenheimer *et al.*, 1983: 33–41). Undeniably, the SAP's electoral success in this period both manifested and consolidated a high degree of popular support for the process. In fact, close association with educational reform seems to have enhanced the political fortunes of Swedish leaders. Sweden's three post-war SAP Prime Ministers, Tage Erlander, Olof Palme, and Ingvar Carlsson, all first served as ministers of education. By comparison, this phenomenon was entirely absent in West Germany (Heidenheimer *et al.*, 1983: 39).

Despite their popular support, the reforms have raised several serious questions. Did they in fact produce a very much changed educational system? Have they lived up to their original goals? Have they engendered negative side-effects as critics had warned? Along with the question posed throughout this book, namely the relationship of the policies under consideration to the solidaristic market economy's capacity to reconcile equality and efficiency, these are the questions to be addressed in our survey of the Swedish educational system.

Education is a significant aspect of the life of today's Swede. Eleven per cent of all Swedes (up from 8 per cent in 1968, Ringen 1987: 127) are enrolled somewhere in the system of formal education comprising comprehensive (or compulsory) school, upper-secondary school (gymnasia), and university (or post-secondary) education. To these we must add pre-schools and a wide range of para-educational courses aimed at adults outside the formal system of education. All levels of government are involved, from the Ministry of Education and national and regional boards of education down to the regional and municipal authorities and local school boards. The latter are appointed by the municipal councils, with each party represented proportionally. The basic unit is the 9-year comprehensive school, compulsory for children aged 7 to 16, and divided into three 3-year levels, junior, intermediate, and senior. English is obligatory from the beginning of the intermediate level, and options are introduced into the curriculum at the senior level among which one other language must be chosen. The general guidelines for the entire school system are set through a curriculum specifying the number of periods per week at each level for each subject. In addition, students from immigrant families are entitled to be taught their mother tongue from pre-school through upper-secondary school. All aspects of schooling, including books, transport, and lunches, are free.

The old educational system had been highly competitive: a child's future dependent on the results of early examinations. Reforms in the sixties and seventies sought to play down competitiveness as much as possible. There are no formal examinations; no numerical marks are awarded except at the end of each term in grades 8 and 9. Such an attitude has not proven incompatible with a practical job-oriented approach to education, the need for which reasserted itself in response to the economic recession of the late 1970s. During their compulsory schooling, students must acquire between six and ten weeks of practical working life experience. At the senior level this takes the form of actual on-the-job experience with local employers. In accordance with another goal of Sweden's educational system, the practical work settings must be such that the students are acquainted with occupations in which the other sex predominates.

Integration of schooling and community life is a principle manifested at many levels. We noted this in discussing labour market programmes aimed at the young in chapter 4. In this context, we should mention the local planning councils on which sit representatives from local schools, labour, and business to arrange for placement of students in the upper compulsory and secondary levels in local enterprises for on-the-job training and, later, possible employment, and to advise school boards concerning curriculum content to complement this training. Another example is found in many larger municipalities which have introduced an integrated school day combining curricular and extra-curricular activities. Where children up to 11 years of age are concerned, the integrated school day is organized through neighbourhood *fritids* (leisure-time centres), while for older children it is co-ordinated with youth recreation centres, public libraries, municipal schools of music, and recreational and cultural associations.

Though not compulsory, upper-secondary schooling is practically universally attended today by young people either immediately after compulsory school at the age of 16, or following an interlude on the job market. Although there are no qualifying examinations for entry, there are certain entrance conditions associated with specific science and technology-oriented programmes of study in the upper-secondary schools. When there are too many applicants for a specific programme in a given county, the selection procedure based on grades attained at the end of comprehensive schooling treats separately those who have been out working at least six months, facilitating the admission of pupils who chose not to continue their schooling immediately as well as those who were not admitted on their first try.

Before 1971, students were divided into three separate streams for purposes of upper-secondary schooling: an academically oriented three-year 'gymnasium', a less demanding two-year continuation school (Fackskola) with a mixed vocational–academic orientation, and a variety of vocational schools. Though there were exceptions, as a rule only gymnasium graduates were eligible to go on to higher levels. With the merging of the three in the new gymnasia, the situation has changed. There are now altogether 23 educational programmes in the upper-secondary school, divided along lines that somewhat parallel the earlier streams. The two-year lines largely follow the earlier Fackskola and vocational school lines, except that they can be prolonged to three and four years, while the academic three-year lines are modified versions of the theoretical programmes of the gymnasium. Establishing the new gymnasia opened access to higher education to those in the non-academic stream; it also—through recently instituted annual 1–3-week subject-related work-experience programmes—gives those in the academic stream closer contact with the world of work. Tripartite committees set up for that purpose in each locality place students in the vocational programmes at the upper-secondary level in on-the-job study periods in local firms for 10 to 20 per cent of the school year in the first and second years, and 60 per cent in the third.

Extending access to further education to graduates of the different upper-secondary programmes has necessitated changes in the system of higher education. The latest major reform came in 1977 when the Riksdag passed a new Higher Education Act. It thereby created a single higher education system (*högskola*), integrating the previously separate universities and institutes and establishing new criteria for admission applying to the entire system so as to assure equal access to students throughout the country. To further widen accessibility, Sweden's system of upper-secondary and higher education operates on the principle that all students are entitled to financial assistance during their studies in the form of study grants and loans. The grants are means-tested, but only the student's income and assets—never the parents'—is taken into account.

Eligibility is based on a number of criteria including previous work experience. Twenty-five per cent of places are guaranteed to those 25 years of age and over with at least four years' work experience. The only academic requirement is that they demonstrate a sufficient knowledge of English and the chosen subject of specialization. Another rule reserves a certain percentage of places in a given programme for recent secondary-school graduates. Since applicants with both secondary-school credits and work experience tend to come out ahead, the system has a built-in incentive for people to alternate periods of work and schooling. According to *The Economist* (11 July 1982: 22), 'more than half of Swedish entrants to higher education are over 25 years old'.

Despite these efforts to value practical education and lessen

disparities in educational achievement, Swedish students, li
those in other developed societies, have increasingly chosen
academic programmes at the upper-secondary level (though
the tendency to devalue professions based on technical skills
is far less prevalent). While this tendency has resulted in a
highly educated workforce, it has caused little in the way of
labour market distortion because the reforms succeeded in
synchronizing the system of education to the needs of the
greater society. As at the lower educational levels, mechanisms
were established to link the intake capacity of the various
post-secondary programmes to labour market demand. The
direct representation of trade unions and employers along with
the educators on the boards of higher education institutions
facilitated this process. At the central level, the National Board
of Universities and Colleges (UHÄ), which supervises the
higher education system comprising 11 universities as well as
other institutions of higher education, has on its 13-member
board of governors a majority of representatives from relevant
interest organizations.

The new procedures rationalizing selection methods in order
to balance preferences against societal goals and needs were
instituted in conjunction with an intensification of educational
counselling on selecting university programmes geared to
career prospects. The unified system of study programmes and
single courses in universities serves to facilitate the student's
path from education to working life and, when required, back
to studies. In a 1976 study commissioned by the West German
Ministry of Education, when it came to getting students
into and out of educational programmes in line with job
requirements, 'Sweden was identified as most successful'
(Heidenheimer *et al.*, 1983: 49). The Swedish system is able
to identify 'bottlenecks' before they become serious. For
example, when the bureau of statistics predicted a shortage of
engineering graduates, especially in data processing and
electronics, of up to 1,000 annually to the end of the century,
the Academy of Engineering was commissioned to propose
solutions which have since been implemented. These went
from extra funding for engineering studies to providing
market-based salary supplements to professors, right down to
detailed methods of emphasizing technical education at the

lowest comprehensive-school levels aimed especially at attracting female students. The stress was on closer co-operation between industry and government to provide research assignments in industry for students close to their place of study, with Sweden's 'silicon valley', the Stockholm suburb of Kista which has attracted companies like ASEA and Ericsson, serving as model (Klevard and Sternerup, 1986). The largest of the new technological centres linking education and industry, Electrum, opened in Kista in March 1988. Electrum employs 650 people from industry and academe to provide under the same roof hands-on training in microelectronics and computers to students and refresher courses to industrial scientists and engineers.

General university degrees are uncommon in Sweden. Study programmes, which total roughly 100, are comparatively quite specialized. These full-degree programmes vary in length from one to five-and-a-half years. In addition there are local study programmes, individual study programmes, and short-cycle study programmes designed for advanced professional training. The orientation is distinctly practical and goal-directed. The students tend to be older, the boys also having all done their compulsory military service. While there are still ritual activities associated especially with the coming of spring and graduation, there is little in the way of a rarefied campus life atmosphere common elsewhere. 'School spirit' is quite absent; university students are more integrated into the life of the wider community. With the exception of a few highly specialized institutions, notably the Stockholm School of Business (Handelshögsklolan), the universities do not have good or bad reputations; students apply to a given university mainly because of the availability of the desired programme, as well as location.

The enormous changes have brought significant gains. Nearly 100 per cent of young people now attend secondary school. Moreover, most of the increase in the proportion of pupils in the academic three-year programmes is made up of young people from working-class backgrounds. Nevertheless, according to a survey by the Central Bureau of Statistics, in 1972 youngsters from university-educated families were six times more likely to register for academic programmes than children of unskilled workers. Similarly, while the reforms increased the proportion of students from working-class homes in higher education, it was only from 15 per cent in 1970 to 20 per cent in 1976 (Rehn and Petersen, 1980: 164). This latter figure seems to have remained fairly steady since then, indicating that social background continues to have significant influence over participation in higher education. In sum, the reforms have brought a positive, but limited, change with respect to equalizing educational achievements among social strata. In the concluding section of this chapter we will return to the paradoxical explanation for this persisting fact.

The reforms have also sought to equalize the educational participation of the sexes. In the 1970s, the proportion of female students in secondary schools came to equal that of males, but the profiles in programme choices still tend to reflect traditional sex-role patterns. Compared to boys, girls choose the liberal-arts and social-sciences rather than natural-science programmes at the upper-secondary level and in university more frequently. Only 7 per cent of all students accepted to the two- and three-year technical programmes in 1978 were girls.

We have noted a de-emphasis on competitiveness in which everyone undergoes the same examination at the same time. The de-emphasis expressed another aim of the reform which came to the fore in the late 1960s, one that might be termed individualization: a stress on student-centred teaching based on co-operation and self-motivation. The extent to which changes in this direction have been real and the effect they have had on the overall quality of Swedish education has been the subject of an ongoing public debate, one which also raises the question of equal accessibility. Is there any possible contradiction between serving the individual pupil's needs and desires and making the system truly accessible to the sons and daughters of blue-collar workers? A concrete manifestation of this issue is raised by the 'specialization' of upper-secondary schools: to what extent is it consistent with Swedish educational philosophy for these schools[1] to have a vocation of their own? To judge by the debate so far, the answer seems to be 'yes'

---

[1] These are all public schools, it should be noted. With practically no exceptions, education in Sweden at every level is public.

when it comes to sports—one gymnasium is known as the 'hockey school', another produces its world champion tennis players—but only 'maybe' when it comes to music, ballet, experimental science, and mathematics. We shall return to these questions at the end of the chapter.

EDUCATION FOR LIFE

The 'fit' between Sweden's societal goals and its educational system is manifested most dramatically in the extension of the boundaries of formal schooling in both directions. Sweden's pre-school system is among the most developed in the world. This development is closely linked to the nation's high level of participation on the job market which results in the great majority of Sweden's adults spending most of the day away from home (though the various leave arrangements are such that 48 per cent of all children below the age of seven spend the best part of their days at home with one parent).

Public child-care services break down as follows. Twenty-three per cent of all children between the ages of one-and-a-half and seven years attend municipal pre-schools while 15 per cent are enrolled in municipally financed family day nurseries, 280,000 in all in 1985 (Herrström, 1986: 3). For the remaining children, especially those 3 to 7 years old, there are part-time arrangements available. The typical pre-school has 40-50 children divided into groups with a maximum of 15 children aged 3-7 per group, and 12 per group of children aged under 3. In the family day nursery, a salaried child-minder ('daymama') takes up to six children into her or his own home. As mentioned above, many children go to *fritids* before and after school where they can eat and spend time on various hobbies and social activities, and do their homework. At any given time 12 to 15 per cent of children aged 7-10 use these services.

The (1987) proportion of 77 per cent of pre-school-aged children of gainfully employed parents in one or another programme is more than respectable. Nevertheless, there has been much dissatisfaction with the inability of the system to deliver on the promise of universal access to pre-schools with their small child-to-adult ratio and ultra-modern equipment. In response to the criticism, the government in 1987 committed itself to rectifying the situation, naming 1991 as the date universal access would be achieved. For reasons related to the entire philosophy underlying the Swedish 'welfare state' (discussed in the chapter to follow), it rejected the non-socialists' proposal for a parallel private day-care system as a means of meeting this commitment, thus making it a major issue of the 1988 election.

Post-schools, to coin a phrase, are almost as well attended as pre-schools. In any given year, it is estimated that one-third of Sweden's adult population pursues some form of organized studies—an extraordinarily high figure. Some institutions, in particular the folk high schools and study circles with their roots in the popular movements, have long been in existence. Newer arrivals include the correspondence courses provided by the broadcasting media, the different forms of labour market training, and a municipally sponsored adult-education system set up in 1968 to make it possible for adults to study at the senior-comprehensive and upper-secondary levels.

Since 1976, employers pay a special payroll tax to regional adult-education boards. The money covers allowances paid to employees returning to study, and also finances courses provided by the popular education associations in civics and in the native languages of immigrants, as well as in other subjects aimed primarily at people having less than the nine years of schooling.

All employees enjoy an unconditional right to take leaves of absence to upgrade skills, and are eligible for allowances to compensate for loss of income. This right is above and beyond that of union members to participate in union-run courses to assist them in their roles as representatives on different bodies. In association with ABF, LO gives a basic sixty-hour course stressing organizational skills and interpretation of financial documents as well as up to an additional 13 weeks of study of various aspects of economic and social policy aimed at employee members of corporate boards and other trade-union officers. Over 20,000 LO members annually take part in these courses, which is less than one-twelfth of the number of members who participate in some form of adult education.

Some of these workers take courses at one of the folk high schools. Like other institutions originally established to provide a service unavailable to ordinary people, the folk high schools have receded in importance with the expansion of the role of the state. In 1986 there were 110 such schools and roughly 28,000 students attending. A much larger share of adult education is in the hands of the eleven popular education associations which in 1985-6 ran nearly 300,000 study circles which attracted 2,540,000 participants. As noted in chapter 3, the largest of them is that associated with LO and SAP, namely the ABF. About one-third of all study circles are organized by ABF, about one-half of which it makes available through one of its 45 member organizations (including the SAP, LO, the co-operatives, the pensioners' organization, even the temperance groups known as the Verdandi) and the other half directly through its 158 local branches. Four others are associated with the TCO and the three 'bourgeois' parties respectively. Courses are normally offered in school buildings or community centres, except for those sponsored by LO and TCO which are commonly given at the worksite.

To be eligible for a subsidy, a study circle must have 5 to 20 members and meet for at least 15 sessions spread over a minimum of four weeks. The subsidy covers about 40 per cent of the costs, except for civics, Swedish, mathematics, and those in the native languages of immigrants, where the percentage is considerably higher. The remaining costs are covered by fees and municipal grants. These highly subsidized courses supplement those given directly by the municipalities. Of the almost 190,000 persons registered in municipal adult-education courses (in 1985-6), approximately half pursued studies at the upper-secondary level, 25 per cent received vocational instruction, and 25 per cent were making up missing years of compulsory school. The mainly elderly people with primary schooling incomplete in this latter 25 per cent, along with immigrant workers entitled to 240 hours of Swedish lessons during working hours with full pay, are specifically targeted groups. Others include the handicapped, parents remaining at home, and inmates at penal institutions. At certain prisons, studies can be pursued on a full-time basis, while one prison, in Uppsala, is limited to inmates pursuing studies.

One-tenth of the total national expenditure on education, which in Sweden is the highest in the world per capita (Heidenheimer *et al.*, 1983: 19), goes to the various kinds of adult-education programmes described here. As a result, although in other nations participation in adult education has been declining due to the inroads of television, the opposite has been the case in Sweden. Based on a sample of 6,500–7,000 Swedes surveyed in 1968, 1974, and 1981 (in the 'level of living' study discussed in the next chapter), Ringen concluded that 'participation in free time courses and study circles increased markedly. . . . In 1981, every third person in the sample was a regular participant in courses or study circles, and 12 per cent were frequent participants, up from one in five and 7 per cent in 1968. Participation in courses at work has increased in much the same way, from 27 to 36 per cent of workers between 1975 and 1979' (Ringen, 1987: 127).

The high level of expenditure and the special recruitment efforts succeeded in bringing one-sixth of those with less than nine years of primary schooling to take part in adult studies in the 1970s. Still, in numerical terms, the chief beneficiaries of the various courses continue to be the already well educated. Before we use this fact to conclude that it is impossible to surmount existing obstacles to using education to achieve egalitarian goals, we should note that unlike the the municipal adult-education courses or the labour training sessions, a large proportion—about half—of the study circles are 'extra-curricular' in content, teaching handicrafts, music, and the like.

CULTURE AND MASS COMMUNICATIONS

The dissemination of knowledge extends beyond the various networks that comprise adult education to a variety of cultural institutions. As might be expected, overall cultural policy is set by national, local, and regional committees with representatives from appropriate organizations. The National Council for Cultural Affairs has four working subcommittees, one for theatre, dance, and music, another for literature and libraries, a third for museums and exhibitions, and the fourth for popular education. Operating independently are the Central Board of National Antiquities and the National Archives Board. Together with the press subsidies discussed below, these organizations in 1981 disbursed a total of 4,300 million kr. on cultural activities and institutions, 59 per cent at the central level, 37 at the municipal, and 4 at the regional. In addition, the National Film Institute receives funds from a 10 per cent surcharge on all box-office revenues to promote the production and distribution of Swedish cinema which, in 1982, totalled 60 million kr. (Kleberg, 1984).[2]

One-third of municipal cultural expenditures, 1,050 million kr. in total, went to 2,200 municipal libraries, 125 bookmobiles, and the various specialized regional libraries which together lent out 76.5 million volumes in 1982-3. A large number originated as people's libraries set up by the ABF in working-class districts in the 1930s. Many others opened in the past 25 years are typically located at the hub of public transportation, recreation, and commerce in the new suburban communities. An annual borrowing rate of almost 10 books per capita reflects the fact that libraries are a significant element in community life in Sweden, yet it leaves out the much larger number of visits to use library periodicals, slides, records and cassettes, and other services. Library services are provided where needed, in hospitals, homes for the elderly, and in 500 places of employment. Many local unions have designated 'book ombudsmen' to facilitate reading among employees. In addition home delivery and pick-up is free for those unable to visit the libraries (Törngren and Alexanderson, 1984).

The above does not include the state-supported Royal Library and the other research libraries at various institutions of higher learning and research open to the public which in 1984-5 received 353 million kr. There are 15 national museums as well as hundreds of regional and local museums of which 26 receive central state funds. In 1981-2 expenditures on museums totalled 184 million kr. Museums are designed to

---

[2] Rather than repeat references *ad nauseam*, the reader is informed that 1981-2 figures cited in this section are from this source (Kleberg, 1984), while more recent ones are taken from the 1988 Swedish Statistical Abstract, published by the SCB (Swedish Bureau of Statistics), unless otherwise noted.

serve the needs and interests of Swedes (rather than tourists) and are very much frequented by them. Attendance is widely promoted. In 1985 there were 219 million visitors to Swedish museums. LO and TCO are, along with SAF, members of the Society for Art Promotion, which disburses more than 4 million kr. to encourage the production, exhibition, and sale of paintings, prints, and cultural products among Swedish working people. The products of many artists and craftsmen are marketed primarily through co-operatives in each area of specialization. In fact there are now nine different such co-operatives also serving those in theatre, dance, film, music, and photography as well as writers, illustrators, and translators. Between them they received 3.2 million kr. from the Council of Cultural Affairs and a similar amount from the AMS in 1985-6 (Nilsson, 1986: 2).

The Council directly subsidizes theatrical, dance, and musical performances and makes available grants and income guarantees to artists. Many of the performances, concert recitals, and readings are organized by the popular education associations which, in 1981-2, spent 500 million kr. on 73,400 such events which attracted an audience of 8.8 million, a total that rose to 96,000 events and 10.6 million people in 1985-6. In all, theatre received 750 million kr. in subsidies in 1981-2, 10 million of which went to Skadebanan, an organization set up to promote popular theatre on which are represented the trade unions, the artists' organizations, and SAF. The 'level of living' survey in 1981 found that 49 per cent of its sample went to theatres, museums, or exhibitions, up from 41 per cent in 1974 (R. Erikson, 1985: 14). Music schools, which gave lessons to a total of 370,000 children, and other music-related activities, received 650 million kr. in 1981-2. Among the subsidized concerts were a number especially aimed at children, reflecting the priority evident in the emphasis on children's theatres, libraries, and museum displays and exhibitions.

Swedish pre-schools and after-school programmes co-operate closely with these cultural organizations in these different pursuits. Indeed far more co-operation among the various institutions takes place to meet special needs, such as those of children or the elderly or to achieve certain objectives, than the separate treatment provided above implies. One such objective is to familiarize children and adults with their past, national and local. Museums, libraries, and various other organizations work together continuously to arrange walking tours, restoration projects, and special exhibitions, displays, and presentations. Despite the modernity of the economic landscape around them, new generations of Swedes are not cut off from their past. Moreover, from all accounts, children are still reading much the same children's literature, such as the works of Elsa Beskov, that their parents and grandparents did—a phenomenon that seems quite uncommon among modern nations.

As we have seen, books and reading are very much part of Swedish popular culture. The 1981 level of living survey found that 78 per cent of Swedes read books regularly. Writers are greatly respected and their work encouraged. Authors receive a certain compensation for borrowing from libraries from a fund of 40 million kr. In addition, the labour movement promotes literary activity through scholarships subsidized by a famous 'book-lottery' and a publishing house for low-priced quality books. There are about 200 publishing houses operating on a regular, commercial basis. They are eligible for subsidies to aid in publication and distribution of worthy non-commercial projects, such as popular-scientific works discussed below, as well as those aimed primarily at children, immigrants, inmates of care institutions, and the disabled. This latter category includes works in braille, 'talking' books and newspapers,[3] and, indeed, theatre for the deaf. For a nation of eight million speaking a non-international language, Sweden has a remarkably large and varied book market: every year some 7,000 to 8,000 titles appear, three-quarters of which are by Swedish writers and one-quarter translations. A great many books are also imported.

The step from culture to communications is even a shorter

---

[3] Talking newspapers, according to an article by Tomas Nilsson in *Sweden Now*, (Jan. 1988), are also an example of the most up-to-date technology being used to aid the handicapped through the efforts of the R & D community. With the aid of the Chalmers Institute (discussed in the next section of this chapter), the text of the *Göteborg Posten*, once set in computer-stored text, is transmitted via radiowaves to the homes of blind subscribers and stored in their own computer equipped with an artificial voice to be 'read' when summoned the next morning.

one than from education to culture. Like books, newspapers are taken seriously and read widely, unsurprising when one recalls that Sweden is a nation that attained universal reading literacy in the seventeenth century, and that freedom of the press and free access to public documents were enshrined in law in 1776. Nowadays everyone has the right to see any public document, a right jealously guarded by the Parliamentary Ombudsman as well as the media. Recent amendments have reinforced the protection of sources and the anonymity of informants. Public discussion is a sacrosanct principle. As one foreign observer described it, 'I most admire their [the Swedes] desire for self-analysis, their unending critical dialogue. . . . Year after year, an endless procession of debates rolls across the screen of Swedish television and the columns of Swedish newspapers' (Jensen, 1986). Swedes themselves are less impressed: one observer complained that 'only' 10 per cent of Swedes actually contribute to newspapers (S. Johanssen, in Fry, ed., 1979: 283).

Sweden is among the countries with the largest newspaper readership per capita. In 1986, there were about 100 daily newspapers with a combined circulation of about 4.4 million or about 525 copies per 1,000 inhabitants, tying Sweden with Finland for OECD honours. The level of living survey found 13 per cent of Swedes to be without a daily paper in their homes in 1981, a number that had in fact risen from 9 per cent in 1974. There were also another 85 weekly newspapers and 46 magazines and periodicals with combined circulations of 500,000 and 5.2 million respectively. One comparative study found that the main difference between levels of readership of political news in daily newspapers in Sweden and those in the US was the perceptibly higher correlation with educational level in the US (Miller and Asp, 1985).

To ensure the survival of newspapers in an era when mass circulation concentrates the advertising revenues that count on the bottom line in a smaller number of hands, starting in 1969 direct subsidies were allocated to 'low-coverage' newspapers, that is, those with not more than 50 per cent household coverage in their place of issue. In 1984 these totalled approximately 360 million kr.,[4] averaging 20 per cent of total expenditures for the subsidized papers and amounting to some 5 per cent of the net revenues from advertising and circulation of all Swedish newspapers (K. E. Gustafsson, 1984). In addition, since 1977 subsidies have been paid to some 400 journals of societies and organizations. The attempt to preserve pluralism in the printed media is associated with a wider recent trend.

During the first few decades of the century, opinion-molding was largely organized along party lines. The expansion of the party system was intimately connected with the establishment of a party press. . . . Party newspapers functioned as local organizers. Social issues were reflected in ideological, partisan terms. This first phase, that of the party press, faded as a wave of newspaper closures and mergers swept over Sweden. The second phase, let us say from the 1940s to the 1960s, was characterized by centralization of the media. Broadcasting media, first radio and later television, assumed a central position. Homogenization and national standards were promoted. . . . The third phase, which seems to have begun recently, is the age of electronic fragmentation. Media fare is scattered, the public is no longer homogeneous, life styles and separate cultures become important (Petersson *et al.*, 1987: 88).

Radio and television programmes in Sweden are broadcast by four autonomous subsidiaries of the Swedish Broadcasting Corporation (SR). The four are responsible for television, national radio, local radio, and educational broadcasting. The share capital in SR is apportioned between private industry holdings (20 per cent), the press (20 per cent), and various national popular organizations (60 per cent). The 15-member Board of Governors includes the director general, the chairman and six other government-appointed members, five shareholder and two employee representatives.

The educational broadcasting corporation produces a certain number of programmes each week for Swedish radio and television, and supplies educational materials directly to schools, pre-schools, adult study circles, libraries, and

---

[4] It should be noted that these were largely papers opposed to the SAP government, as only 21 per cent of newspapers with only 20 per cent of circulation support the SAP compared to 60 per cent of papers with over 70 per cent of circulation which support one of the bourgeois parties.

museums. It specializes in language training, teaching aids, special programmes for the handicapped, children's programming, and correspondence courses.

The average Swede watches a low 104 minutes of daily television (SVT, 1985), compared to, for example, the average French man or woman at 192 and Canadian at 225. The two television channels are separately organized as to programming, but share technical and administrative facilities and co-operate closely, to the extent of providing a signal on the screen when a new programme begins on the other channel. Of the 103 hours telecast weekly (as of 1983–4), excluding specialized programmes for children and other selected groups, 40 per cent of weekly hours are information rather than entertainment oriented. Shows produced in other nations make up a similar percentage. There are 7 weekly hours of closed-caption television programming (in addition to the 36 hours of regular subtitled programming of foreign language transmissions) every week. Swedish television operates on a principle established in Swedish cinema: avoid dubbing. Removing a film's own words in its own language is viewed as depriving the audience of something valuable. All foreign television is presented in its own language and subtitled in Swedish. Apart from retaining the vital link between a particular programme and the national culture it depicts, this practice also contributes notably to literacy and an active rather than passive disposition toward electronic information.

Swedes listen to radio slightly more than they watch television. There are now three radio channels, each with its own character. The channels are managed by three independent subsidiaries: P1, nation-wide radio specializing in news and culture; P2, specializing in serious music and minority language broadcasts in co-ordination with educational radio; and P3, local community-access radio, specializing in light music, entertainment, sports, local activities, and youth broadcasts. Any person or organization engaged in non-profit, charitable, political, or other promotional activity has the right to broadcast over these stations. There are also a large number of independent short-range radio stations. Radio and television is financed from revenues obtained from annual licence fees paid by the 3.75 million owners of television receivers. Commercial advertising is prohibited in all Swedish broadcasting. Foreign sources of cabled-in television, notably Sky-Channel, exist but have a limited number of subscribers, though some consideration is being given to the extension of cabled-in television. The airwaves, it is felt by most Swedes— but not all, as the Conservatives' platform for the 1988 election reminds us—are too important as sources of popular culture and information to become subject to the distortions of commercialism. Despite the fact that the 1987 SAP congress went even further than its executive, voting to reject any consideration of radio and television advertising, the debate is not over, and will surely intensify if a new bourgeois coalition comes to power.

RESEARCH AND ITS DEVELOPMENT AND DISSEMINATION

Scientific and technological research and development is the aspect of knowledge dissemination most closely linked to the world of industry; but it is not alone. All aspects we have looked at have their place in maintaining Sweden's economic progress, and, equally important, are understood as such and funded accordingly. Even more than for these other aspects, support for R&D funding has been non-partisan. The proportion of government spending for R&D was augmented both by the non-socialist government in 1982 and by the SAP government in 1984 and again in 1987.[5] The latter, upon returning to office in 1982, had placed responsibility for co-ordination in the hands of the Deputy Prime Minister, with the Prime Minister serving as chairman of the Research Advisory Board, which, on occasion, meets at his summer residence at Harpsund.

The State finances R&D either directly, through institutional funding of higher education, or indirectly, through project funding from research councils and sectorial agencies, a good part of which also goes to institutions of higher education.

---

[5] The sources for the facts and figures cited in this section are either specific descriptive publications of the agencies in question or the Swedish Institute, or one of two more general compilations: Dyring (1985), or a government publication entitled *Science and Technology Policies in Sweden*, published in 1986.

Three research councils report to the Ministry of Education and Cultural Affairs: the Medical Research Council (MFR), the Natural Science Research Council (NFR), and the Council for Research in the Humanities and Social Sciences (HSFR). The councils allocate funds according to criteria defined by the researchers themselves who elect seven of the eleven members; the chairman and three others are appointed by the government. A fourth agency structured along similar lines, the Council for Forestry and Agricultural Research (SJFR), falls under the Ministry of Agriculture. While the research councils are dominated by researchers, the Swedish Council for Planning and Co-ordination of Research (FRN), a new organization set up in 1977 to monitor societal research needs and to initiate new research programmes, is composed mainly of organizational and community representatives. Its board includes representatives of the political parties, SAF, the trade unions, and the associations of municipal and county councils.

Allocations for 1985–6 were as follows (in million kr.): National Science Research Council 260, Medical Research Council 183, Council for Research in the Humanities and Social Sciences 85, Council for Forestry and Agricultural Research 60, and Council for Planning and Co-ordination of Research 124. Despite the importance of these councils, R&D organization is quite sectorized with each government department, agency, and regional administrative body taking responsibility for building up the appropriate infrastructure. There are about a hundred sectorial agencies which plan, finance, and sometimes carry out R&D activity, most of which are quite small.

The largest and most significant government agency involved in technological, as opposed to scientific, research is the National Board for Technical Research (STU). Thirty per cent of its funding, which totalled 644 million kr. in 1985–6, goes to projects at universities and technical institutes. The second largest chunk of this funding goes to finance almost 50 per cent of the work of Sweden's collaborative technological research institutes. There are thirty-one of these institutes, some more narrowly focused toward one industry like textiles or pulp and paper, others stressing research into problems that affect many industries such as corrosion, waste disposal, optics, and water use. STU also supports the work of individual inventors and a number of projects within specific firms. In all, it backs approximately 3,000 projects annually.

Despite the importance of these state agencies, only 30 per cent of R&D is conducted in universities, institutes, and sectorial agencies. Seventy per cent of R&D in Sweden is carried on within industry, 59 per cent of all R&D is financed by it. The OECD reported that in 1986 a high 10 per cent of value added in Swedish industry went to R&D, up from 4 per cent in 1973. This growth has not been uncoordinated. R&D has been seen as a major axis on which long-term regional development must be based. Growth poles in each county were identified and institutions linking research and industrial development established and promoted. An important role in this process is played by SIND, the National Industrial Board, a branch of the Swedish Ministry of Industry with its board of directors as well as advisory board on regional policy made up primarily of representatives of business and labour. LO has its own permanent standing committee (LOFO) mandated to co-ordinate labour's participation in R&D policy-making and application.

Industrial research is thus becoming more closely linked with the institutional research community. Industrial parks and development institutes have mushroomed in recent years— especially in the vicinity of institutions of higher education. For example, in the early 1970s, Luleå College's Institute of Technology in northern Sweden incorporated into its charter a commitment to assist the development of local industry. A decade later, Växjö University College, in Småland, a south-eastern region known for its small entrepreneurs, established a centre for small business research and innovation. Both are following a path broken by the Chalmers Innovation Centre in Göteborg, the first successful enterprise incubation centre within higher education.

Lund's research village Ideon adds another dimension to the integration of university and industry, creating a research environment as a setting for major corporate operations. By 1985, there were altogether about 80 such research settings linking academe, business (and labour), and local government, many of them founded in the 1980s. In fact, all Swedish institutions of higher learning are involved at least to some degree in systematic co-operation with industry.

The success of Swedish 'high-tech' industry is due to planning and expenditures but also to the existence of an appropriate research environment able to respond to challenges that arise. For example, because of rapid technological development, engineers must return regularly for further education. The university–industry link-up facilitates this, as does the practice of university lecturers engaging in full-time research at regular intervals. At the decision-making level, the integrated structure facilitates the direction of funding toward promising or socially valuable sectors of research. Traditionally, research in the fields of engineering, materials, the environment, energy, and medicine have been priority sectors for both industry and state agencies. More recently, micro-electronics, especially information technology and man–machine interfaces, have been stressed, along with biotechnical research, with new centres for information and biotechnical technologies research planned for Linköping and Göteborg Universities respectively.

Other priority areas for industrial research include the Swedish space programme, launched in 1972 in conjunction with the European Space Agency, and, funded by a sectorial agency, the National Board for Space Activities (DFR) with a (1985–6) budget of 435 million kr. The Swedish energy programme was initiated in 1975 in response to concern over nuclear power, becoming the largest single public R&D programme with an annual budget of 400 million kr. Apart from basic research, it studies energy supply as well as energy use in industry, transportation, and buildings. Another, funded by the Council for Building Research (BFR), carries out research in community planning and construction with a (1985–6) budget of 225 million kr., the bulk of which goes to the (collaborative) Building Research Institute. A separate programme is funded by the Environment Protection Board (SNV), concerned mainly with the ecological and public-health effects of air and water pollution, acidification, environmentally hazardous substances, and depletion of flora and fauna.

We have already noted the high level of investment in

R&D, recently estimated at 2.5 per cent of GNP by the OECD (compared to 2.3 per cent for West Germany and 1.8 per cent for Japan, SIP News, 8 Sept 1988). Per capita expenditures on industrial research in fact now exceed even those of Japan. Not surprisingly, then, the OECD examiners' review of Swedish science and technology policies was glowing in its praise. 'In several fields, it is remarkable that Sweden has held international eminence over decades, with world leadership in some cases . . . [such as the] . . . pharmaceutical and biomedical industry which spends 17–18 per cent on R&D, and Government allocates 15 per cent of its R&D outlays to this branch, with a total per capita expenditure on biomedical research higher than in the USA. . . . The examiners could equally well have chosen the technology of communication or of paper-making, or the development of robots, or environmental research, or energy-saving. . . .' (OECD, 1986: 5–6). Recognition from such an authoritative source is evidently welcomed, but more important is the domestic consensus on the value of R&D investment to which such recognition surely contributes.

The pay-offs from R&D are there to be seen; moreover, they are seen by the population at large because the required knowledge—about science and technology in this case—is not kept within narrow circles but diffused widely in a continuing effort to bridge the gap between expertise for the few and knowledge for the many. Scientific journalism is quite pervasive in Sweden: there are science departments in the major newspapers and the radio and television channels. The association of scientific journalists has 200 members (Dyring, 1985: 71). Among the periodicals that are substantially subsidized are popular-scientific journals, the most famous of which is *Forskning och Framsted* (Research and Progress) with 50,000 subscribers. Since 1978 the research planning council (FRN) has run programmes to foster public understanding of science in co-operation with the universities, providing services to teachers, museum and library staff, journalists, and researchers.

Moreover, in an effort to bring researchers into public debate over controversial issues, two series of publications are widely distributed. *The Fount* has so far published debates between leading scientific investigators on over 50 controversial issues including nuclear energy, the impact of computers, food and cancer, and genetic screening, in an easy-to-read format edited by leading journalists. The second series is called *The Frontiers of Science* and consists of popular books with a scientific bent. Finally, operating in a related area are two organizations worth mentioning: the Secretariat for Futures Studies and the internationally known Stockholm Institute for Peace Research (SIPRI).

CONCLUSION

Having glimpsed the parts, we can better comprehend Sweden's approach to the dissemination of knowledge as a whole viewed in the context of Swedish economic, social, and political life. The following case serves to illustrate the complementarity of knowledge and action. Since 1980 the FOSAM Division of the University of Lund, Sweden's largest university, located in the south-west, has arranged a series of courses providing a multi-disciplinary presentation on a given country or world region intended primarily to suit the needs of export-oriented firms. Courses cover the Arab world, Japan, China, the ASEAN countries, India, Northern Africa, Latin America, the USSR, and USA. When 200 Canadianists gathered at Lund in August 1987 for an academic conference on 'Canada and the Nordic countries', FOSAM took advantage of their presence to organize a one-day seminar for executives on 'Doing business in Canada.'

Consumer awareness, which comprises aspects of nutrition, home economics, ecology, and the like manifests the same complementarity. The communications media, from popular-science magazines to television, play an important role in building consumer awareness into the popular culture. But the process is not merely a passive one. KF and ABF (and other associations) collaborate with the finance ministry's consumer division, the parliamentary commission on consumer affairs, as well as the local consumer information bureaux established in 230 (of 284) municipalities to prepare materials and organize conferences on subjects such as 'computers and consumers', 'spending money wisely', and 'the food revolution'.

But what of the critics? Already mentioned is the claim that 'declining standards' are the legacy of a democratized system of education and culture. Has excellence in fact been sacrificed? Though the call for a return to the old standards and values grew louder in the 1980s, the verdict is not in yet as to whether and to what extent Swedish education suffered from the reforms. Outside observers sometimes get a wrong impression unconsciously taking the text of the reforms and applying it to conditions back home. Comparatively speaking, Swedish schools are not anarchic; discipline is not breaking down. Students' work in the first seven years continues to be evaluated even in the absence of formal exams; parents receive regular progress reports from teachers comparing their child's performance to the mean of the other students. According to the results of a comparative assessment of educational performance in 1970 by the International Education Association, 'Swedish pupils more than held their own' (Rehn and Petersen, 1980: 120). More specific comparative studies show, for example, that high-school seniors tend to score lower on science tests in countries like the United States and Sweden, where larger proportions stay in school at senior levels, than in more selective countries such as West Germany. Yet if the average grades of the top either 1 or 5 per cent are compared, the scores turn out to be quite similar (Heidenheimer *et al.*, 1983: 45).

A second concern speaks to the possible invasion of privacy as sophisticated data gathered in research programmes associated with certain sectorial agencies are linked with the provision of services discussed in chapter 7. Early in 1986, controversy was stirred by a newspaper exposé of a 'secret' sociological study that kept detailed profiles of 15,000 Swedes over a 20-year period. In the end, it turned out that fears had been somewhat exaggerated; except for the identity of the 15,000, the study had never been secret. Moreover, Sweden already had rather strict rules, such as those barring different public authorities from examining and comparing the data in their respective computerized registers without special permission (Heckscher, 1984: 133). Nevertheless, in early 1987, the government announced legislation to tighten up procedures even further. Responsible authorities are required to correct not only erroneous but misleading information in personal files, appoint liaison agents to assist any person suspecting inaccuracies, and pay compensation for any inconvenience caused by a leak of sensitive information.

More thorny is the question of equality through education, a shibboleth of 'progressive' thinking throughout the Western world. It is assumed that as you remove obstacles to educational achievement, the differences between the various strata will decline proportionately. Yet, just as Sweden has shown that the economic 'law' that equality leads to inefficiency need not apply, so Swedish experience demonstrates that in an egalitarian system, educational level achieved correlates only partially with the degree of accessibility. As we shall see in the next chapter, the economic distance between the classes is lowest in Sweden, where all education is free. Yet while people from blue- and white-collar worker backgrounds are much better represented among graduates at the higher levels than a generation ago, they are still markedly underrepresented and signs point to them remaining so.

The continued involvement of labour movement representatives in the elaboration of educational policies means that Sweden will not rest on its laurels in this matter; nevertheless, there are limits to the upward mobility attainable through education. Surely, in a society where ordinary workers have access to the same services as the highest paid, and can expect only limited financial pay-offs for higher academic studies, then aspirations toward mobility become less important than home environment in instilling motivation to pursue advanced studies. Parents with higher educations are more likely—even if only unconsciously—to instil an ambition for academic achievement *per se* than parents who have completed only compulsory or secondary schooling.

Swedish labour's response is twofold: non-institutionally acquired knowledge is stressed—as we have seen—and given respect; at the same time, higher education is not denigrated and every class-based obstacle to attaining equality in the dissemination of educational resources is doggedly opposed. In summarizing the results of a Swedish Bureau of Statistics' study, a recent LO publication deplored as unacceptable the fact that only 30 per cent of LO members read books every week and 45 per cent regularly used the library compared with 70 and 81 per cent respectively for the university-trained SACO/SR members (LO News, 1985).

Yet the LO members' figures would be eminently respectable transposed, say, to middle-class, college-educated Americans. The level of living survey asked respondents if they had books taking up two metres of shelf space in their homes; 62 per cent of manual workers said yes (Erikson, 1985: 13). Placed in a wider comparative framework, what stands out is not the distance between the classes in Sweden but the absence of such distance when it comes to the circulation of knowledge. By any standards, the labour movement has successfully promoted popular culture and education and thereby broken down the cultural and informational barriers between those who work in jobs requiring university-level training and those who do not. This may not conform to everyone's standard of egalitarianism, but it is a significant accomplishment in its own right.

One area where such barriers have come down that merits special mention concerns the awareness of economic realities. An explanation for this lies in the fact that academic Swedish economics has traditionally been of a practical bent. There is also the traditional linkage between the academic world, the state, and journalism. A world-famous economist like Bertil Ohlin found it quite natural to put his ideas to work in leading a Swedish political party. 'Swedish economists move effectively in the front rooms of power', *The Economist* put it in 1962. Unlike in many other nations, the Swedish labour movement has continuously sought out outstanding economists and put them to the task of planning and explaining policy, the LO going so far as to set up its own economic think-tank, FIEF, to compete with SI's prestigious Industrial Institute for Economic and Social Research (IUI) in the 1980s. We have seen the importance given to practical economics in the trade-union courses given by the LO. A similar emphasis pervades the curricula in the schools and in the media generally. If there is any aspect of knowledge that manifests the breakdown of class-based barriers to the circulation of information and knowledge, it is practical economics, and, given the operations of the solidaristic market, it is not a coincidence. To take a current example, Stockholm's second-largest morning paper, *Svenska Dagbladet,* in its issue for Sunday, 7 Feb. 1988, published an eight-page section providing a wealth of information relevant to Swedish exports, including a detailed listing of upcoming trade fairs around the world. In the light of all this we should not be surprised that Sweden was placed first in a geography test conducted by Gallup in the Summer of 1988 among people in Canada, France, Germany, Italy, Japan, Mexico, the US, and the UK.

In chapter 1 we argued that Swedish solidaristic market economic relationships prove effective because they lower information and transaction costs. In the chapters that followed, the actual system of labour market relationships and the norms that guided them were set out. Here we have added another piece to the puzzle; the fact that decisions of mass organizations, trade unions, co-operatives, etc. are taken by a membership informed of the practical economic consequences of the various alternatives and therefore less vulnerable to demagoguery and the distortions of sales campaigns. The effect of the latter are well portrayed by a contemporary American critic of television:

The distance between rationality and advertising is now so wide that it is difficult to remember that there once existed a connection between them. Today, on television commmercials, propositions are as scarce as unattractive people. The truth or falsity of an advertiser's claim is simply not an issue. . . . The television commercial is not at all about the character of products to be consumed. It is about the character of the consumers of products. Images of movie stars and . . . happy families packing their station wagons for a picnic in the country—these tell nothing about the products being sold. But they tell everything about the fears, fancies and dreams of those who might buy them. What the advertiser needs to know is not what is right about the product but what is wrong about the buyer. And so the balance of business expenditures shifts from product research to market research. The television commercial has oriented business away from making products of value and toward making consumers feel valuable (Postman, 1985: 128).

Of course there is a thin line between informing people about the economic consequences of policy decisions, thus enhancing their capacity to make the necessary distinctions, and manipulating them to one's own particular perspective. Foreign critics not infrequently infer that the Swedish labour movement subtly engages in such manipulation. For example: 'The prolific study circles, party press, commune conferences, party ombudsperson, the seemingly endless supply of debate materials, labour's ceaseless internal conversation to find the "right line"—all this constitutes an enormous mechanism for absorbing internal dissent without forfeiting a sense of identity and direction to mere reformist expediency' (Heclo and Madsen, 1987: 324). One can indeed presume that if ordinary people act reasonably they must be being manipulated, and therefore dismiss much of what has been described here as an elaborate mechanism for 'absorbing internal dissent'. The alternative, however, is leaving the mass of the people 'free' to be manipulated by advertising hype and political demagogy, dependent for the basic information on which they make everyday choices on someone wishing to profit from those choices. An élitist answer is no answer at all to the question of dissemination of necessary knowledge, not if one is both a democrat and an egalitarian. Sweden does seem to be producing an answer, though not without raising some fundamental long-term questions. Ultimately how much can a nation keep radio and television content within any kind of nationally set parameters, given the internationalization of the airwaves with the advent of the latest mass communications technology—especially in a country where practically everyone is fluent in English?

Nevertheless, if anyone can respond to the challenge, it will probably be the Swedes. Two recent events are suggestive of this and provide a convenient closing to this chapter. Early in 1987, the plans for Stockholm's fifty-seventh museum, believed to be the first museum of the economy in the world, were unveiled: a new means of disseminating necesssary knowledge in an active form will soon be in operation. Second: in the summer of 1987, more than 70 Swedish members of parliament from all political formations (up from 45 in 1986) went 'back to the workplace' for a few weeks, building cars, baking bread, selling kitchen utensils . . . that is, learning practical economics. If the Swedes seem somehow able to agree on what are the main problems to be confronted as a nation, and rationally debate the alternative practical solutions, perhaps it is because, whatever their positions in society, they operate in the real world and have the intellectual tools for seeing the world for what it is.

7

Social Policy and Social Democracy

Five of the six principles of social democracy—economic well-being, work, democracy, participation, and access to knowledge—have so far found concrete expression in this book. Policies expressing the social solidarity which lies at the moral core of social democracy are the subject of this chapter. Social solidarity links individuals with their communities through reciprocal rights and obligations over and above the right of all human beings to be treated fairly, without distinction as to race, sex, disability, etc. In the much-repeated words of the SAP leader Per Albin Hansson in 1928, 'the good society is a society which functions like a good home . . . where equality, consideration, cooperation, helpfulness prevail. . .' (Hedborg, 1986: 6). The analogy of social democracy with a 'people's home' may sound unsophisticated, even maudlin: it is none the less a reality in Sweden.

The two pillars on which social solidarity is founded are the values of social responsibility and equality. Respecting each other not as winners and losers in a competitive jungle, but as members of a community living together in the people's home, citizens in a social democracy respect their common institutions, and put effort into trying to make them work as they should. They regard them as their own constructs to be consequently adhered to, eschewing the 'free ride' on the backs of others. Understood thus, social solidarity has been present in much of what has already been discussed, from the traditional values underlying Sweden's political culture to its wage-setting mechanisms, to the expectations Swedes place upon each other with regard to organizational participation in economic, political, and cultural life. Indeed, given our approach to social democracy as a social system, it is only once social solidarity has been placed in its wider context that we can turn to its embodiment in the specifics of social policy.

We cannot, of course, expect to do justice to the wide

network of social programmes for which Sweden is famous in one chapter. Nor can a book such as this give more than a glimpse of the many less tangible aspects of Swedish society that make social solidarity a matter of everyday living. A case in point: somewhere in the 1960s Swedes abandoned the formal 'Ni' (analogous to the German 'Sie' or the French 'vous') in addressing each other. Or another: Stockholm's (or Göteborg's, Malmö's . . .) phone book lists not only addresses and phone numbers but names in full—both women's and men's—and occupation. The fear that making such information public might leave one's privacy open to invasion, let alone one's person to physical danger, remains absent from public consciousness.

An unthreatening and harmonious living environment is something that defies easy quantification. In our original listing, we identified insistence on an unspoiled living environment as a seventh principle of social democracy. But, as noted then, environmental preservation did not need to be discussed at length in this book, since, like armed neutrality and generous foreign aid, it enjoys such widespread support that policies such as guaranteed freedom of access to nature (even on privately owned land) are sacrosanct. Guaranteed universal access to the many unpolluted beaches, recreation areas, and unspoiled green spaces—notably in Sweden's metropolis archipelago of Stockholm—is intrinsic to the unquantifiable 'quality-of-life' side of social well-being.

Of course, some achievements are revealed in figures. Life expectancy in Sweden is 80 years for women and 74 for men which puts it just below the top rank occupied by Japan and Iceland; infant mortality at 5.9 per thousand ties Sweden for lowest with those same two nations plus Finland. Other aspects emerge in the policies described below through which the weak and the vulnerable—the young, the old, the handicapped, and the sick—are not only well cared for but integrated into—rather than excluded from—community life.

While limited, the discussion of social policies in this chapter will serve the required purposes: first, to set out the operating principles of Sweden's system of social insurance and social services; second, to link these to the economic relationships we have seen as essential to Swedish social democracy; and third, to evaluate the results of sixty years of social reforms in the context of claims made for the Swedish welfare state and (especially) against it—and thereby set the stage for the concluding chapter. Our perspective toward these policies is a positive one, though it is not uncritical; it is also one that corresponds fairly closely to the prevailing views among Swedes in 1988, more closely, probably, than would have been the case, say, five years earlier.

While Swedes continue to complain over high taxes and view with concern the high cost of state programmes, underlying Swedish social policy and public spending is a far sturdier consensus than outsiders sometimes perceive. For example, a 1985 LO study which compiled various opinion surveys found that while a majority, 52 per cent, of Swedes felt the public sector to be too expensive, 62 per cent wanted its role maintained or extended (LO News, July 1985), and, as many studies have shown, the percentage is higher when the question addresses specific programmes.

Though initial implementation of certain social reforms has proven controversial over the years—the ATP pension plan is a case in point—the overall pattern has been one of incremental and widely accepted changes. And while the neo-conservative attack on the welfare state gained some ground in Sweden early in the decade, that gain proved largely ephemeral. As elsewhere, there were fears at the end of the seventies that the increase in state services was outstripping the growth of the economy needed to sustain it. These fears have since receded. Present demographic projections show that, unlike a number of other Western societies, Sweden's population is no longer increasing in average age: the 15–64 wealth-producing age group will continue at least to hold its own until at least the year 2015 (Gidlund *et al.*, 1985: 81). In addition, the new housing stock, schools, hospitals, and other modern facilities constructed since the 1950s mean a decrease in demand for new capital expenditure on services until at least the year 2000 (Snickars and Axelsson, 1984). These conditions made it possible to limit the belt-tightening brought on by the recession, so that there was no appreciable retreat on egalitarian policies and services.

This chapter sets out the main programmes in the policy

areas of income security, health, and housing. These are then evaluated from the standpoint of the system's own redistributive goals, briefly comparing level and quality of services in Sweden with those of other nations. Finally, the effects of these programmes *per se* and as part of a comprehensive social-welfare system are considered from the standpoint of the critics, testing for evidence of a 'dark side' of social democracy, a breakdown in the system of incentives, and, more widely, in societal institutions and values. It is argued that rather than there being a necessary contradiction between social welfare and economic progress, there is rather the challenge of developing policies based on social solidarity that complement the workings of the productive sectors of the economy.

As in education and communications—the King's children attend public (state) schools—where we noted a relatively narrow difference between the cultural pursuits and informational resources of the worker and those of the professional and manager, so in social policies and institutions. The corporate executive's wife, if not a teacher, is probably a health worker in a public institution; they use the same public hospitals, clinics, and recreational centres as the workers who clean their work premises. Indeed, the distinction between those policies discussed in the previous chapter under the dissemination of knowledge, and those here labelled social policies is largely arbitrary. Where do pre-schools, or training allowances fit? Moreover, in each case, the principles are set nationally, in law, to be applied by local authorities in concertation with the relevant voluntary client-run service organizations. One distinction is an administrative one: public health is the concern, practically the only concern, of the county or regional level of government, while the municipal level of government is primarily involved with education and culture (but also social welfare).

SOCIAL POLICY: SOCIAL SOLIDARITY APPLIED

A commonly used definition in Sweden views welfare as consisting of one's command over the resources with which one can direct one's own life (Erikson *et al.*, 1987). Two central principles in the delivery of social services in Sweden emerge from that definition. The first is universality: Swedish (or Nordic) social policy is distinguished by being comprehensive, institutionalized, solidaristic, and divorced from market criteria (Esping-Andersen and Korpi, 1987). All Swedes, whatever their position in society, rely on the same network of services and consequently have a stake in their quality. The second is participation in decision-making and policy administration by organizations composed of recipients of services. Both, we have suggested above, are not only complementary but integral to the workings of the solidaristic market economy. Universality makes possible adjustment to new economic conditions without fear of losing social rights tied to specific employment status. Participation means that individuals are assured that their own interests and concerns are integrated into the adjustment policies developed and adopted.

The social services act of 1982 consolidates a number of previously separate programmes in one coherent legal framework. Four goals are set forth that guide the provision of social services: economic and social security, equalization of living conditions, active participation in community life, and self-determination and respect for individual privacy. This fourth principle, that of self-determination, is increasingly taking the form of de-institutionalization, the replacement of institutionalized care with care that permits the recipient to live at home, in an environment he or she can control. In order to live up to the first goal, that of economic and social security, the law also stipulates that over and above the specific services public agencies are obliged to provide under the various programmes, there exists a general obligation upon all of them to assist anyone in need.

While Sweden has made impressive progress in de-institutionalizing the provision of care, it is for its universality that Sweden's social insurance system is still best known.[1] Universality, it should be noted, does not mean without cost

---

[1] When not identified by name, the sources for the facts and figures cited in this section are either specific descriptive publications by the agencies in question or the Swedish Institute or secondary sources referred to—but not repeated in each relevant case—in the text, such as Olsson (1987).

to the recipient. As a general rule, a fee of about 50 kr. up to an annual maximum total is charged each time for medical, psychiatric, physical, or occupational therapy. The same applies to daily hospital charges and prescription drugs. The principle is that the client should contribute toward the cost of the treatment, but not according to the dictates of the market: the charge should not discriminate against those who require professional services, drugs, tests, and facilities that happen to be more costly to provide. Not only is the charge the same in each case, but, to ensure this, the transportation costs of getting to the health-care centre are included in the expenses reimbursed.

Birth control, alcohol and drug counselling, and related services are free. Dental services for those up to the age of twenty are also free, while adults receive subsidies of 40 per cent of charges up to 2,500 kr. and 75 per cent above that amount. Statutory sick benefits are 90 per cent of income lost due to illness up to a maximum amount of 180,000 kr. per year, while non-working persons receive a small daily allocation. Victims of industrial injuries receive the sickness benefits and are exempt from fees for all services including dental ones. Those permanently impaired due to occupational injury get a pension covering total lost earnings up to a maximum financed by payroll taxes levied on the employers. Sweden is able to afford such generous workers' compensation largely because industrial safety programmes have brought occupational injuries down to less than 3 per 100 workers annually (according to ILO statistics for the 1970s), compared to West Germany and France which average between 8 and 10.

A different kind of pension equivalent to the basic retirement pension is paid to those with permanent or long-term disabilities that reduce their capacity to work by more than 50 per cent. Given these and other benefits discussed below, a recent finding that average household income for the severely handicapped was only slightly below that of households without handicapped members (Olsson, 1987: 47–8) should come as no surprise.

Payroll charges finance almost two-thirds of the funds of pensions paid to Swedes upon retirement, the age for which is normally 65 but can be moved forward to 60 or back to 70 through appropriate payment adjustments by the employee. The 1987 budget set basic pensions at 23,000 and 37,000 kr. for single pensioners and couples respectively. The same budget raised pension payments for those choosing to retire on a part-time basis between the ages of 60 and 65 from 50 to 65 per cent (it is 100 per cent in cases where their work is considered especially strenuous). Most Swedes also benefit from supplemental pensions under the ATP system discussed in chapter 5, from which they receive 60 per cent of average income earned during the highest-paid 15 years. Those who do not qualify for ATP pensions receive an increment of about one-half the basic pension. Pensioners are also entitled to a housing supplement up to a monthly maximum for those without earned incomes set for 1987 at 1,500 kr. for single pensioners and 1,650 for couples. There are also special provisions for widows' and children's pensions. In total, Sweden spent an average of 11.7 per cent of GDP on pension payments between 1960 and 1983, sixth highest in the OECD (Kohl, 1988).

Another universal scheme is the child allowance which, in 1987, was set at 5,820 kr. per year for each of the first two children 16 and under, and more thereafter. A family with four children receives 35,500 kr., and 5,820 kr. is also awarded in the form of study assistance to those still in school between 16 and 19 years. (There is also a small stipend for young men during their compulsory military service period.) The state also provides an annual minimum of 9,800 kr. per child to single parents as maintenance advances to be repaid, where feasible, by the other parent. In addition, on the birth or adoption of a child, parents are entitled to split between them nine months' leave at 90 per cent of pay and another three months' leave at a lower flat daily rate. The idea of child allowances came to the fore in the 1930s, in large part to meet the long-term economic dangers associated with a declining birth rate. Alva and Gunnar Myrdal led the campaign, taking their case also to the royal commission, on which Gunnar Myrdal was a prominent member, set up in that decade to survey housing conditions. While the introduction of child allowances had to await the end of the war, rapid implementation followed the commission's recommendation of housing subsidies (discussed below) to enable families with children to move into less crowded quarters.

Aid to the handicapped is a significant aspect of Swedish social policy. In fact, the very terms underscore the approach taken. Unlike an 'impairment' or 'disability', a 'handicap' is a function not of the individual's personal traits, but of the social context in which that individual operates. Changing that context so that the handicap is overcome is, by definition, the responsibility of the society at large, a responsibility above and beyond that of the designated public agencies. In chapter 4 we noted the impressive range of labour market measures aimed at enabling the handicapped to work. To this should be added the various leisure activities organized by the Swedish sports association for the disabled (Ewander and Miller: 1982). Hand in hand with these measures are obligations upon local authorities to provide without charge technical aids to those whose mobility, sight, hearing, or other faculties are impaired, which the associations of the handicapped assure are distributed to all who require them. In 1986 1,500 million kr. was spent in this area (Strömgren, 1987). These measures are complemented by certain services, such as special telephone operators who relay messages to allow the deaf to use their telecommunication devices to place or receive ordinary phone calls, and a subsidy to allow the handicapped to use taxicabs at the cost of a public transit fare. It might be added that the existence of these programmes has stimulated a great deal of research into, and development of, living aids of all kinds, from the most elaborate wheelchairs to the simplest cutting tools, which in several cases have grown into industries with impressive export capacity. Again here, as in the development of sophisticated technology in industrial safety and environmental protection, we see the complementarity of economic and social objectives.

The primary objective is the third of the four: to facilitate active participation in community life. The attempt to integrate the handicapped into mainstream institutions begins well before working life. A special child allowance is allocated to parents of the disabled, who are also eligible for subsidized job-leave to attend to the special needs of their children. Handicapped children have priority access to pre-schools; the law requires that every effort be made to integrate them into regular schools. In 1987, 25 million kr. was spent by a special body, the National Board of Attendant Services, to aid severely handicapped pupils to attend post-secondary institutions. Finally, as noted earlier, a special concerted effort throughout the adult-education network is directed at the disabled.

Integration of the handicapped has in recent years gone hand in hand with de-institutionalization, the fourth guiding principle of Swedish social policy. A special housing allowance goes toward redesigning apartments to meet the needs of the disabled, while for the extremely disabled there are service flats with help available on a 24-hour basis. For example: one unit of such flats was integrated into a housing project built at Falun in central Sweden in 1980. Indistinguishable from the exterior, the unit contains 12 flats with underground parking and elevator service up to each of them. The entire housing area including the shopping and recreational centre is closed to motor traffic and accessible by wheelchair (HI, 1982). The municipalities provide regular transport for the mobility-impaired, and home helpers to aid in cleaning, food preparation, shopping, clothing, and personal hygiene. Most also provide escorts to cultural activities, and a number of additional personal services, including hairdressing and laundry. (It is worth adding here that de-institutionalization has similarly been put into practice in the 'correctional care' system. For youth offenders especially, group homes and the like substitute for penal institutions which themselves are closely integrated into community life through work, education, retraining, and cultural and recreational programmes. The size of the correctional staff employed reflects this concern. According to *The Economist* (6 Feb 1987: 20), Sweden is highest in Europe with 147 penal employees per 100 prisoners compared, say, to 112 for the Netherlands, 53 for the UK and 42 for West Germany.)

Evidently, the same approach infuses programmes aimed at those whose impairments are due to advanced age. Just as, in accordance with the third principle, the handicapped organizations (HCK) have a lot to do with the content and application of programmes designed for their members, so the pensioners' organizations look after their constituents' interests. The key operating principle is plainly spelled out in the social services act: the elderly must be treated in such a way as to be able to live as normal lives as possible in keeping with their own goals and choices.

About 90 per cent of pensioners live in ordinary dwellings, as a rule in modern apartment complexes, aided by housing subsidies. Half the remaining 10 per cent reside in special service apartments and most of the rest, usually those aged over 80, in residential homes. In all, 5 per cent of those aged seventy or over were patients in long-term care institutions in 1983. In that year, 63,000 home helpers provided services to about 285,000 elderly persons in the towns and cities, while nursing assistance was provided to 48,000; in rural areas, letter carriers double as home visitors to the elderly. Pensioners benefit from a whole gamut of discounts: especially impressive are the off-peak transportation discounts which encourage them to travel frequently. Given these programmes, and given that their incomes have grown at a faster pace than the average (79 per cent compared to 19 per cent between 1967 and 1980—Olsson, 1987: 47), Swedish pensioners can no longer be regarded as in any way underprivileged.

Sweden's extensive network of health and income security programmes is not without its critics. They point to the fact that while the provision of health and social services is the responsibility of local and regional governments, a good part of the money spent by them is transferred by the central government according to pre-set formula, and for which they are called to account only well after the fact. Moreover, inefficiency is attributed to the narrowing of wage differentials which demotivates nurses and other experienced professionals. Finally, it is widely believed that because its primary orientation is toward the chronically or acutely ill, the system places too low priority on, and thus causes delays in, elective surgical operations such as cataracts and hip-joints. This latter concern was addressed at the 1987 SAP congress which pledged the government to relieve the situation with a number of long-term measures as well as an immediate additional budgetary expenditure.

It is hard to judge the overall validity of the first two criticisms. The system has its flaws, but, even at its worst, care in Sweden could hardly be described as inadequate. In general, the direct participation of representatives of different organizations and the close relationship of local and central government through the political parties serves to limit the impact of the above-described tendencies. Moreover, the process of de-institutionalization through local clinics and at-home services of a large proportion of the out-patient care formerly provided by hospitals and senior citizens' homes appears to have met with some success in breaking down excessive bureaucratization and inefficiency. Health-care expenditure, which amounts to 9 per cent of GNP, is high in Sweden but has been declining slightly in the 1980s and is in fact lower than in the US with its significantly higher infant mortality rates and shorter life expectations (Heidenheimer *et al.*, 1983: 79). And recent studies have found that the degree of contact with physicians and nurses no longer correlates with social class in Sweden (Lundberg and Kjellström, 1987)— undeniably a remarkable achievement. Leaving aside until the end of this chapter the more general criticisms directed at the welfare state as a whole, and the levels of taxes needed to pay for it, we may conclude this section by stating that if it is conceivable to condemn a society for bending over too far to meet the needs of its elderly, its handicapped, its children, and its disadvantaged at the expense of its healthy, educated, and able-bodied adults, then Sweden stands condemned.

DECENT, AFFORDABLE HOUSING FOR ALL

The success of many of the programmes designed to assist elderly and handicapped persons and families with children is contingent on an adequate supply of suitable housing. Swedish housing policy is a remarkable story of a successful— if problematic—effort at reconciling egalitarian redistribution and free market choice. Foundations for future achievements in housing were laid in the decision of Stockholm's town fathers to land bank the surrounding green space early in this century. Later, in the 1930s, inspiration came from the highly publicized commission report which described and deplored the often appalling living conditions of working-class families with children. The commission called notably for rent subsidies to help these families, and low-interest loans to non-profit building societies to get the needed housing built.

It was not until after the war that these two policies were implemented on a significant scale. In the 1950s housing was almost entirely privately owned, housing construction dependent on the private capital market. Rent controls had been introduced in the 1930s in order to help poor tenants, but this hardly spurred housing construction. The post-war programme of the SAP included a resounding call for decent affordable housing for all, a commitment its office holders took quite literally. Government planners translated this commitment to mean an affordable apartment or flat (costing no more than 20 per cent of income) with all the necessary conveniences, and a maximum of two persons per bedroom. The private market could not be expected to make such housing available to everyone; the co-operative and public home builders had already been designated for the job. The question was how to finance it.

The answer lay in collective capital accumulation. Legislation kept mortgage rates down below returns on investment in commercial lending. Thus private capital gradually moved elsewhere to be replaced by collective investment primarily through the ATP funds, which, as described in chapter 5, rapidly accumulated a great deal of capital which was restricted from direct commercial investment. Local government projects and housing co-operatives were given priority for construction loans. A housing boom ensued. In the early 1960s, the government undertook to see to the construction of a million dwellings within ten years, and proceeded to put it into effect starting in 1965. In a decade, the majority of Sweden's housing stock was renewed, and a typical Swedish family paid 15 per cent of gross income for (good-quality) housing. A social transformation had taken place: privately owned, multi-unit housing was now more frequently the

exception than the rule: the bulk of such units being owned
by co-operatives and municipal housing authorities.[2]

The availability of the new housing units, naturally enough,
complemented the economic effects of wage solidarity and
active labour market policies by facilitating geographic mobility. Just as enhanced mobility to the cities of the South gave
rise to prótests that the northern rural communities' way of
life was being wiped out, so critics objected to the housing
complexes mushrooming in the suburban green belts the town
fathers had set aside. Their lack of aesthetic beauty, and the
failure to time their opening to coincide with the availability
of public transit and other services, spurred a sometimes
intense public debate. Yet, in retrospect, the defects proved
not to be widespread and were seldom repeated (Daun, 1985).
From the perspective of visiting observers generally, the
typical suburban community constructed during this period,
surrounded by green space, linked up to rapid public transit,
and providing decent housing and services to all, easily stands
comparison.

In 1967 a major shift in policy took place. Instead of
providing subsidies to builders, funds were directed toward
various housing allowances to low-income families to ensure
that the moneys found their way toward supplying housing
to those in need. (In 1987, maximum housing allowances were
set at 1,285 kr. monthly for a family with one child, climbing
an average of 500 kr. for every additional child.) The shift
was based on the realization that market forces had to be
compensated by other forces if decent housing was to be
regarded as a necessity rather than a privilege. Rent controls
were evidently inappropriate since they ignored the tenants'
ability to pay, and were removed in 1976 once the new
housing stock was in place. However, rents are not left free
to be set by market forces. Collective bargaining over rents

---

[2] The structural arrangements governing Swedish housing co-ops are quite original,
furnishing good examples of buffer-zone institutions. Swedish co-operative dwelling
holders have great freedom of disposal, including renovation and sale of the dwelling,
and are responsible for its upkeep. Guidelines are set by an assembly of all the
dwelling holders and applied by a board elected by it (Lundqvist, 1984). The same
is true of the pattern of collective bargaining over rents that takes place between the
tenants' associations and the municipal housing authorities and associations of
co-operatives.

takes place between the tenants' associations on the one side and the municipal housing authorities and associations of co-operatives on the other, the resulting 'solidaristic' rents setting the standard for the private market. As a result, residents of older apartment buildings frequently complain that taking actual construction costs into account, they subsidize those moving into newly built units. In fact, it is they who are often the privileged owners of spacious central-city flats no longer to be had except by the fortunate few.

The problem has proven complex, perhaps ultimately intractable. Assessing the actual value of housing is far more a subjective process than determining a solidaristic level of wages and fringe benefits. Despite the painstaking efforts of Swedish planners to establish objective standards for the 'use-value' of housing based on square metres, availability of services, location, etc., it has not proven possible in fact to distribute housing in a fully fair and satisfactory fashion over the long run. In Stockholm, especially with its current labour shortage, though the problem remains small compared, say, to London, more people want to live in the central city than it can hold—especially given the very tough zoning regulations in this environmentally sensitive nation. Since market forces are held back, queueing results, with accusations of hoarding and black-marketeering, especially in cases of organization-owned flats, and the danger—though seldom (yet?) the manifestation—of favouritism or corruption. Moreover, the higher-income (or rather, smaller-family) tenants tend to feel especially mistreated since they benefit neither from housing subsidies nor from income-tax deductions for money spent on privately owned dwellings. These tax breaks are in fact estimated to cost the state more, in lost revenues, than any of the other housing-related programmes.

The problems are often difficult to tackle, since doing so can give rise to more complex issues. Attempting to predict future demand for new housing can be hazardous, since making low-cost dwellings available in itself raises the level of demand, especially among young people previously content to live with their families. Thus housing policies raise a social-policy question, namely the desirability of encouraging young people to leave their parents' home. An even more complex issue raised is the apparently increasing desire of Swedes, including many SAP voters, to become owners of detached cottages. The proportion of owner-occupied dwellings is slowly rising, having passed 40 per cent in the 1980s compared to 30 per cent in the mid-sixties. This trend is worrisome to social democrats not only on ecological grounds, but also because the debt incurred to meet mortgage payments and the inequalities caused by rapid rises in the market value of housing in the city centres makes people less sympathetic to the kinds of transfers built into social democratic programmes, and, ultimately, the solidaristic values underlying them.

Yet 40 per cent home ownership is very low by comparative standards. The overall picture at this writing is far from a bleak one. Largely due to interest subsidies annually amounting (in the mid-1980s) to roughly 13 billion kr. yearly, home construction and renovation continues apace, averaging 30,000 units in each category. The amount allocated for these subsidies is roughly equivalent to that received by home owners through tax breaks and almost twice as large as that paid out in housing allowances. Though these policies may ultimately provoke serious conflicts over the distribution of housing, they continue to assure what was only dreamt of in the 1930s: decent affordable housing for all. The above-cited surveys provide a positive picture of housing conditions in Sweden. Less than 1 per cent of Swedish housing is substandard and only 5 per cent lacks modern stoves and refrigerators. In 1981, only 5 per cent of Swedes considered themselves to be living in overcrowded housing, compared to 40 per cent in 1968 (Olsson, 1986: 53-5).

SOCIAL EQUALITY: PRO AND CON

These housing conditions are the direct result of a comprehensive programme dedicated to reducing inequalities and eliminating poverty. A whole range of other figures could be cited to similar effect. Sweden remains the Western society with the highest proportion of GDP in total public expenditures on health, education, and related programmes. A careful analysis of the results of the level of living study, which, as we noted, was based on a series of intensive surveys carried out in 1967, 1973, and 1980 with a sample of 6,000–7,000 Swedes—replacing only those no longer present—reported a 'clear equalization of income during this period' (Erikson and Åberg, 1987: 150).

In a detailed comparative study of Canada, West Germany, Israel, Norway, Sweden, the UK and the US, the population of families below the poverty line was found to be highest in the US at 17 per cent, and lowest in Sweden and Norway at about 5 per cent (Ringen, 1986: 26), with a poverty rate among single-parent families of 60 per cent in the US compared to 10 per cent in Sweden. Redistribution, the average change between gross and disposable income, was highest in Sweden, a startling fact given that Sweden had the lowest rate of inequality in gross income to begin with (Ringen, 1987: appendix G). 'The most notable aspect of the data is the strikingly low degree of inequality in Sweden' (O'Higgins *et al.*, 1985: 21). Given the breadth of the various programmes described, none of these figures should bring surprise.

Statistics, however impressive, do not do justice to the idealism and determination underlying the policies behind them. Official documents are also often similarly dry, but not always. A significant clarion call was sounded in the 1970 Alva Myrdal report on equality which was unanimously adopted at the same SAP congress that welcomed Olof Palme as the new leader. The Myrdal report's tone reflected the aggressive reformism of the day, its theme combining a pride of achievement with a determination to take up the main challenge that still lay ahead. According to Alva Myrdal, social security and full employment had been won; it was time for the labour movement to turn to achieving fundamental social equality. 'Equalization must be carried by a true popular movement and be asserted everywhere—in every assembly of persons, in every school, in all places of work, in all organizations, in every home . . . [to redress the balance in favour of] those who for some reason are badly equipped to assert themselves in the competitive struggle' (cited in Heckscher, 1984: 228, 230).

The report inspired many of the reforms of the 1970s such

as dental insurance, industrial safety legislation, parental leave, and extended housing subsidies and day care. Linked in the public mind with the fiery and outspoken Palme (who had publicly attacked the US over Vietnam when minister of education), it also fostered misgivings as to the intentions of the new government. Its aggressive tone bears contrasting with the report on the welfare state prepared in large part by the economist Anna Hedborg, junior author of the Meidner plan, for the 1986 LO congress. The very title of the report, 'Welfare State Resources Now Fully Developed: Now They Must Be Utilized Correctly', heralds a clear shift in the attitude of the labour movement from that of the early 1970s. These changes reflect both the fact that many of the goals of the 1970s had indeed been met, and the changed intellectual climate.

The report begins with a summary of historical trends. In 1900, public expenditure constituted about 12 per cent of GNP; in 1946 it was still less than 20 per cent. It then jumped dramatically to attain nearly 70 per cent by 1983.[3] This rate, the report suggests, is high enough. Even with only a moderate rate of economic growth, the welfare state can be maintained— and shortcomings corrected—on its existing slice of the pie. A telling analogy is drawn at some length: the welfare state apparatus stabilized its share of GNP around 1980 in the same way that industry, which had been growing rapidly, stabilized its share of employment late in the fifties. Just as industry did not stop being dynamic, managing to transform itself in the intervening years, so the maturity of the welfare state should not mean stagnation and standstill. Attention could and should now be diverted from enlarging the slice of social programmes to improving and, where necessary, reshaping them. Indeed, de-bureaucratization had an important place in the process. The report signals reductions in activities and expenditures under the Swedish National Board of Health and Welfare and the National Board of Education, enabling each to reduce

---

[3] This figure is now (1988) reduced to 63 per cent. Moreover, given Sweden's social welfare arrangements, a certain amount of double counting is inevitable. For example, a pensioner with private earnings equal to his total pension pays a good part of that amount in income taxes. Though he receives his pension from the state, he is thus in fact transferring most of that amount to himself.

staff by several hundred while de-institutionalizing mental-care patients and the elderly to be cared for in more homelike conditions.

Of course the LO is not about to have the Swedish welfare state simply rest on its laurels. Much remains to be done in a number of areas to achieve real equity. The report cites the educational statistics noted in chapter 6 which highlight the far greater proportion of university graduates' children who continue on to higher education compared to those of unskilled workers. Furthermore, of LO members' children, it reports that an intolerably low 18 per cent attend day nurseries, compared to 43 per cent for those of SACO/SR members.

The conclusion is that the system must be made to work even better. And that means in the first place, LO reminds us, that the market economy must function well. In order to maintain market efficiency, special efforts are required of the public sector to prevent it from inhibiting the dynamism and thus international competitiveness of Swedish industry, while at the same time continuing to equalize resources among people. Yet, cautions the report, such competitiveness would not be served by privatizing public services as some—even in Sweden—propose: the emphasis must remain on the spirit of solidarity that universal public systems engender. However, unlike the Myrdal report, the language is quite moderate: the 'no' a qualified one. Room is made 'on the margins' for private efforts that are inexpensive and of good quality to, for example, handle peaks in the workload of public-service delivery agencies.

The Swedish welfare state, as we noted, came under serious attack both domestically and internationally at the beginning of the 1980s. As the LO report illustrates, proponents of the welfare state are taking up this challenge with reasoned and moderate arguments, quite different from the defiant triumphalism of the preceding decades heralded by the Myrdal report. Political debate in the 1980s has tended to focus primarily on 'freedom of choice', the absence of an alternative system of private schools, medical facilities, old people's homes, and day-care centres. Indeed this was the major theme of the Conservatives' 1985 campaign. In the course of the debate, the labour movement came to realize that it again had to demonstrate the validity of its traditional opposition to private-based operations in social services. The fundamental argument is the same: profit maximization in the long run leads to segregation because market considerations force the companies to try to push out the groups that are the most expensive to serve, that is those that need the service most. This argument is extended into a defence of the fundamental principle of universal accessibility. As Anna Hedborg and Rudolf Meidner recently put it:

It is a short step from imposing charges on those who can pay to the demand for personal freedom to choose. And when the well-off separate themselves in, for example, special schools, separate doctor visits, or senior citizens' homes, then broad public support for a common high-quality social welfare system is put into jeopardy. Then for the better-off it becomes true that their standards and security are dependent on paying low taxes. The universal system by which high taxes offer high benefits for all is undermined (in Heclo and Madsen, 1987: 198).

The issue is ultimately moral, one of values. A marginal type of social policy, as in the United States, effectively draws a 'poverty line' in the population and thus separates the poor from the majority. Programmes are directed primarily at those below the poverty line. This marginal system generates implicit coalitions between the better-off workers and the middle class. It creates the constituency of a welfare backlash, making it a rational political stance for the majority of the citizens. In contrast, a Swedish-style institutional type of social policy leaves a much smaller constituency for a potential welfare backlash. The poor need not stand alone (Korpi, 1980).

The leaders of the Swedish labour movement know full well that the principled defence of the welfare state must also be a pragmatic one based on a proven record of performance. That they have achieved such a record can be largely explained by the fact that workers in competitive manufacturing industries have an important numerical part, and an even more important symbolic part, in the LO and TCO. They thus constitute an antidote to the 'toujours plus' attitude to which public-sector workers are prone when it comes to public spending. The reasonably high level of cost efficiency of

Swedish public services (see Ringen, 1987) made it possible to successfully meet the conservative counter-offensive against the welfare state on its own ground in 1985 and, in so doing, make manifest to all concerned that few Swedes were prepared to call into question the fundamental goals or achievements ·of the welfare state (Tilton, 1985). Indeed, the tone of political debate became more subdued the following year as a result of the departure of the old battlers, Palme, the Centre party leader Fälldin, and Ulf Adelsson of the Moderates. The fact that their nation spends over 30 per cent of GNP on social services (widely defined), compared to 14 in the US, and 24 in West Germany, it seems fair to say, is a matter of practical but not ideological concern to Swedes, especially as this proportion is no longer rising. It is in this context that the criticisms aimed at Swedish social policy are to be addressed and assessed.

ECONOMIC INCENTIVES AND THE WELFARE STATE

We have now come around almost full circle to where we left off in the Introduction and can return to the questions raised by the attack on the Swedish welfare state. Some of the opposition can be dismissed as based on ignorance and myth, amounting to a .misreading of the Swedish penchant for solitude and public self-criticism as evidence that Swedes are not happy. Cited facts often turn out to be based on partial, false, or misinterpreted statistics on such matters as rates of suicide, alcoholism, drugs, crime, and family break-up (e.g. Shenfield, 1980). To the extent that statistics do count in these matters, the facts portray quite the opposite picture.

Let us begin with suicide simply because Sweden's supposed high suicide rate is a widely believed myth that has somehow retained its credibility for several decades. Eighteen per 100,000 Swedes commit suicide annually (Statistical Abstract of Sweden, 1988: 327), a figure typical of advanced nations (or rather non-Catholic ones, since the data on suicides in Catholic and other nations where suicide is regarded as sinful are often unreliable). Moreover, the link between the rate of suicide and social well-being is more complex than it would appear, especially when Sweden's longevity is taken into account, as shown by the following breakdown of World Health Organization figures. In 1982, among those over 65, the Swedish suicide rate was 26 compared to 18 for the US; but for the 15- to 24-year-olds, the Swedish rate of 8 was lower than the US's 10 (Erikson and Fritzel, 1987).

Sweden's rates of drug use, prostitution, crime and delinquency, and alcohol use and abuse are well below the OECD average. For instance, the consumption of alcoholic beverages in Sweden (1977) was 7 litres per person over 15 years of age compared to an average of 13 litres for the US and Europe; reported violent or serious crimes were 21 per 100 thousand in Sweden versus 250 in the US (Rehn and Petersen, 1980: 41).[4] The Swedish family unit appears in some danger if defined as cohabitation by married persons—the annual marriage rate per capita is half that of the US—but not if defined by, for example, the proportion of adolescents living with their biological parents (see Erikson and Fritzel, 1987). A Japanese study which interviewed 2,000 young people in each of the five major Western countries plus Sweden, Switzerland, and Australia found the Swedes to rank highest in satisfaction with home life, choosing a parent as confidant, and having close friends (Rehn and Petersen, 1980: 28).

Indeed, a meaningful assessment of the social consequences of the welfare state begins with the fact that the very success of Sweden's policies opens up new choices not even imaginable before, but which potentially bring new 'problems'. If housing and employment is available, young people will move out earlier. If women are economically independent, they are under less pressure to enter or remain in marital relationships. And with these tendencies, and with people living longer, family units become smaller and more people live alone. Statistical decreases in average family size in recent decades therefore prove nothing. Meaningful assessment requires analysing the extent to which institutions have been able to respond appropriately to the new conditions. The level of living survey concluded that social isolation, measured as the

---

[4] These numbers are merely suggestive, since the crimes defined in this manner are not fully comparable in the two countries.

proportion of people lacking the necessary level and intensity of interaction with others, had not increased between 1968 and 1981 (Erikson and Åberg, 1987: 231). In general, Sweden's ability to adapt has proved encouraging. For example, while the process has not been entirely smooth, the intensive effort put into the integration of refugees, through such means as the institution of an ombudsman against ethnic discrimination (Hirschfeldt, 1986), has succeeded in Sweden as well as anywhere in Europe, despite the fact that the highest proportion of refugees per capita have found asylum in Sweden in recent years.

A more credible criticism concerns the fact that for the wife (or husband) of any Swede to choose not to work outside the home but to stay home with the children is also to invite poverty. This is the direct result of income equalization policies and the fact that—apart from the parental leave and various family support programmes—governments have deliberately chosen not to subsidize full-time housewives. According to critics (e.g. Lindbeck, 1987), the result is a loss of freedom, a theme echoed by the bourgeois parties' campaigning in their preparation for the September 1988 election. They proposed an annual taxable voucher worth 15,000 kr. to be used by Swedish families to pay for day care; the SAP countered with a proposal to extend parental leave to 18 months and, by 1991, to guarantee places in public day-care centres for all children over 18 months old. It is uncertain that this theme of freedom of choice struck a responsive chord in the electorate; many Swedes—including especially Swedish women—feel strongly that the sexual equality gained far outweighs any freedom lost.

A last and innocuous-seeming criticism is perhaps the most pernicious. It is often intimated that Swedes have lost compassion: content to pay bureaucrats to deal with other people's problems, they deny their own responsibilities and end up indifferent to the plight of others. There is no evidence to support this contention (Ringen, 1987), which simply confuses respect for privacy and individual autonomy with lack of caring. Moreover, it is ultimately egoistic, as it looks at the world from the point of view of the charity giver, not the needy. It implicitly views the less fortunate as a second order of humanity to be regarded with sympathy—if not pity—by the healthy and wealthy members of the first order. Would any handicapped person trade the respect as a full-fledged contributing member of a society he or she receives as a matter of course in Sweden for private charity and benevolence? As noted, to be old is no longer to be poor in Sweden. Does anyone affected regret this fact?

It is really only when we turn to the economic consequences of these social policies that more substantial criticisms are encountered. The concern focuses primarily on the methods of financing these programmes and their consequences, an understandable concern given that Sweden has the highest proportion of tax revenues over GDP in the OECD (*The Economist*, 19 Sept. 1987: 119). One charge that does not stick is that the revenues raised by high taxes are dissipated in the bureaucracy needed to collect them. According to one estimate, only 1 per cent of Swedish taxes goes toward the administrative cost of raising them (Ringen, 1987: 93). A fact that does appear worrisome on the face of it is that in Sweden 26 per cent of the electorate are public employees and another 28 per cent live mainly on state transfers (Lindbeck, 1985: 324). Nevertheless, there is no evidence that the Swedish electorate acts more irrationally when it comes to public spending than electorates elsewhere; indeed, we shall argue in the concluding chapter that the Swedish electorate is unusually sophisticated about economic reality.

A related concern is that of overburdening employers. In 1950, government taxes financed 85 per cent of social insurance with employee contributions covering 10 per cent, leaving only 5 per cent for employers' charges. Since then, much of the burden of the cost of the social insurance system has been transferred to payroll charges on employers. An average Swedish employer today pays payroll charges of 43 per cent of wage costs, among the highest in the OECD. It is also true, however, that these charges are taken into account not only by government in setting corporation taxes, but by the unions in setting wage demands, as well, of course, as being passed on in higher prices. On the whole, as argued by *The Economist* (1 Aug. 1987: 73–5), the tax structure does not inhibit Sweden's large multinationals, but, if the charges as well as the numerous regulations affecting business do have disincentive effects, these are upon the small service-oriented entrepreneurs. But there is another side to it. The effects of payroll charges and bureaucratic impositions are the 'down' side of a coin on the 'up' side of which are extensive public services to business, most notably on-the-job and other AMU training programmes, which give most small businesses access to skills and resources they could otherwise not afford.

The most important and difficult questions raised by critics of the welfare state concern the system of rewards resulting from the combination of wages, taxes, transfers, and other sources of income on individuals and, ultimately, its effect on the workings of the economy. They are perhaps most fully explored in the work of the distinguished and increasingly critical Swedish economist Assar Lindbeck. In Lindbeck's recent work is found perhaps the most sophisticated expression of the often-made argument that somewhere in the 1970s the excessive redistributiveness of Swedish welfare policy began to actually decrease the aggregate quantity of socially useful work by significantly increasing leisure through shorter work years and absenteeism and pushing activity into the 'unofficial economy' in the form of barter, do-it-yourself work, and other forms of tax avoidance (Lindbeck, 1981).

Statistics appear to give credence to this concern. By the end of the 1970s, a marginal income-tax rate for a middle-income skilled blue-collar or white-collar employee had risen to almost 60 per cent, 10 per cent higher than at the beginning of the decade. And, according to a 1986 report by the Swedish engineering employers' association, after all absences are taken into account, Swedish blue-collar workers average 1,546 yearly hours compared to 1,654 in West Germany and 1,930 in the US (US Dept. of Labour, 1987). Absenteeism has indeed increased in Sweden since the 1960s, though the extent to which this is due to high marginal taxes rather than the fact that many categories of people who elsewhere do not work at all entered the Swedish labour force, is uncertain (Viklund, 1978). Tax avoidance and economic crime has also increased, though estimates of the degree of the problem vary. A royal commission set up to study economic crime assessed the proportion of goods and services produced 'unofficially' at 5 to 6 per cent in 1983 (Berke, 1984). However, an American observer estimated that between 12 and 25 per cent of income in Sweden was unrecorded. He claimed, thus, that Sweden 'was the only country on the downward sloping portion of its long-run Laffer curve', its tax rate pushing so much income into the unrecorded economy that a tax reduction would in fact not reduce state revenues (Feige, 1986: 127).

In light of such claims, Lindbeck arrives at a harsh diagnosis: in Sweden, 'economic well-being' does not serve to reward households for their contributions to the official production system. Going beyond the already low pre-tax and even lower post-tax income disparities, Lindbeck weighs households according to the number of 'consumer units' (i.e. 1 adult = 1; 2 adults = 1.8; plus children depending on age = from 0.3 to 0.6) and then compares real income disparities between the deciles of the population according to pre-tax income. He finds practically no real income difference at all per consumer unit per household—with the exception of households in the highest decile of income. Moreover, he adds, the breadwinners in the upper deciles work longer with no additional reward. Taking hours of work into consideration, since 'economic inequality is drastically exaggerated when income data is not adjusted for differences in working time, provided that the length of working time reflects "free" (unconstrained) choices', he concludes:

Disposable income per consumer unit per hour of work falls rather than rises by factor income of households. . . . The capital value of life-income does not seem to vary much between various levels of education, except for specific professions like masters of business administration, graduate engineers, etc. . . . Thus, we would expect that a considerable part of the differences in income standards today are connected with differences in demographic variables, success in 'jumping' queues for rationed public services, 'smart' asset trans-actions, real capital gains due to speculation in inflation, various types of dishonest activities etc., rather than with differences in productive efforts. The problem, then, for those who want to increase their income, or even become rich, in a Welfare State like Sweden is not that it is impossible, but rather that it is difficult to achieve by way of honest and productive effort (Lindbeck, 1983: 253–4).

These are worrying thoughts, but to what extent are they justified by real rather than expected behaviour? Do taxes really so discourage productive effort? According to the level of living survey, dissatisfaction with taxes in fact receded between 1973 and 1981. And further, 'some relatively low-tax countries, like Italy, the United States and Spain, have been shown to have larger underground sectors than the Scandinavian countries' (Heidenheimer *et al.*, 1983: 191). Public disapproval of cheating on taxes is stronger in Sweden than in comparable societies (Vogel, 1974). The filmmaker Ingmar Bergman's tribulations with the tax man provided vivid evidence of an attitude that, as Swedish political leaders know especially well, refuses to tolerate tax offences that would be overlooked elsewhere. Indeed, according to *The Economist*'s comparison of executive 'perks' in Western nations, Swedish managers, already just about the lowest paid, faced 'a top marginal [income-tax] rate of 80 per cent on $46,000. In theory this should create an armful of perks in Sweden. It doesn't because the tax man is so vigilant there' (11 Feb. 1987: 73).

Still, there is no doubt that the high levels of marginal taxation constitute a problem. Indeed, the powerful minister of finance, K.-O. Feldt, has made it a priority to bring them down somewhat. In a position paper on tax reform presented to the SAP and the public in April 1987, Feldt argued that steps had to be taken to eliminate aspects of the tax system that encourage people to evade contributing to the common welfare and thus erode public morals and social solidarity. He proposed three main guidelines for reform: lower income-tax rates (30 per cent for the lowest bracket, 45 per cent for the middle, and 60 per cent for the highest), as well as restricting deductions and fairer and more uniform tax on capital gains, especially from real-estate transactions. Though Feldt emphasized the urgency of the task he did not suggest the problem has reached the crisis proportions intimated by the critics. Indeed, if it had, we would see more among educated Swedes emigrating than we do. In 1987, 22,000 persons emigrated, while 43,000 immigrants were welcomed. Evidently, dissatisfaction is lower than expected. One explanation lies in the common knowledge that the billions of kr. in transfers—29 per cent of all individual income (O'Higgins *et al.*, 1985: 14)—are, in effect, paid by the Swedes to themselves and their loved ones, for services they use, for their pensions upon retirement, or the allowances that they receive. Swedes know that if they operate outside the regular economy, they may get away without paying taxes on revenues incurred, but they won't be eligible for many of the appertaining inflation-protected benefits either.

Altruism, indeed, begins at home: in helping others one helps oneself. Despite the grumbling, few Swedes so resent not being able to realistically aspire to become rich legally that they regularly violate the relational norms underlying their institutions. They continue to work and study—not ferociously like many in the emerging South-East Asian economies—but quite seriously none the less and are rewarded for it by a decent income, top quality services, a harmonious living environment, and a sense of well-being that comes from pride of place. A recent meticulous study of the costs and benefits of the welfare state in Sweden and elsewhere concluded:

Inefficiencies . . . both in the production of social services and arising from the structure of taxation . . . compared to the strength of much contemporary criticism, are relatively moderate. . . . The serious assertion that we pay for redistribution by sacrificing activity and compassion in our way of life is dismissed. . . . The prevailing critical view of the welfare state is that it is low on effectiveness and high on side-effects. On the basis of the present study, I would turn this around and say that it is high on effectiveness and low on side-effects. . . . The power of reform is not unlimited but it is quite considerable (Ringen, 1987: 206–7).

Conclusion

For the present, then, the dire predictions of critics have proven unfounded and Swedish social democracy appears secure. But what of its future; what, if any, are the lessons to be drawn that are likely to be valid for generations beyond the present one? Before proceeding to answer this question, a note of caution raised in the Introduction bears repetition. The social system of contemporary Sweden is not presented as *the* model of social democracy but as one real-world expression of the basic principles underlying it. Norway would serve as another (and similar) such expression, as would Austria. Other candidates include Finland and Denmark—though these appear to be less clearly social democratic.

That said, we can return to the question posed when we began. We asked: is it possible to be social democrats in our heads as well as hearts, to ground our convictions on proof that social democracy delivers the goods, that it can and does work? The key to the answer was hypothesized to lie in a complementary rather than contradictory relationship between the competitive and co-operative aspects of social existence, the culturally rooted understanding that the very possibility of maintaining a community based on social solidarity is conditional upon its 'fitness' at surviving in the international economic jungle. The rest of the book amplified, opera-tionalized, and tested this basic hypothesis, identifying how the main features of social democracy fit together as a working whole, a social system. The following fictional news story serves to highlight those features.

It was before the assembled delegates that the president of the major national trade-union confederation rose to speak. After eloquently invoking the vision of the egalitarian and democratic society which the labour movement had always made its own, and recalling the great steps taken towards its realization, he warned that the realization of that vision would be endangered if labour chose to ignore its responsibilities, blaming employers for any problems. 'Our historical task is to channel the efforts of business toward increasing overall wealth while maintaining the fundamental principles guiding its distribution, to mobilize innovative energies toward useful production rather than speculation and financial manipulation, and to consolidate a people's culture that values shared achievement based on knowledge and skill.'

With the power, resources, and experience at its disposal, it was the labour movement's responsibility to keep not only its own institutions, but those of the nation as a whole, firmly on the path it had staked out. 'Those of you from our most successful export-oriented manufacturers' companies must not be seduced by your employers' blandishments. If there are excess profits, you must help us institute legislative and contractual means to oblige their being channelled toward productive investment from which all workers will benefit and not just a few.'

Public-sector workers were then singled out: 'Indeed you should keep pace with your private-sector comrades. But the international market from which you are sheltered forces them to be productive. And, following their lead on wages must mean following it equally well on productivity. Service-sector wage increases that are less tied to productivity gains than those in the export sector will raise costs which will be borne by our industry in lost competitiveness, and, ultimately, by every worker in lowered living standards.'

Finally he addressed the government ministers in the audience, summoning them to redouble efforts to ensure the fairest possible redistribution of wealth, and to remind them that achieving social justice at home and abroad was two sides of the same coin. 'A society living under the threat of poverty and unemployment is an inflexible society: each sector acts to preserve the relative privilege it enjoys; change is instinctively resisted. How does one reduce the production of weapons when those producing them face unemployment as a result? How does one reduce environmental pollutants or preserve forests when such actions would destroy people's livelihoods? How does one welcome immigrants and imports from developing countries when these are perceived as a threat to those with jobs?'

In returning to his main point, he summoned politicians and trade unionists alike. 'Do not be tempted to take the easy route of stimulating demand by lowering taxes on consumption. Our laws should enable us to consume more and better by stimulating us to *produce* more and better. The greatest threat to our way of life is becoming uncompetitive internationally through too high consumer spending, or public-sector wages unsupported by productivity rises, or wage drift in the most profitable industries that forces us trade unionists to bid up wages among competing employers. By serving our narrow, short-term interests, we disserve our wider long-term needs as workers and the interests of the nation of which we are part.'

The above report is fictional, but were it to be published in a newspaper in Sweden (or Norway, Austria . . . as opposed to Britain, the US, or Canada), it would provoke some thoughtful comment but probably little controversy and no surprise. In these pages we have explored in concrete terms how Swedish labour leaders have traditionally acted in a socially responsible manner and retained the confidence of their membership in so doing. LO members expect to be called upon to act responsibly, even when doing so conflicts with their immediate interests. And their knowledge of the wider economic reality and their place in it tells them that this concern with the 'big picture' has paid off over the years.

SOCIAL DEMOCRACY TODAY

Having come this far, the attentive reader will not interpret the above illustration as intimating that to achieve social democracy one need only recruit socially responsible labour leaders. If it were simply a matter of rationally choosing the appropriate course upon consideration of possible alternatives, a trade-union leader would conclude that the kind of socially responsible stance characteristic of social democracy described herein is the best practical approach to realizing democratic egalitarian objectives, and act accordingly. But, as Mancur Olson's pitiless 'public choice' logic forced us to concede, good intentions in themselves count for little: broad, rational considerations in the public interest give way to organizational interests—unless the two are complementary rather than contradictory. To be meaningful, actions by social-democratic trade-union and government leaders must be such as to reconcile immediate organizational considerations with overall societal objectives. The first prerequisite is thus an organizational base described in chapter 1 as an encompassing labour movement. Only an encompassing labour movement can be expected to actively, rather than merely rhetorically, support long-term social-democratic policy commitments. Conversely, such policy commitments must serve also to foster encompassing labour movement structures and legitimize socially responsible behaviour.

Encompassing trade unions are hardly sufficient: large and powerful unions in Britain and elsewhere have frequently abused their position. Throughout this book we have seen how in a social-democratic social system, as illustrated by Sweden, the complementarity of culture, institutions, and policies creates a context for socially responsible choices at different levels of activity on the part of labour as of other strategic groups. If an egalitarian social system is to be adaptable enough to prove resilient in the face of external shocks, it will not be because an enlightened minority within it finds its logic attractive, but because in their everyday organized activities people choose to act in ways that complement that logic.

It was further suggested in the Introduction that a 'small country mentality' characteristic of small independent nations with open economies is conducive to the development of a social-democratic social system. A small country mentality may characterize larger countries—Japan, for example—but only exceptionally.[1] Trade unions and other strategically placed interest organizations operating within such a cultural context are constantly reminded—as in the fictional speaker's comments—that the nation's prosperity depends on their collaboration to respond effectively to external challenges. This does not imply that they necessarily act in the national interest; it does mean that they normally operate within a widely shared set of references and facts making national consensus possible.

Swedish cultural values were explored in chapter 2. A small country mentality must be reinforced by societal values

[1] The term 'small country mentality' is used literally as well as figuratively. In a recent discussion, the author asked a Japanese official about his country's economic achievements: the answer began with 'Japan is a small country; every Japanese school child knows this'. This statement vividly brought back the fact that in virtually every one of the scores of interviews held with Swedish business, trade-union, academic, and government representatives, they would, at some point, point out: 'Sweden is a small country, therefore . . .'

emphasizing contribution to the public good through work and organizational participation. While no one historical factor is pre-eminent, such factors as the importance of the free peasantry, the late and rapid arrival of the commercial and industrial revolution, the society's status as neither colony nor colonizer, its early attainment of literacy, even the adoption of a proportional-representation system of elections, affect relevant cultural attitudes. These factors are conducive to the development of more centralized forms of organization on the labour market and elsewhere in the society, greater regional co-ordination, and, in general, a tendency toward compromise and consensus in the national interest.

The early chapters stressed the micro-level relationships and expectations underlying such consensus. The 'social contract' that characterizes relations between business and labour is the highest and most visible expression of a network of agreements and shared assumptions at the local and sectorial levels. It is through these institutionalized relationships among individuals and organizations that the values underlying social democracy are reinforced. The metaphor is that of a buffer zone composed of the activities and relationships of representative groups which constitute a web governed by—and shaping—the fundamental values of the society. Representatives of unions, business, and other interest organizations are members of public boards, agencies, and commissions investigating and implementing policy decisions; these organizations themselves provide important services in employment, adult education, housing, etc.

A wide buffer zone is thus another feature associated with social democracy as a social system. The assumption by 'private interest' organizations of public responsibilities is a concrete expression of those cultural values seen to be linked to the nation's size, independence, and geographical position. That these attitudes and practices have endured in Sweden up to this day testifies to the fact that they not only reflect traditional values but also meet immediate practical requirements. In chapter 1, a theoretical explanation of the economics of micro-level co-operation and macro-level concertation was presented. The fundamental notion was that socially re-sponsible consensual actions in keeping with the prevailing 'social contract' reduced the information and transaction costs of economic activity in ways which were seen to pay off to micro-level actors. It was argued that the kinds of relations that thus emerged at both the micro and macro levels were qualitatively different from those of both the competitive market and the command economies: a special term was proposed, the solidaristic market economy.

The middle chapters spelled out at length the practices and conventions of the solidaristic market economy in Sweden, and the principles that guided the trade-union economists who developed them in the middle of this century. That they formed the basis of a societal consensus might best be illustrated by here citing the 'other side's' perspective on what the head of the Swedish Federation of Industry's (SI) prestigious Industrial Institute for Economic and Social Research (IUI), Gunnar Eliasson, calls the 'old Swedish policy model'.

The old Swedish policy model, as understood by implicit contracts (and some documents) between the unions, business and the social democratic governments, was one of (1) non-intervention on the part of the central authority in the productive process of firms, (2) so-called solidaric wage policies, (3) an active labor market policy to stimulate mobility, (4) a 'low interest rate' policy to stimulate growth in manufacturing and (5) redistribution through taxes and public sector growth. . . . The key notions were efficient production through free trade and competitive entry, decentralized production and ownership, efficient structural adjustment through active labor market policies and efficient (equitable) distribution through public sector growth. The objective was to maximize the growth of the total output cake and to appropriate as much as possible of output—through the tax system and public sector growth—for redistribution, but without violating the basic growth premise (Eliasson, 1985).

With the exception of the stress on low interest-rate policies and the use of the term 'solidaric' rather than 'solidaristic', business's understanding of the traditional macro-level social contract as expressed in this passage is the same as that of labour.

While the preconditions for arriving at a lasting social contract in a small open economy lie in the existence of the appropriate encompassing organizations operating within a wide buffer zone, the existence of such preconditions is no guarantee that the right decisions will be taken at the right time. This is especially true with regard to full employment, as the Dutch (and, to some extent, Danish) examples illustrate. Crucial choices by LO, SAF, and other key actors at pivotal historical points were very much a factor. These include the measures specifically aimed to secure full employment, such as the active labour market and wage-solidarity policies, as well as two other types of policy commitments discussed in the last two chapters. The first concerns the manner in which services are provided to citizens: that they must be universal rather than marginal, since their delivery is certain to be inefficient if limited to serving those scorned by the market-place. Moreover, as well as undermining social solidarity, the existence of private service agencies renders the economy less flexible: for example, compared to transferable public social security arrangements, employer-based secondary pensions and sick benefits impede labour mobility.

The second commitment concerns education, research, culture, and communications. In chapter 6, we found a profound lessening of the distance between the classes in Sweden when it came to the circulation of knowledge. By vigorously promoting popular culture and education, the Swedish labour movement has broken down cultural and informational barriers between those who work in jobs requiring university-level training, and those who do not. Informed mass participation in buffer-zone activities was facilitated, decisions of mass organizations, trade unions, co-operatives, etc. being taken by a membership informed of the economic consequences of the various alternatives and therefore less vulnerable to demagoguery and commercialism.

Each chapter reinforced the principle of complementarity from another angle. In chapter 5, the emphasis was on employee involvement in corporate decision-making. Industrial democracy, combined with greater access to practical knowledge, security through nation-wide universal social insurance schemes, and a number of other factors discussed at some length, creates the required context for socially responsible behaviour. Each actor is predisposed to making economic choices that complement the workings of the economic system when it comes to employment, mobility, training, investment, use of technology, and participation in policy planning and implementation. In short, the message delivered by our fictional labour leader reflects the reality of Swedish workers as revealed in their day-to-day experiences.

These then are the main pieces in the social-democratic puzzle. They explain how equality and efficiency can be complementary and why, Mancur Olson and Marxists notwithstanding, the resilience of the Swedish system in the face of the external shocks witnessed in recent years comes as no surprise. Short-term, narrow interests need not win out, social democracy has proven itself not merely as a moral vision, but as a practicable social system.

But what of the future? Can the prophets of doom still be proven right? Perhaps the words of our labour leader are not likely to prove pertinent in light of future trends, some of which have already been noted. As industry continues to computerize its organization and robotize production, the distinction between blue- and white-collar work will continue to lose significance. LO's blue-collar industrial federations will continue to decline numerically in comparison to white-collar and public employees' organizations in and outside of LO. One manifestation of intra-union tensions occurred in the summer of 1987 when crane operators in three Swedish ports went on a wildcat strike to protest at 11 of their members being transferred from the LO's municipal workers' union to its transport union. Yet, while the stoppage embarrassed the LO, it would be foolhardy to see it as indicative of things to come. Indeed, it served to emphasize a counter-tendency to the strengthening of public-sector unions at the expense of private-sector ones, since the workers in question were being transferred because their employer was no longer the municipality but rather a city-owned company. Moreover, tensions exist within the public sector itself, as illustrated by the fact that in this same period, TCO nurses and hospital technicians broke ranks with other members of their negotiating cartel, demanding special wage increases.

Though, as noted at the end of chapter 3, the rifts are not as clear-cut as is sometimes made out, tensions will continue to arise. Trade-union solidarity will not be easy, especially in the face of continued pressure to keep wage increases down to a level comparable to their trading partners—among whom the tight-fisted West Germans set the pace. At the same time, calls to close ranks will be less automatically heeded by a generation of union members that knows little of the struggle for recognition and solidarity their parents experienced. Yet, when all is said and done, for all the internal tensions, the labour movement can be expected to be able to surmount the divisions and continue to play the role portrayed in the opening words of this concluding chapter. As long as Swedish export-oriented, engineering-based manufacturing remains at the economic and symbolic core of Sweden's continued prosperity—as it shows every sign of doing—then those LO trade unions associated with it—and thus LO as an institution—will continue to play a leading, if evolving, role. We have seen in recent years that the public-sector unions, though numerically strong, have by and large been successfully constrained by the absence of public sympathy from using their numbers and strategic infrastructural position to move ahead of their private-sector confrères.

What of Swedish business? Where will it stand? Gunnar Eliasson's use of the word 'old' in outlining the Swedish policy model is not accidental. It indicates that business, although generally satisfied with the SAP's rather conservative fiscal policy under Mr Feldt, is not persuaded that the 'Swedish policy model' has indeed been restored. For business-oriented economists like Eliasson, the government's violation of what he listed as the first principle of the model—'the non-intervention on the part of the central authority in the productive process of firms'—in the co-determination laws and wage-earner funds, and its direct involvement in wage bargaining, has added a new and unwelcome element to Swedish economic decision-making. As empirical confirmation of the inappropriateness of this new element, Eliasson points to indications that under the new constraints, solidaristic wages impede growth by introducing added rigidity to the labour market, thus discouraging workers from moving to new jobs: the IUI's 1985 long-term survey calculated that due to the new guarantees, to fill the average vacancy at the 1960s rate today requires 4 per cent unemployment, double the rate at that time (IUI, 1985).

While many employers share this concern, they are also aware that even if the average time for filling a vacancy has lengthened, it remains—at less than four weeks—impressive by international standards. Indeed, those who find themselves on the job market for lengthy periods consist almost solely of inexperienced young people and inappropriately educated refugees, both groups which wage solidarity tends to price too high for the market (Holmlund, 1986; Flanagan, 1986a; Åberg, 1988), and for whom, as we saw at length, specific training and 'relief work' programmes have been put into operation. Moreover, mobility statistics fail to count those workers who have taken advantage of opportunities for mobility and flexibility *within* their own firms enhanced by wage solidarity as well as the job redesign and worker-participation schemes described in chapter 5. Today, an L. M. Ericsson employee can be classified in one of only six occupational categories; in a comparable American communications firm, the number is 100.

As far as laws on employee participation and government participation in wage setting are concerned, setting aside the excessive rhetoric of the 1970s, these have, objectively speaking, largely been in keeping with the natural evolution of business-labour relations under the 'old' policy model in response to changing conditions. Of course, some business spokespersons do not accept the old model for ideological reasons—though these are still few—or because, following Assar Lindbeck, they foresee an irreversible rise in the degree of inefficiency in the allocation of labour, and in the tendency of productive employees to work less than they might otherwise, taking more vacations and part-time leaves, and retiring earlier.

As we concluded in chapter 7's discussion of the question, Lindbeck's fears appear exaggerated since they pay scant attention to the lowered transaction and information costs on the other side of the equation, the benefits of a secure, stable, and co-operative working environment complemented by the existence of efficient, dependable, complementary services. The most intensive study of the Swedish economy ever made by outsiders, that of the prestigious Brookings Institution of Washington, DC in 1986, found 'no evidence that Sweden cannot sustain domestic growth and international competitiveness if the economy is managed well. Despite the heavy commitments to wage equalization and high employment, the economy has proved responsive to the need for structural change' (Rivlin, 1986: 19). If the Brookings economists are unimpressed by the fears that have been raised, then we are surely on safe ground in seeing little possibility of their being realized.

But realized or not, does the very existence of these fears not bode ill for the future of SAF as an encompassing organization and the central role it plays? And what of new technological developments? There are indications that a new breed of entrepreneur is emerging outside of SAF. Typical are firms run by a handful of university graduates selling the most advanced financial and informational skills to big and slower-moving corporations. If this trend were to accelerate, it would eventually alter the fundamental equilibrium on the labour market. But that point is still far off and, given past experience, it would seem more likely that many of these companies will be integrated into the larger, unionized manufacturing corporations with which they work just as others emerge to take their place.

A related phenomenon is tied to recent moves to integrate Sweden's capital markets with those outside its borders, and the rapid rise of share prices on the Stockholm exchange in the mid-1980s. Swedes suddenly witnessed the appearance of a crop of instant millionaires, a phenomenon outside their experience and in contradiction with the norms of their society. As the price of keeping successful enterprises intact, the solidaristic market economy allows for the concentration of corporate control in a small number of hands through inherited corporate ownership. The (heavily taxed) income and wealth derived therefrom is legitimate because it is directly linked to production and employment. But wealth from stock or currency speculation—like that derived from gains in central-city real-estate values—is not the same. As the volatility of the speculative markets returned after the crash of October 1987—

which wiped out a few of those instant millionaires—new strains upon the business–labour partnership appeared. But we are not there yet and, judging by past experience (and ongoing discussions noted at the end of the last chapter), appropriate fiscal mechanisms limiting the acquisition of wealth from capital gains and stock-market and real-estate speculation will likely be devised to keep the problem within manageable bounds.

As noted in chapter 3, contractual negotiations from 1986 to 1988, though far from smooth, do not reflect the negative trends Olson foresaw. In general, wage bargaining seems to have moved on to a rather predictable course with the government setting the targets for wage increases (awaiting agreement on a new generation EFO formula—FOS—on which the partners have been working), relying on its taxation powers as well as its close links to the LO. Parliament went so far as to temporarily control prices early in 1987 to keep inflation below the level agreed to for reopening the wage settlement during the second year of the collective agreement. (In fact, the rate went just over the stipulated rate of 3.2 per cent, but the unions did not press the point.) And the government set clear cash limits for wage increases in the state sector for 1988. Moreover, there were signs of centripetal tendencies on the labour market to balance the centrifugal ones. In the 1986 collective agreement, SAF, LO, and PTK managed for the first time to include the provision that wage drift in the first year be subtracted from the wage increase for the second year in the collective agreement. And the next year the labour federations persuaded the government to regard profit-sharing bonuses paid out by companies to their employees as equivalent to wages for taxation purposes.

With government's role in wage policy increasing, one senses that SAF is playing a more secondary role in negotiations, as a kind of arbiter attempting to slice an already baked pie in a manner to satisfy both blue-collar LO and white-collar PTK. On another front, there was a move on the part of SAF and SI to contest the long-accepted principle of lay members being named to the boards of public agencies that implement state policy. While it is hard to conceive SAF and SI actually refusing to nominate representatives to these agencies, the mere floating of the idea indicates that as far as business is concerned, the days of the glorious SAF–LO partnership are gone and will not be resurrected. But it would appear that business's public unhappiness is also a matter of skilful lobbying. It seems unlikely that SAF's central position would be willingly abandoned by Swedish industry. In a social-democratic system with its centrally focused political institutions and communications networks, employers know full well that they cannot forgo recourse to an organization through which they can centrally co-ordinate and mobilize their resources and energies, especially since the business-oriented political parties are chronically weak and divided.

Early in 1986, the *International Labour Review* published the views of L. G. Albåge, the SAF deputy director general, on trends in Swedish collective bargaining. The article concludes:

Whether the social partners will be able to act in concert in order to get the economy moving again is something we cannot yet tell. . . . We can only express the hope that out of the present labour pains a new Swedish model will be born, resembling its forerunner. There are, in fact, good chances of this. Despite the adverse trends mentioned above, there are many sound elements of the Swedish economy and industrial relations system that have survived and can be built on. . . . In their hearts the Swedes share a deep community of values. The representatives of labour and management can still mix with each other centrally and locally in a spirit of trust and are capable of working together on matters of common interest. Promising signs are the agreements that have been concluded in recent years on such collaboration and, above all, the fact that the debate on wage policy is now being conducted in the broader context of the nation's economic health.

In a rejoinder in the same issue, Harry Fjällström, a member of the central bureau of LO, commented:

Many people in Sweden see . . . the frequent breaches of labour peace as linked to the departure from the centralized bargaining system. At the same time there is widespread agreement that prosperity must be safeguarded and equitably shared. This is why I believe that the pressures favouring the return to co-ordinated central negotiations will prevail, even if slight changes may be expected in the unions' distribution policy. The bargaining system that has come to be known as the Swedish model of industrial relations has stood the test of time and I am confident that given the opportunity it will continue to serve both sides of industry well for many years yet.

In the end, then, despite the strong and continual pressure on Sweden's collaborative labour-market system to keep down wage costs under full employment, if these views are as representative as they give every indication of being, system failure is not a likely prospect for years to come. What of the dangers of success? As noted in chapter 7, the image of Sweden as a nation driven to suicide, alcoholism, and sexual excess by the absence of personal challenge is pure myth. However the very success of social democracy does raise fundamental questions. We noted in chapter 6 how the lack of financial incentives for pursuing one's studies (Björklund, 1986) probably largely explains the stubborn fact that even in egalitarian Sweden the offspring of university-educated parents disproportionately go on to university. We noted in chapter 7 that the securing of financial independence for women and young people has removed artificial ties keeping families intact. Yet, rather than worrisome, these are exactly the challenges on which the Swedish policy makers thrive. On the basis of their past record, there is no convincing reason to doubt the capacity of the people through their political parties, representative organizations, and public agencies to come up with appropriate solutions together.[2]

Indeed, the essential political rationality of the citizenry in its expectations upon policy makers is reassuring in this regard. A recent study of Norway showed, confirming an earlier study of Sweden, that voters were sophisticated enough not to be bribed with their own money, that is, to judge governments on their long-term achievements rather than be swayed by attempts to manipulate macroeconomic conditions for electoral purposes (Sørensen, 1987: 31). And recent figures indicate that Sweden's birth rate, once among the very lowest, has risen above those of France, Germany, and Italy.

---

[2] Outsiders speaking to Swedes often come away with a different impression. But this seems largely due to cultural misperceptions. Swedes have little use for euphemisms: they describe things as they see them or not at all. For Americans especially, who sugar-coat things almost as a matter of course, Sweden can only be in bad shape. The opposite is usually the case: problems can be resolved only if faced up to.

More serious is perhaps the opposite danger, that the system itself will come to be seen as humdrum, taken for granted, stripped of its overriding vision. The rising popularity of the 'Greens' is one such indication. There is a lingering sense that the administration of Mr Carlsson and Mr Feldt, while competent, is too technocratic; the 1987 SAP Congress seems to have been especially businesslike and uninspiring. Some yearn nostalgically for Mr Palme's galvanizing personal style. Evidently the lessons of the past decade have not been forgotten: better to err on the side of caution, the labour movement today is saying, than to indulge again in the new leftist adventurism of the 1970s and provoke another neo-conservative backlash.

The balance is clearly a delicate one. Social democracy is a fine blend of idealism and pragmatism which must be renewed in each generation. As its realizations are consolidated at home, its vision will increasingly be manifested in actions and initiatives outside its borders, an area of discussion outside the scope of this book. Sweden's international position is generally well known in its broad contours. It combines neutrality based on security with a fundamental solidarity with Third World nations. Security is achieved through the production of sophisticated defensive weapons and the capacity to rapidly mobilize a large military force; solidarity with the poor nations is expressed in the form of a commitment to 1 per cent of the GNP for development assistance—higher than virtually every nation—a commitment it has lived up to for a number of years. Sweden's international vocation has been the subject of internal debate in recent years, sparked by the assassination of Olof Palme who had incarnated that vocation. The nagging suspicion that his still unsolved murder might have something to do with Swedish arms apparently finding their way to warring Middle-East nations in violation of Swedish law, and controversies surrounding the murder investigation, have led to attempts to focus Sweden's international role more clearly. Yet the main thrust of Sweden's objectives in international action remains certain, in Third World development, the struggle against apartheid, and de-nuclearization. Efforts to realize these objectives through state and organizationally based Swedish agencies (such as those of the trade unions and co-operatives) seem likely to help keep the flame of social-democratic idealism burning in the years to come.

Those directly involved will be the minority. Others, young people especially, will continue to be attracted by the excitement of New York's neon glitter or the opulence of the Côte d'Azure. But when it comes time for them to settle down, build their lives and families, and contribute their energies and talents to a wider community, few will have been seduced by the 'get-rich-quick and buy-happiness' culture; they will return to their caring—if somewhat predictable—homeland.[3] And in playing their part and keeping informed through their jobs and their participation in political parties and voluntary organizations, they will be contributing to the continued functioning of the solidaristic market economy that underpins their country's international efforts.

In his address to the 1987 SAP Congress, Ingvar Carlsson ended on words he attributed to the American rock singer Bruce Springsteen: 'There is no winner unless we are all winners'. We too shall leave Swedish social democracy on those well-chosen words. What others choose to learn from it is not for the Swedes to say—nor for me. Swedish social democracy is intact and likely will remain so. Its success is not accidental, nor mysterious; it can be comprehended as long as the various parts are understood in the context of the whole. Such an understanding should provide to social democrats elsewhere some guidelines as to what can and cannot be reasonably expected to be accomplished in their own settings.

Beyond that . . .

---

[3] From all reports, this is the case for the scores of Swedish ice-hockey players who have found fame and fortune in North America, as well as its world-champion professional tennis players, who return as soon as they can to their pristine red-brown stugas by the Baltic, the North Sea, or one of the many inland lakes.

BIBLIOGRAPHY

Åberg, Rune (1984). 'Market-Independent Income Distribution: Efficiency and Legitimacy', in Goldthorpe (ed.), *Order and Conflict in Contemporary Capitalism*.

—— (1988). 'Economic Work Incentives and Labor Market Efficiency in Sweden', in Olsen (ed.), *Industrial Change and Labour Adjustment in Sweden and Canada*.

——, Selen, Jan, and Tham, Henrik (1987). 'Economic Resources', in Erikson and Åberg, *Welfare in Transition*.

Adler-Karlsson, Gunnar (1967). *Functional Socialism: A Swedish Theory for Democratic Socialization*, Stockholm: Bokförlaget Prisma.

AIC (undated). *The Swedish Labour Movement*, Stockholm: AIC.

Alapuro, Risto, *et al.* (1985). *Small States in Comparative Perspective*, Oslo: Norwegian University Press.

Albåge, Lars-Gunnar (1986). 'Recent Trends in Collective Bargaining in Sweden', *International Labour Review*, vol. 125: 1.

Allardt, Erik (1984). 'Representative Government in a Bureaucratic Age', in *Daedalus*, vol. 113: 169–96.

Amnå, Erik (1986). 'Increased Participation and Effectiveness through Decentralisation and Integration', in Sven Wiberg (ed.), *Ledarskap och decentralisering*, Göteborg, Sweden: University of Göteborg.

AMS: National Labour Market Board (1985). *Labour Market Training*, AMS: Solna.

Andersen, Bent Rold (1984). 'Rationality and Irrationality of the Nordic Welfare State', in *Daedalus*, vol. 113: 109–39.

Anton, Thomas J. (1969). 'Policy Making and Political Culture in Sweden', in *Scandinavian Political Studies*, IV.

Arvedson Lennart, *et al.*, eds. (1985). *Economics and Values*, Stockholm: Almqvist and Wiksell.

Åsard, Erik (1980). 'Employee Participation in Sweden 1971–1979: The Issue of Economic Democracy', in *Economic and Industrial Democracy*, vol. 1: 3.

—— (1986). 'Industrial and Economic Democracy in Sweden: From Consensus to Confrontation', in *European Journal of Political Research*, vol. 14: 3.

Auer, Peter (1985). *Industrial Relations, Work Organization and the New Technology: The Volvo Case*, Berlin: Wissenschaftszentrum.

Auer, Peter (1988). 'Recent Labour Market Trends in Selected OECD Countries', in Olsen (ed.), *Industrial Change.*

Axelsson, Christina (1987). 'Family and Social Integration', in Erikson and Åberg (eds.), *Welfare in Transition.*

Bäckström, Anders (1984). *Reduction of Working Hours and Employment,* Stockholm: LO.

—— (1988). 'The Role of the Automotive Industry for the Swedish Economy and Labour Market', in Olsen (ed.), *Industrial Change.*

Barbash, Jack (1972). *Trade Unions and National Economic Policy,* Baltimore: The Johns Hopkins Press.

Bellan, Ruben (1986). *Necessary Evil: An Answer to Canada's High Unemployment,* Toronto: McClelland and Stewart.

Bengtsson, Lars, Eriksson, Ann-Charlotte, and Sederblad, Per (1985). *The Associative Action of Swedish Business Interests,* Berlin: Wissenschaftszentrum.

Berger, Suzanne, Hirschman, Albert, and Maier, Charles, eds. (1981). *Organizing Interests in Western Europe,* Cambridge, Cambridge University Press.

Berggren, Christian (1986). 'Top Management and Co-determination in Swedish Companies: Greater Union Influence Results in Better Decisions', in *Economic and Industrial Democracy,* vol. 7: 1.

Berke, Lena (1984). 'Economic Crime in Sweden', in *Current Sweden,* No. 322: Aug. 1984, Stockholm: Swedish Institute.

Björklund, Anders (1986). 'Assessing the Decline of Wage Dispersion in Sweden', in Gunnar Eliasson (ed.), *The Economics of Institutions and Markets,* Stockholm: IUI.

Blais, André (1986). 'Industrial Policy in Advanced Capitalist Democracies', in Andre Blais (ed.), *Industrial Policy,* vol. 44 of the research studies prepared for the Royal Commission on the Economic Union and Development Prospects for Canada, Toronto: University of Toronto Press.

—— and McCallum, John (1986). 'Government, Special Interest Groups, and Economic Growth', in David Laidler (ed.), *Responses to Economic Change,* vol. 27 of the research studies prepared for the Royal Commission on the Economic Union and Development Prospects for Canada. Toronto: University of Toronto Press.

Boalt, Gunnar, and Bergryd, Ulla (1981). *Political Value Patterns and Parties in Sweden,* Stockholm: Almqvist and Wiksell.

Bosworth, Barry P., and Rivlin, Alice M., eds. (1986). *The Swedish Economy,* Washington: Brookings Institution.

Brennan, G., and Buchanan, J. M. (1980). *The Power to Tax,* Cambridge: Cambridge University Press.

Brittan, Samuel (1979). *The Economic Consequences of Democracy,* New York: Holmes and Meir.

Burtless, Gary (1986). 'Taxes, Transfers, and Swedish Labor Supply', in Bosworth and Rivlin (eds.), *The Swedish Economy*, Washington: Brookings Institution.

Burton, Jeffrey (1980). 'The Swedish Steel Merger: Government and Worker Participation', in *Working Life in Sweden*, No. 21, Ottawa: Swedish Embassy.

Calmfors, Lars (1984). 'Stabilization Policy and Wage Formation in Economies with Strong Trade Unions', in Michael Emerson (ed.), *Europe's Stagflation*, Oxford: Oxford University Press.

Cameron, David R. (1978). 'The Expansion of the Public Economy: A Comparative Analysis', in *American Political Science Review*, Dec. 1978.

—— (1982). 'On the Limits of the Public Economy', in *Annals*, No. 459: Jan. 1982.

—— (1984). 'Social Democracy, Corporatism, Labour Quiescence, and the Representation of Economic Interest in Advanced Capitalist Society', in Goldthorpe (ed.), *Order and Conflict in Contemporary Capitalism*.

Carnoy, Martin, *et al.* (1983). *A New Social Contract*, New York: Harper and Row.

Castles, Francis G. (1978). *The Social Democratic Image of Society*, London: Henley and Boston.

Catherine, Robert, and Gousset, Pierre (1965). *L'État et l'essor industriel; Du dirigisme colbertien a l'économie concertée*, Paris: Berger-Levrault.

Chandler, M. A. (1986). *The State and Industrial Decline: A Survey*, in Andre Blais (ed.), *Industrial Policy*, vol. 44 of the research studies prepared for the Royal Commission on the Economic Union and Development Prospects for Canada. Toronto: University of Toronto Press.

Childs, Marquis (1936). *Sweden: The Middle Way*, New Haven: Yale University Press.

—— (1985). *Sweden: The Middle Way on Trial*, New Haven: Yale University Press.

Christensen, Anna (1982). 'Wage Labour as Social Order and Ideology', in the Secretariat for Futures Studies, *Shifts in Values within Swedish Society*, Stockholm: Secretariat for Future Studies.

Crosland, C. A. R. (1956). *The Future of Socialism*, London: Jonathan Cape.

Dahl, Hans F. (1984). 'Those Equal Folk', in *Daedalus*, vol. 113: 93–107.

Dahl, Robert A. (1970). *After the Revolution: Authority in a Good Society*, New Haven: Yale University Press.

Dahlberg, Åke (1986). 'Actual Policies, Programmes and Cost of Sweden's Labour Market Policies', paper presented at conference on Industrial Adjustment, Dec. 1986, York University, Toronto, Canada.

Daun, Åke (1985). *Setbacks and Advances in the Swedish Housing Market*, Stockholm: Swedish Institute.

DeGeer, Hans, *et al.* (1986). *In the Wake of the Future*, Stockholm: Faradet.

Douglas, Mary, and Wildavsky, Aaron (1983). *Risk and Culture*, Berkeley: University of California.

Dyring, Annagreta (1985). *Swedish Research*, Stockholm: Swedish Institute.

Dyson, Kenneth, and Humphreys, Peter, eds. (1986). 'The Politics of the Communications Revolution in Western Europe: Special Issue', *West European Politics*, vol. 9: 4.

Eiger, Norman (1983). 'The Education of Employee Representatives on Company Boards in Sweden', in *Working Life in Sweden*, No. 27: May 1983. New York: Swedish Information Service.

Einhorn, Eric S., and Logue, John A. (1986). 'The Scandinavian Democratic Model', in *Scandinavian Political Studies*, vol. 9: 3.

Eliassen, Kjell A. (1981). 'Political and Public Participation', in Erik Allardt *et al.* (eds.), *Nordic Democracy*, Copenhagen: Det Danske Selskab.

Eliasson, Gunnar (1983). *Policy Making in a Disorderly World Economy*, Stockholm: Industriens Utrednings-Institut (IUI).

—— (1984). *The Micro-Foundations of Industrial Policies*, Stockholm: IUI.

—— (1985). *Is the Swedish Welfare State in Trouble?*, Stockholm: IUI.

—— (1986). *International Competition Productivity Change and the Organisation of Production*, Stockholm: IUI.

—— and Ysander, Bengt-Christer (1982). 'The End of Welfare', in *Journal of Economic Literature*, vol. xx: 1.

——, Sharefkin, Mark, and Ysander, Bengt-Christer (1983). *Policy Making in a Disorderly World Economy*, Stockholm: Almqvist and Wiksell.

Elster, L. (1982). 'Marxism, Functionalism, and Game Theory', in *Theory and Society*, 11: 453–82.

Elvander, Nils (1974), 'Interest Groups in Sweden', in *Annals of the American Academy of Political and Social Science*, No. 413: 27–43.

Engberg, Jan (1986). 'Folkrörelserna i vålfarssamhellet', Ph.D dissertation: Universitet Umeå.

Engström, Peter, and Levinson, Klaus (1982). 'Industrial Relations in the Swedish Auto Industry: Developments in the Seventies', paper presented at the workshop on 'Recent Developments in Automobile Industrial Relations', 26–27 Mar. 1982, Berlin: International Institute of Management.

Erikson, Robert (1985). 'Welfare Trends in Sweden Today', Stockholm: Swedish Institute.

—— , and Åberg, Rune, eds. (l987). *Welfare in Transition: A Survey of Living Conditions in Sweden 1968–1981*, Oxford: Clarendon Press.

—— and Fritzeil, Jonan (1987). *Sweden: Transfers and Programs: an institutional social policy against the life cycle of poverty*, Stockholm: Swedish Institute for Social Research (SOFI).

—— , Hansen, Erik Jørgen, Ringen, Stein, and Usitalo, Hannu, eds. (1987). *The Scandinavian Model: Welfare States and Welfare Research*, New York: M. E. Sharpe.

Esping-Andersen, Gösta (1985). *Politics Against Markets*, Princeton: Princeton University Press.

—— and Korpi, Walter (1987). 'From Poor Relief to Institutional Welfare States: the Development of Scandinavian Social Policy', in *International Journal of Sociology*, vol. xvi: 3–4.

Ewander, Anders, and Miller, Sam (1982). 'The Disabled in Sweden: Handicaps and Recreation', Stockholm: Swedish Institute.

Fägerlind, Ingemar, and Saha, Lawrence (1983). *Education and National Development*, London: Pergamon Press.

Faxén, K.-O., Faxén, C.-E., and Spånt, R. (1988). 'The FOS Report—a new model for wage formation', in *Inside Sweden*, No. 2 (May–June 1988).

Feige, Edgar L. (1986). 'Sweden's "Underground Economy"', in Gunnar Eliasson (ed.), *The Economics of Institutions and Markets*, Stockholm: IUI.

Fjällström, Harry (1986). 'Recent Trends in Collective Bargaining in Sweden: an Employer's View', in *International Labour Review*, vol. 125: 1.

Flanagan, Robert J. (1986). 'Compliance and Enforcement Decisions under the National Labour Relations Act', paper presented at FIEF, June 1986, Stockholm.

—— (1986a). 'Efficiency and Equality in Swedish Labor Markets', in Bosworth and Rivlin (eds.), *The Swedish Economy*.

—— , Soskice, David W., and Ulman, Lloyd (1983). *Unionism, Economic Stabilization, and Incomes Policies*, Washington: Brookings Institution.

Forsebäck, Lennart (1980). *Industrial Relations and Employment in Sweden*, Stockholm: Swedish Institute.

Foy, Nancy, and Gadon, Herman (1976). 'Worker Participation: Contrasts in Three Countries', in *Harvard Business Review*, May–June 1976.

Fraser, Neil (1987). 'Economic Policy in Sweden: Are there lessons from the Swedish model?', in *International Review of Applied Economics*, vol. 1. 2: 209–24.

Fry, John, ed. (1979). *Limits on the Welfare State*, Farnsborough: Saxon House.

Furness, Norman, and Tilton, Timothy (1979). *The Case for the Welfare State*, Bloomington: Indiana University Press.

Gidlund, Gullan (1988). 'The Costs of Party Performance in Sweden', presented at the XIVth International Political Science Association Congress, Washington, DC.

Gidlund, Janerik, Ekman, Ann-Kristin, *et al.* (1985). *Choosing Local Futures: Introduction to a Swedish study and an outline of scenarios 2000*, Stockholm: Secretariat for Futures Studies.

Gilder, George (1981). *Wealth and Poverty*, New York: Bantam.

Ginsburg, Helen (1983). *Full Employment and Public Policy: The United States and Sweden*, Lexington, Mass.: Lexington Books.

Glotz, Peter (1985). 'Let's stop waiting for the right to fail', in *Socialist Affairs*, vol. 1: 85.

Goldthorpe, John H. (1984). 'Introduction', in John H. Goldthorpe (ed.), *Order and Conflict in Contemporary Capitalism*, London: Oxford University Press.

Gramlich, Edward M. (1986). 'Rethinking the Role of the Public Sector', in Bosworth and Rivlin (eds.), *The Swedish Economy*.

Gustafsson, Agne (1983). *Local Government in Sweden*, Stockholm: Swedish Institute.

—— (1986). 'Rise and Decline of Nations: Sweden', in *Scandinavian Political Studies*, vol. 9: 1, 35–50.

Gustafsson, Bo (1985). 'Conflict, Confrontation and Consensus in Modern Swedish History', in Lennart Arvedson *et al.* (eds.), *Economics and Values*, Stockholm: Almqvist and Wiksell.

Gustafsson, Karl Erik (1983). 'Mass Media Structure and Policy in Sweden in the Early 1980s', in *Current Sweden*, No. 301: June 1983, Stockholm: Swedish Institute.

—— (1984). 'Press Subsidies in Sweden Today—Structure and Effects', in *Current Sweden*, No. 318: June 1984.

Gustavsen, Björn (undated). *A Decade with Employee Representation on Company Boards: Experiences and Prospects for the Future*, Stockholm: Arbetslivscentrum.

Gustavsson, Carl G. (1986). *The Small Giant: Sweden Enters the Industrial Era*, Athens, Ohio: Ohio University Press.

Gyllenhammar, Pehr G. (1977). 'How Volvo adapts work to people', in *Harvard Business Review*, vol. 55, No.4.

Hadenius, Axel (1985). 'Citizens Strike a Balance: Discontent with Taxes, Content with Spending', in *Journal of Public Policy*, 5: 3.

—— (1976). *Facklig organisationutveckling. En studie av Ländsorganisation i Sverige*, Stockholm: LO.

Hadenius, Stig (1985). *Swedish Politics during the 20th Century*, Stockholm: Swedish Institute.

Hancock, M. Donald (1972). *Sweden: the Politics of Postindustrial Change*, Hinsdale, Ill.: Dryden Press.

Haskell, Barbara (1987). 'Paying for the Welfare State: Creating Political Durability', in *Scandinavian Studies*, vol. 59.2: 221–53.

Heckscher, Gunnar (1984). *The Welfare State and Beyond*, Minneapolis: University of Minnesota Press.

Heclo, Hugh, and Madsen, Henrik (1987). *Policy and Politics in Sweden: Principled Pragmatism*, Philadelphia: Temple University.

Hedberg, Bo (1979). *Worker Participation in Structural Change*, Stockholm: Arbetslivscentrum.

Hedborg, Anna (1986). 'The Swedish Welfare State Model', presented at conference on Industrial Adjustment, York University, Dec. 1986, Toronto, Canada.

Hedström, Peter (1986). 'The Evolution of the Bargaining Society: Politico-Economic Dependencies in Sweden', in *European Sociological Review*, vol. 2: 1.

—— (1986a). 'From Political Sociology to Political Economy', in Ulf Himmelstrand (ed.), *The Sociology of Structure and Action*, London: Sage Publications.

—— and Swedberg, Richard (1985). 'The Power of Working Class Organizations and the Inter-Industrial Wage-Structure', in *International Journal of Comparative Sociology*, vol. xxvi: 1–2.

Heidenheimer, Arnold J. (1985). 'Comparative Policy at the Crossroads', in *Journal of Public Policy*, Vol. 15: 4.

——, Heclo, Hugh, and Teich Adams, Carolyn (1983). *Comparative Public Policy*, New York: St Martin's Press.

Heisler, Martin, and Kvavik, Robert B. (1974). 'The European Policy Model', in Martin Heisler (ed.), *Politics in Europe*, New York: David McKay.

Hernes, Gudmund (1987). 'Karl Marx and the Dilemmas of Social Democracies: The Case of Norway and Sweden', paper presented at the Nordisk Förbund for Statskundskap, Copenhagen, 20–23 Aug. 1987.

—— and Selvik, Arne (1981). 'Local Corporatism', in Berger *et al.*, *Organizing Interests in Western Europe*.

Herrström, Staffan (1986). *Swedish Family Policy*, Stockholm: Swedish Institute.

HI (Handikapp Institutet, 1982). *Housing with Day and Night Service for the Severely Disabled*, Stockholm: HI.

Hibbs, Douglas A. Jr. (1986). 'Party Goals and Macroeconomic Policies and Outcomes in the United States', paper presented at European Consortium for Political Research, 1–6 Apr. 1986, Göteborg, Sweden.

Higgins, Winton (1985). 'Political Unionism and the Corporatist Thesis', in *Economic and Industrial Democracy*, vol. 6: 3.

Himmelstrand, Ulf, *et al.* (1981). *Beyond Welfare Capitalism*, London: Heinemann.

Hirschfeldt, Johan (1986). *An Ombudsman Against Ethnic Discrimination*, Stockholm: Swedish Institute.

Hofstede, Geert (1985). 'The Role of Cultural Values in Economic Development', in Arvedson *et al.* (eds.), *Economics and Values*.

Holmberg, Sören (1988). 'Political Representation in Sweden', presented at the XIVth International Political Science Association Congress, Washington, DC.

Holmlund, Bertil (1986). 'Comment', in Bosworth and Rivlin (eds.), *The Swedish Economy*.

Huntford, Roland (1971). *The New Totalitarians*, London: Allen Lane.

Isberg, Magnus (1982). *The First Decade of the Unicameral Riksdag: the Role of the Swedish Parliament in the 1970s*, Stockholm: Forskningsrapporter.

IUI (1985). *Long Term Survey*, Stockholm: Industrial Institute for Economic and Social Research.

Jangenäs, Bo (1985). *The Swedish Approach to Labour Market Policy*, Uppsala: Swedish Institute.

Jensen, Brikt (1986). 'The Dream of Sweden', in *Inside Sweden*, Jan. 1986.

Johannesson, Jan (1985). *Financing Active and Passive Labour Market Policy—The Swedish Case*, Stockholm: Institutet för social forskning (SOFI).

—— and Persson-Tanimura, Inga (1978). *Labour Market Policy in Transition: studies about the effects of labour market policy*, Stockholm: SOU.

—— and Persson-Tanimura, Inga (1984). *Labour Market Policy Under Reconsideration*, Stockholm: SOU.

—— and Niklasson, Harald (1974). *Evaluating Labour Market Policy*, Stockholm: SOU.

Jones, H. G. (1976). *Planning and Productivity in Sweden*, Totowa, NJ: Rowman and Littlefield.

Jönsson, Berth (1980). 'The Volvo Experiences of New Job Design and New Production Technology', in *Working Life in Sweden*, No. 19, Ottawa: Swedish Embassy.

Jonsson, Janne (1987). 'Educational Resources', in Erikson and Åberg (eds.) *Welfare in Transition*.

Jonzon, Björn (1986). 'Evaluation of Labour Market Policy Measures: Some Short Reflections', presented at conference on Industrial Adjustment, Dec. 1986, York University, Toronto, Canada.

Jordan, Grant (1984). 'Pluralistic Corporations and Corporate Pluralism', in *Scandinavian Political Studies*, vol. 7: 84.

Katzenstein, Peter (1985). *Small States in World Markets*, Ithaca, NY: Cornell.

—— (1984). *Corporatism and Change: Austria, Switzerland, and the Politics of Industry*, Ithaca, NY: Cornell.

Keck, Otto (1986). 'The Information Dilemma', paper presented at the American Political Science Association, Annual Meeting, Sept. 1986, Washington, DC.

Kelman, Steven (1981). *Regulating America, Regulating Sweden*, Cambridge, Mass.: MIT.

Keman, Hans (1984). 'Politics, Policies and Consequences: A Cross-national Analysis of Public Policy-formation in Advanced Capitalist Democracies (1967–1981)', in *European Journal of Political Research*, 12: 147–69.

Kesselman, Mark, Krieger, Joel, *et al.* (1987). *European Politics in Transition*, Lexington, Mass.: D. C. Heath and Company.

KF: Konsum (1985). *Consumer Cooperatives in Sweden*, Stockholm: KF/Konsum.

King, Anthony (1973). 'Ideas, Institutions and the Policies of Governments', in *British Journal of Political Science*, vol. 3.

Kleberg, Carl-Johan (1984). 'Cultural Policy in Sweden', draft version of article published in M. Cummings and R. Katz (eds.), *Government and the Arts in the Modern World*, Baltimore: The Johns Hopkins Press.

Klevard, Åsa and Sternerup, Christina (1986). *The Engineer Shortage and Engineering Studies—What Is Sweden Doing?*, Stockholm: Swedish Institute.

Kluckholm, Florence, and Strodbeck, Fred (1961). *Variations in Value Organizations*, Evanston, Ill.: Row, Peterson.

Köhl, Jürgen (1988). 'Public/Private Mixes in Pension Policies: Some Examples from Western Europe', presented at the XIVth International Political Science Association Congress, Washington, DC.

Korpi, Walter (1978). *The Working Class in Welfare Capitalism*, London: Routledge and Kegan Paul.

—— (1980). 'Social Policy and Distributional Conflict in the Capitalist Democracies: A Preliminary Comparative Framework', in *West European Politics*, vol. 3: 3.

Korpi, Walter (1985). *Economic Growth and the Welfare State: Leaky Bucket or Irrigation System?*, Stockholm: SOFI.

—— (1985a). 'Economic Growth and the Welfare State: A Comparative Study of 18 OECD Countries', in *Labour and Society*, vol. 10: 2.

Kraus, Sidney, and Perloff, Richard M., eds. (1985). *Mass Media and Political Thought: an Information-Processing Approach*, Beverly Hills: Sage Publications.

Kuttner, Robert (1984). *The Economic Illusion*, Boston: Houghton Mifflin.

Lange, Peter, and Garrett, G. (1985). 'The Politics of Growth: Strategic Interaction and Economic Performance in the Advanced Industrial Democracies', in *Journal of Politics*, vol. 47: 792–827.

Larsson, Allan, ed. (1979). *Labour Market Reforms in Sweden: Facts and Employee Views*, Stockholm: Swedish Institute.

Lash, Scott (1985). 'The End of Neo-corporatism? The Breakdown of Centralized Bargaining in Sweden', in *British Journal of Industrial Relations*, vol. 23.

Laxer, Gordon (forthcoming). *Open for Business*, Toronto: Methuen.

Lehmbruch, Gerhard (1984). 'Concertation and the Structure of Corporatist Networks', in Goldthorpe (ed,), *Order and Conflict in Contemporary Capitalism*.

Lewander, Anders, and Miller, Sam (1982). *The Disabled in Sweden: Handicaps and Recreation*, Stockholm: Swedish Institute.

Lewin, Leif (1977). 'Union Democracy', in *Working Life in Sweden*, no. 3, Ottawa: Swedish Embassy.

Lewis, Donald E. (1986). 'Sweden's Manufacturing Sector: A Modern Success Story', in *The Australian Quarterly* Vol. 58: 1.

Lijphart, Arend (1968). *The Politics of Accommodation: Pluralism and Accommodation in the Netherlands*, Berkeley: University of California.

Lindbeck, Assar (1981). *Work Disincentives in the Welfare State*, Stockholm, IIES (Institute for International Economic Studies: Stockholm University).

—— (1983). *Interpreting Income Distributions in a Welfare State*, Stockholm: IIES.

—— (1985). 'Redistribution Policy and the Expansion of the Public Sector', in *Journal of Public Economics*, vol. 28: Dec.

—— (1986). 'Limits to the Welfare State', in *Challenge*, vol. 28: Jan./Feb.

—— (1987). 'Individual Freedom and Welfare State Policy', paper presented at Schumpeter Lecture, EEA Congress, 23 Aug. 1987.

Linton, Martin (1984). *The Swedish Road to Socialism*, London: Fabian Pamphlet: 503.

Listhaug, Ola, and Miller, Arthur H. (1985). 'Public Support for Tax-Evasion: Self-Interest or Symbolic Politics?', in *European Journal of Political Research*, vol. 13: 3.

LO: Swedish Confederation of Trade Unions [1951]. *Trade Unions and Full Employment*, Stockholm: LO.

LO (1985). *LO's Role in the Framing and Implementation of School and Educational Policy Reforms in Sweden*, Stockholm: LO.

LO (1986, Feb.). 'Report to the Congress: Welfare State Resources Now Fully Developed; Now They Must Be Utilized Correctly', Stockholm, LO News.

Logue, John (1981). 'Saab/Trollhätten Reforming Work Life on the Shop Floor', in *Working Life in Sweden*, no. 23, Ottawa: Swedish Embassy.

Lundberg, Erik (1985). 'The Rise and Fall of the Swedish Model', in *Journal of Economic Literature*, vol. xxiii: 1–36.

Lundberg, Olle, and Kjellström, Svenake (1987). 'Health and Health Care Utilization', in Erikson and Åberg (eds.), *Welfare in Transition*.

Lundh, Tina (1986). *Computerization at Work*, Stockholm: Swedish Institute.

Lundqvist, Lennart J. (1984). 'Housing Policy and Alternative Housing Tenures: Some Scandinavian Examples', in *Policy and Politics*, vol. 12: 1.

Lyon, Vaughan (1985).'Citizen Funds', in *Policy Options/Options politiques*, vol. 6: 1.

Maier, Charles S. (1984). 'Precondition for Corporatism', in Goldthorpe (ed.), *Order and Conflict in Contemporary Capitalism*.

March, James G., and Olsen, J. P. (1976). *Ambiguity and Choice in Organizations*, Oslo: Universitets förlarget.

Marklund, Sixten, and Bergendahl, Gunnar (1979). *Trends in Swedish Educational Policy*, Stockholm: Swedish Institute.

Marks, Gary (1986). 'Neocorporatism and Incomes Policy in Western Europe and North America', in *Comparative Politics*, 1986: Apr.

Martin, Andrew (1978). *Employee Investment Funds: An Approach to Collective Capital Formation*, London: Allen and Unwin.

—— (1984). 'Trade Unions in Sweden: Strategic Responses to Change and Crisis', in Peter Gourevitch *et al.*, *Unions and Economic Crisis*, Boston: Allen and Unwin.

Meidner, Rudolf (1985). *The Role of Manpower Policy in the Swedish Model*, Stockholm: Arbetslivscentrum.

—— (1987). 'A Third Way—The Concept of the Swedish Labour Movement', mimeographed paper.

—— and Ohman, Berndt (1972). *Fifteen Years of Wage-Policy*, Stockholm: LO.

Meyerson, Per-Martin (1982). *The Welfare State in Crisis: the Case of Sweden*, Stockholm: Swedish Institute.

Micheletti, Michele (1984). *The Involvement of Swedish Labor Market Organizations in the Swedish Political Process* (SNS occasional paper No. 18), Stockholm: SNS.

—— (1985). 'Organizing Interest and Organized Protest', Ph.D thesis, University of Stockholm (Dept. of Political Science).

—— (1987). 'Historical Consolidation and Present Complications of Farmer Organization in Sweden', mimeographed paper: University of Stockholm (Dept. of Political Science).

Miller, A. H., and Asp, Kent (1985). 'Learning about Politics from the Media: A Comparative Study of Sweden and the United States', in Kraus and Perloff (eds.), *Mass Media and Political Thought*.

Milner, Henry (1987). 'Corporatism and the Microeconomic Foundations of Swedish Social Democracy: the Swedish Model Revisited', in *Scandinavian Political Studies*, vol. 10: No. 3.

Ministry of Finance (1988). *The Swedish Budget 1988-89*, Stockholm: Government of Sweden.

Muller, Edward N. (1986). 'Distributions of Income in Advanced Capitalist Societies: Political Parties, Labour Unions, and the Industrial Economy', presented at the American Political Science Association, Annual Meeting, Sept. 1986, Washington, DC.

Myrdal, Gunnar (1973). *Against the Stream: Critical Essays on Economics*, New York: Pantheon Books.

Myrdal, Hans-Göran, and Schiller, Göran (1987). *Worker Participation in Sweden: Functioning and Effects—A Case Study*, Stockholm: SAF.

National Institute of Economic Research (1985). *The Swedish Economy Autumn 1985*, Stockholm: Norstedts Tryckeri.

Nielson, Klaus, and Pedersen, Ove (1988). 'The Negotiated Economy: Ideal and History', in *Scandinavian Political Studies*, vol. 11.2.

Nilsson, Karl-Ola (1986). *Cultural Workers' Centres in Sweden*, Stockholm: Swedish Institute.

Nordic Council (1983). *Working Together: An Opinion Poll of the Nordic Countries Spring 1983*, Göteborg: Nordic Council.

North, Douglass C. (1981). *Structure and Change in Economic History*, New York: Norton and Company.

—— (1985). *Institutions, Transactions Costs and Economic Growth* (Political Economy Working Paper), St Louis: Washington University.

OECD (1980). *The Welfare State in Crisis*, Paris: OECD.

—— (1985). *Social Expenditure, 1960-1990: Problems of Control and Growth*, Paris: OECD.

—— (1986). *Living Conditions in OECD Countries: A Compendium of Social Indicators*, Paris: OECD.

OECD Directorate for Science, Technology and Industry (1986). *Reviews of National Science and Technology Policies: Sweden*, Paris: OECD.

Offe, Claus (1981). 'The Attribution of Public Status to Interest Groups: Observations on the West German Case', in Berger *et al.* (eds.), *Organizing Interests in Western Europe.*

O'Higgins, Michael *et al.* (1985). 'Income Distribution and Redistribution: A Microdata Analysis For Seven Countries', Luxembourg Income Study, LIS-CEPS: Luxembourg.

Öhman, Berndt (1980). 'Wage-earner Funds: Background, Problems, and Possibilities', in *Economic and Industrial Democracy*, vol. 1. (1980).

Okun, Arthur H. (1975). 'Inflation: its Mechanics and Welfare Costs', in A. H. Okun and G. L. Perry (eds.), Brookings Papers on Economic Activity, 1975: 2.

Olsen, Gregg, ed. (1988). *Industrial Change and Labour Adjustment in Sweden and Canada*, Toronto: Garamond.

Olsen, Johan P. (1983). *Organized Democracy. Political Institutions in a Welfare State—The Case of Norway*, Oslo: Universitets-förlaget.

Olson, Mancur (1982). *The Rise and Decline of Nations*, New Haven: Yale University Press.

—— (1983). *An Approach to Public Policy that Transcends Outdated Ideologies*, Berlin: Wissenschaftszentrum.

—— (1986). 'An Appreciation of the Tests and Criticisms', in *Scandinavian Political Studies*, vol. 9: 1.

—— (1986a) 'A Theory of the Incentives Facing Political Organizations', in *International Political Science Review*, vol. 7: 2.

Olsson, Sven E. (1985). *Welfare Programs in Sweden*, Stockholm: SOFI.

—— (1986). *Growth to Limits: The Western European Welfare States, the Case of Sweden*, Stockholm: Swedish Institute for Social Research.

—— (1987). *Social Welfare in Economically Advanced Countries: Social Services and Social Security in Sweden*, Stockholm: SOFI.

Örtengren, Johan (1984). 'Sweden: An Economy at the Crossroads', in DOR *et al.*, *Economic Growth in a Nordic Perspective*, Finland: Frenckell.

Paloheimo, Heikki (1984). 'Political Struggle and Economic Development in Developed Capitalist Countries', in *European Journal of Political Research*, vol. 12.

—— (1986). 'The Effect of Trade Unions and Governments on Economic Growth', paper prepared for the Workshop on National Models at the ECPR Joint Session of Workshops, 1–6 Apr. 1986, Göteborg.

Panitch, Leo (1981). 'Trade Unions and the Capitalist State', *New Left Review*, No. 125.

Parkin, Frank (1971). *Class Inequality and Political Order*, London: McGibbon and Kee.

Pestoff, Victor (1983). *The Swedish Organizational Community and its Participation in Public Policy-making: An Introductory View*, Stockholm: University of Stockholm (Dept. of Political Science).

—— (1986). 'The Politics of Private Business, Cooperatives and Public Enterprise in a Corporatist Democracy—The Case of Sweden', paper presented at Society for Co-operative Studies' Conference, 20-21 Oct. 1986, HSB-skolan, Lidingö.

—— (1986a). 'The Politics of Private Business, Co-operatives and Public Enterprise in an Economy of Negotiation—The Case of Sweden', paper presented at the European University Institute, 21-25 Apr. 1986, Florence, Italy.

—— (1987). 'Joint Regulation, Meso-games and Political Exchange', revised version of paper presented at the ECPR Workshop on Corporatism, Apr. 1987, Amsterdam.

Peters, T. J., and Waterman, R. H. (1982). *In Search of Excellence*, New York: Harper and Row.

Peterson, Eric (1977). 'Interest Group Incorporation in Sweden', paper presented at the APSA Annual Meeting, Sept. 1977, Washington, DC.

Petersson, Olof (1981). 'Swedish Social Democracy and French Socialism', in Himmelstrand *et al.*, *Beyond Welfare Capitalism*.

—— *et al.*, eds. (1987). *The Study of Power and Democracy in Sweden: Progress Report 1987*, Stockholm: Regeringskansliets Offsetcentral.

Pontussen, Jonas (1984). *Public Pension Funds and the Politics of Capital Formation in Sweden*, Stockholm: Arbetslivscentrum.

Postman, Neil (1985). *Amusing Ourselves to Death*, New York: Viking.

Przeworski, Adam (1985). *Capitalism and Social Democracy*, Cambridge: Cambridge University Press.

Rasmusson, Ludwig (1982?). 'The Forties Generation', in Secretariat for Futures Studies, *Shifts in Values within Swedish Society*, Stockholm: Swedish Institute.

Rationalization Council (LO and SAF) (1976). *The Volvo Kalmar Plant: the Impact of New Design on Work Organization*, Stockholm: SAF.

Rehn, Gösta (1983). 'The Debate on Employees' Capital Funds in Sweden', paper prepared for the Commission of the European Communities, Aug. 1983, Brussels.

—— (1984). *Cooperation between the Government and Workers' and Employers' Organizations on Labour Market Policy in Sweden*, Stockholm: Swedish Institute.

—— (1984a). 'The Wages of Success', in *Daedulus*, vol. 113: 2.

—— (1985). 'Swedish Active Labour Market Policy: Retrospect and Prospect', in *Industrial Relations*, vol. 24: 1.

—— (1987). 'State, Economic Policy and Industrial Relations in the 1980's', *Economic and Industrial Democracy*, vol. 8, 61–100.

—— and Lundberg, Erik (1963). 'Employment and Welfare: Some Swedish Issues', in *Industrial Relations*, vol. 2: 2.

—— and Petersen, K. Helveg (1980). *Education and Youth Employment in Sweden and Denmark*, New York: The Carnegie Foundation.

Richardson, Jeremy (1986). 'Policy, Politics and the Communications Revolution in Sweden', in *West European Politics*, 9: 4. 80–97.

Ringen, Stein (1986). *Difference and Similarity: Two Studies in Comparative Income Distribution*, Stockholm: SOFI.

—— (1987). *The Possibility of Politics: A Study in the Political Economy of the Welfare State*, Oxford: Clarendon Press.

Rivlin, Alice M. (1986). 'Overview' in Bosworth and Rivlin, (eds.), *The Swedish Economy*.

Rokkan, Stein (1966). 'Norway: Numerical Democracy and Corporate Pluralism', in Robert A. Dahl (ed.), *Political Oppositions in Western Democracies*, New Haven: Yale University Press.

Rose, Richard (1980). *Challenge to Governance*, London: Sage Publications.

Rothstein, Bo (1985). 'Managing the Welfare State: Lessons from Gustav Möller', in *Scandinavian Political Studies*, 8: 3, 151–70.

Ruin, Olof (1974). 'Participatory Democracy and Corporativism: The Case of Sweden', in *Scandinavian Political Studies*, vol. 9: 171–84.

—— (1982). 'Sweden in the 1970s', in Jeremy Richardson (ed.), *Policy Styles in Western Europe*, London: Allen and Unwin.

Rustow, Dankwart A. (1971). 'Sweden's Transition to Democracy, Some Notes toward a Genetic Theory', in *Scandinavian Political Studies*, 6: 1, 10–26.

Ruth, Arne (1985). 'The Second New Nation: the Mythology of Modern Sweden', in Arvedson *et al.*, *Economics and Values*.

Rydén, Bengt, and Bergström, Villy, eds. (1982). *Sweden: Choices for Economic and Social Policy*, London: Allen and Unwin.

SAF (undated). *SAF: Swedish Employers' Confederation*, Stockholm: SAF.

Sainsbury, Diane (1980). *Swedish Social Democratic Ideology and Electoral Politics 1944–1948*, Stockholm: Almqvist and Wiksell.

—— (1985). 'Women's Routes to National Legislatures', paper prepared for the ECPR Joint Session of Workshops, 25–30 Mar., Barcelona.

—— and Castles, Francis G. (1987). 'Scandinavia: the Politics of

Stability', in Roy Macridis (ed.), *Modern Political Systems: Europe* (6th edn.), Englewood Cliffs: Prentice Hall.

Scharpf, Fritz W. (1981). *The Political Economy of Inflation and Unemployment in Western Europe: an Outline*, Berlin: Wissenschaftszentrum.

—— (1983). 'Strategy Choice, Economic Feasibility and Institutional Constraints as Determinants of Full-Employment Policy during the Recession' (unpublished paper), Berlin: Wissenchaftszentrum.

—— (1983a). *Economic and Institutional Constraints of Full-Employment Strategies: Sweden, Austria and West Germany*. Berlin: Wissenschaftszentrum.

Schmitter, Philippe C. (1981). 'Interest Intermediations and Regime Governability in Contemporary Western Europe and North America', in Berger *et al.* (eds.), *Organizing Interests in Western Europe*.

Schwartz, Eli (1980). *Trouble in Eden: A Comparison of the British and Swedish Economies*, New York: Praeger.

Secretariat for Futures Studies (1982). *The Future Works*, Stockholm: Swedish Institute.

Self, Peter (1985). *Political Theories of Modern Government: Its Role and Reform*, London: Allen and Unwin.

Shenfield, Arthur (1980). *The Failure of Socialism: Learning from the Swedish and English*, Washington: American Enterprise Institute.

SI: Federation of Swedish Industries (1983). *The Debate on Collective Wage Earner Funds in Sweden*, Stockholm: SI.

Sik, Ota (1980) 'Towards a Humane Social Democracy', in *Economic and Industrial Democracy*, Aug. 1980: 317.

SIND: National Industrial Board (1987). *Increased Investments: Prospects and Possibilities*, Stockholm: SIND.

SIND (1987). *Storkoncernernas Lönsamhet: En Jämförelse med Svensk Industri*, Stockholm: SIND Data.

Snickars, Folke, and Axelsson, Sten (1984). *Om Hundra År*, Stockholm: Regeringskansliet.

Söderström, Hans Tson, ed. (1985). *Sweden: the Road to Stability*, Stockhholm: SNS.

Sørensen, Rune J. (1987). 'Microeconomic Policy and Government Popularity in Norway 1963–1986', paper presented at the workshop Økonomisk politikk och politisk Økonomi, Nordisk Förbund for Statskundskap, 20–23 Aug. 1987, Copenhagen.

SOU: The Swedish Ministry of Public Administration (1985). *The Central Government, the State Agencies and their Management and the Public Service Corporations and their Companies*, Stockholm: Civildepartementet.

Statistical Abstract of Sweden 1988. Stockholm: Statistics Sweden.

Stephens, John D. (1979). *The Transition from Capitalism to Socialism,* London: Macmillan.

Strömgren, Jan-Peter (1987). *The Disabled in Sweden: the Provision of Technical Aids,* Stockholm: Swedish Institute.

Sveriges Television (1985). 'Facts about SVT', Stockholm, SVT Information Department.

Swedish Institute (1986). *Fact Sheets on Sweden: Sport and Exercise,* Stockholm: Swedish Institute.

Swedish Post Office (1985). *Annual Report, July 1984-June 1985,* Stockholm: Swedish Post Office.

Tanzi, Vito (1982). *The Underground Economy in the United States and Abroad,* Lexington, Mass.: Lexington Books.

TCO (1985). *TCO 1986-1989: Draft Programme,* Stockholm: TCO.

Therborn, Göran (1986). 'Patterns of Economic Performance and Cycles of Policy: An OECD Overview 1974-85, and a Dutch Case Study', paper prepared for the Workshop on National Models at the ECPR Joint Session of Workshops, 1-6 Apr. 1986, Göteborg.

Thomas, Alister H. (1986). 'Social Democracy in Scandinavia', in William E. Osterson and A. H. Thomas (eds.), *The Future of Social Democracy,* Oxford: Oxford University Press.

Thurow, Lester C. (1985). 'The Dishonest Economy', in *New York Review,* 21 Nov. 1985: 34-7.

—— (1983). *Dangerous Currents,* New York: Oxford University Press.

Tilton, Timothy A. (1974). 'The Social Origins of Social Democracy: the Swedish Case', in *American Political Science Review,* vol. 68: 561-71.

—— (1979). 'A Swedish Road to Socialism: Ernst Wigforss and the Ideological Foundations of Swedish Social Democracy', in *American Political Science Review,* vol. 73: 505-20.

—— (1985). 'Swedish Voters Reject Neoliberalism', *Inside Sweden,* No. 2.

—— (1987). 'Why Don't the Swedish Social Democrats Nationalize Industry?', in *Scandinavian Studies,* vol. 59. 2: 142-66.

Tinbergen, Jan (1985). *Production, Income, and Welfare,* Salisbury: Wheatsheaf.

Tingsten, Herbert (1973). *The Swedish Social Democrats,* New Jersey: Badminister Press.

Titmuss, Richard (1974). *Social Policy,* London: Allen and Unwin.

Tomandl, Theodore, and Fuerboeck, Karl (1986). *Social Partnership: The Austrian System of Industrial Relations and Social Insurance,* Ithaca, NY: ILR Press.

Tomasson, Richard F. (1970). *Sweden: Prototype of Modern Society,* New York: Random House.

Törngren, Margareta, and Alexanderson, Bengt (1984). *The Swedish Library System*, Stockholm: Swedish Institute.

United States' Department of Labor (1987). *Foreign Labor Trends: Sweden*.

Turner, Stephen (1986). 'The Swedish Model: What Went Wrong?', in Gunnar Eliasson (ed.), *The Economics of Institutions and Markets*, Stockholm: IUI.

Verba, Sidney, *et al.* (1987). *Elites and the Idea of Inequality*, Cambridge, Mass.: Harvard University Press.

Viklund, Birger (1978). 'Work Hours in Sweden', *Working Life in Sweden*, No. 7.

Vogel, Joachim (1974). 'Taxation and Public Opinion in Sweden', *National Tax Journal*, vol. 27, No. 4.

Von Otter, Casten (1980). 'Swedish Welfare Capitalism: the Role of the State', in R. Scase (ed.), *The State in Western Europe*, London: Croom Helm.

Wadensjö, Eskil (1980). *Job Creation and Job Maintenance in the Private Sector*, Lund: Nationalekonmiska Institutionen.

—— (1984). *Labour Market Policy towards the Disabled in Sweden*, Berlin: Wissenschaftszcentrum.

—— (1985). 'The Financial Effects of Unemployment on Labor Market Policy Programs for Public Authorities in Sweden', Berlin: Wissenschaftszcentrum.

Wheeler, Christopher (1975). *White-Collar Power: Changing Patterns of Interest Group Behaviour in Sweden*, Chicago: University of Illinois Press.

Wilensky, Harold (1976). *The 'New Corporatism', Centralization and the Welfare State*, Beverly Hills: Sage Press.

—— (1975). *The Welfare State and Equality*, Berkeley: University of California Press.

Wilson, Dorothy (1979). *The Welfare State in Sweden*, London: Heinemann.

Wittröck, Björn (1980). 'Science Policy and the Challenge to the Welfare State', *West European Politics*, vol. 3, No. 3.

Wolinetz, S. B. (1986). 'The Role of Trade Unions in Industrial Policies, 1945–1984', in Andre Blais (ed.), *Industrial Policy*, vol. 44 of the research studies prepared for the Royal Commission on the Economic Union and Development Prospects for Canada, Toronto: University of Toronto Press.

Zetterberg, Hans (1984). 'New Values at the Workplace', paper presented at the Third Annual CROP Report and TRI-SC Subscribers Conference, Montreal, 15 Mar. 1984.

—— (1985). 'An Electorate in the Grips of the Welfare State', Stockholm: SIFO.

Zysman, John (1983). *Governments, Markets and Growth: Financial Systems and the Politics of Industrial Change*, Ithaca, NY: Cornell University Press.

INDEX